Managerial Accounting
Concepts and Empirical Evidence

Fourth Edition

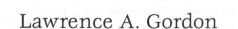

Lawrence A. Gordon

University of Maryland, College Park
Robert H. Smith School of Business

The McGraw-Hill Companies, Inc.
Primis Custom Publishing

New York   St. Louis   San Francisco   Auckland   Bogotá
Caracas   Lisbon   London   Madrid   Mexico   Milan   Montreal
New Delhi   Paris   San Juan   Singapore   Sydney   Tokyo   Toronto

McGraw·Hill

A Division of The McGraw·Hill Companies

Managerial Accounting
Concepts and Empirical Evidence

McGraw-Hill's Primis Custom Publishing consists of products that are produced from camera-ready copy. Peer review, class testing, and accuracy are primarily the responsibility of the author(s).

Materials from the *Certified Management Accountant Examination*, copyright © 1991, 1992, 1993, 1994, 1995, 1996, 1997 by the Institute of Certified Management Accountants, are reprinted and/or adapted with permission.

1 2 3 4 5 6 7 8 9 0   BKM BKM 9 0 9 8

ISBN 0-07-228750-0

Editor: Christine Bowie
Cover Design: Maggie Lytle
Printer/Binder: Book-Mart Press, Inc.

Dedicated to
Hedy, Lauren, Marc, Jessie, and Seymour

CONTENTS

PREFACE

The objective of this book is to provide a conceptual treatment, supported by empirical evidence, of managerial accounting. The book is intended for first year MBA/MS level, and executive level, managerial accounting courses. In addition, the book is appropriate for undergraduate managerial accounting courses, where the focus is on using, rather that preparing, managerial accounting data.

The writing of this book has evolved over several years of teaching managerial accounting courses to a large variety of university and executive level students. Many of these students have had either a direct or indirect influence on the material chosen for coverage, and the approach taken in this book. My deep appreciation is extended to all of those individuals who have influenced the writing of this book.

—*Lawrence A. Gordon*

Permission has been received from the Institute of Certified Management Accountants to use questions and/or unofficial answers from past CMA examinations.

ABOUT THE AUTHOR

Dr. Lawrence A. Gordon is the Ernst & Young Alumni Professor of Managerial Accounting at the University of Maryland at College Park. He earned his Ph.D. degree from Rensselaer Polytechnic Institute, and his M.B.A. and B.S. degrees from the State University of New York at Albany. Prior to joining the University of Maryland, Dr. Gordon was on the faculty of McGill University and the University of Kansas. In addition, Dr. Gordon has been a guest lecturer at numerous other universities in Europe and North America.

Professor Gordon is the recipient of numerous teaching awards, and has written over 60 articles and several books. Further, he is currently the co-editor of the *Journal of Accounting and Public Policy*, an associate editor of the *Journal of Business Finance and Accounting*, and is on the editorial board of several other journals. Dr. Gordon has also served as a consultant to numerous business and governmental organizations.

1

MANAGERIAL ACCOUNTING: CONCEPTUAL FRAMEWORK

CHAPTER OUTLINE

- Information Economics

- Managerial Accounting vs. Financial Accounting

- Management Accountant

- Managerial Economics vs. Managerial Accounting

- Decision Support Systems

- Contingency View of Management Accounting

INTRODUCTION

The primary objective of this book is to provide a conceptual approach to the study of **managerial accounting** for profit oriented organizations.[1] **Managerial accounting** is concerned with the design and use of information systems that support managerial planning and control.[2] Hence, the purpose of a **management accounting system (MAS)** is to support managerial activities via a formal system of gathering, processing, reporting, and evaluating information.

The terms planning and control play a central role in the definition of managerial accounting. **Planning** is a process consisting of the following basic stages: (1) *Setting* organizational objectives; (2) *Identifying* opportunities and/or problems related to these objectives; and (3) *Selecting* a given course of action to be pursued, which will determine the allocation of organizational resources. **Control** is a process which consists of assessing whether the allocation of organizational resources has accomplished the desired objectives and, if not, determining the reallocation necessary to more closely attain those objectives. Thus, control is an evaluative process, which requires feedback and the measurement of performance. Effective control should improve subsequent planning. Figure 1.1 illustrates the planning and control framework discussed above.

In light of the fact that this book's focus is on profit oriented firms, it will be assumed that the overriding objective of these firms is to continually improve profits and, in turn, firm value. This objective is consistent with, although not identical to, maximizing profits and firm value. However, it recognizes that true maximization requires a level of information, and information processing, usually not available (Simon, 1979). Further, unless otherwise specified, it will also be assumed that managers carry out their planning and control activities in a fashion which is consistent with their firm's overall objective of improving profits.[3]

---

1.   Although the primary focus of this book is on profit oriented organizations, management accounting systems are also important to nonprofit private and governmental organizations. As such, many of the topics discussed in this text have direct application to these latter organizations.

2.   The terms **managerial accounting** and **management accounting** are used interchangeably throughout this book.

3.   If managers try to continually improve profits, their observed behavior will be consistent with that of acting as if they are trying to maximize profits. See Friedman (1953) for an interesting discussion on the importance of the observed behavior of managers.

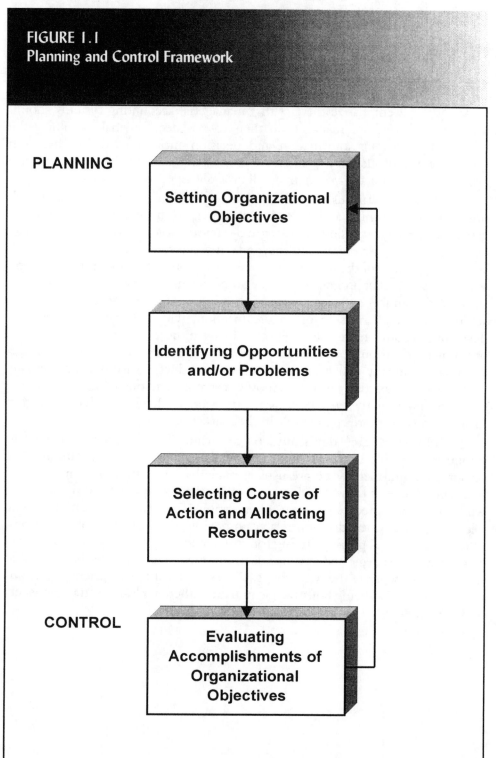

FIGURE 1.1
Planning and Control Framework

PLANNING

Setting Organizational Objectives

Identifying Opportunities and/or Problems

Selecting Course of Action and Allocating Resources

CONTROL

Evaluating Accomplishments of Organizational Objectives

The term **decision making** will be used in this book to include the activities associated with planning and control. These activities are frequently represented by decision models. Decision models provide procedures by which a decision maker pursues managerial activities. The focus of this book will be a decision making, user oriented approach to management accounting. In other words, we will emphasize the fact that managerial accounting systems should focus on the needs of managers in their role as decision makers. Thus, the relationship between information and decision making (with emphasis on specific types of decisions, such as profit planning, pricing, performance evaluation, and capital investments) will be a key aspect of this book.

There are various ways to categorize decision making associated with organizational planning and control. One way is to think in terms of strategic versus nonstrategic decisions. **Strategic decisions** have long-term effects on an organization (e.g., five years and beyond), involve senior executives, impact a significant portion of the organization's resource commitments, and do not lend themselves to a set of programmable (i.e., predetermined, in either a semi or fully structured manner) steps or routines. In essence, strategic decisions relate to setting the overall mission of an organization, with particular emphasis on developing a competitive edge over other firms in the market place. An example of a strategic decision would be the decision to enter a new market by acquiring a subsidiary company which produces a set of products that differ substantially from the firm's existing products. Another example, and one which has become quite prominent in the early 1990s, is the decision to "downsize" an organization in an effort to be more competitive in the market place.

Nonstrategic decisions range from highly programmable to semiprogrammable steps and routines, involve small to medium amounts of resource commitments, and are usually made by lower to upper middle level managers. Some of these decisions may affect the operations for only one year, while others will affect several years of operations. One example of a nonstrategic decision would be the decision related to next year's target level of operations, often referred to as profit planning (or cost-volume-profit analysis). Of course, given that nonstrategic and strategic decisions are related, it could be somewhat misleading to separate the two groups. For example, although pricing decisions are often viewed as being nonstrategic in nature, there is clearly a strategic aspect to these decisions.

Management accounting systems should attempt to support all categories of decision making. However, to the extent that decisions are nonprogrammable, it is certainly more difficult to design an MAS which supports such decisions. Accordingly, the primary focus in this book will be on designing and using management accounting systems for the programmable aspects of the decision making process, regardless of the strategic or nonstrategic labeling of a decision.[4] However, to the extent that management accounting systems gather and process various types of information (as discussed later in this chapter), the MAS will also support the nonprogrammable aspects of decision making.

Information is another term which is critical to our definition of managerial accounting. In concept, we can differentiate data from information. **Data** include all signs and symbols gathered and processed, providing they are understood by the sender. **Information** consists of that subset of data which increases the knowledge of the person receiving the data. Technically speaking, information relates to reducing the uncertainty surrounding an event. Hence, information to one person may only be data to another. For example, assume that two managers, A and B, are formally notified of the fact that the cost of a given service has increased by 10%. Also assume that A had previously heard about the cost increase via the company grapevine, but B had no previous knowledge of this fact. Technically speaking, the formal notice concerning the cost increase would be information to manager B, but only data to manager A. Unfortunately, the distinction between data and information is often illusory. Further, today's information will be tomorrow's data. Hence, the two terms will be used interchangeably throughout this book.

Information can be **financial** (i.e., monetary) or **nonfinancial** in nature. Information may also be characterized as either **ex post** (i.e., historical) or **ex ante** (i.e., future oriented). Further, some information relates to an organization's **internal** operations, while other information relates to factors **external** to the organization. Traditional accounting systems usually emphasize financial, ex post, and internal information (e.g., historical operating costs). Yet, to carry out their planning and control activities, managers require information that is characterized as nonfinancial and/or ex ante and/or external in nature (e.g., forecasting economic trends). This point is especially true for decisions which have a strategic orientation. Hence, it is useful for designers and users of management accounting systems to think in terms of the three-way classification scheme shown in Figure 1.2. In effect, there are eight (i.e., $2^3 = 8$) possible combinations of information characteristics based on this scheme: (1) financial, ex post, internal (e.g., a firm's actual cost of producing a specific product); (2) financial, ex post, external (e.g., a competitor's actual price for a specific product);

---

4. To the extent strategic decisions are supported by the MAS, it is becoming popular to think in terms of strategic management accounting.

FIGURE 1.2
Three-Way Classification Scheme of Information

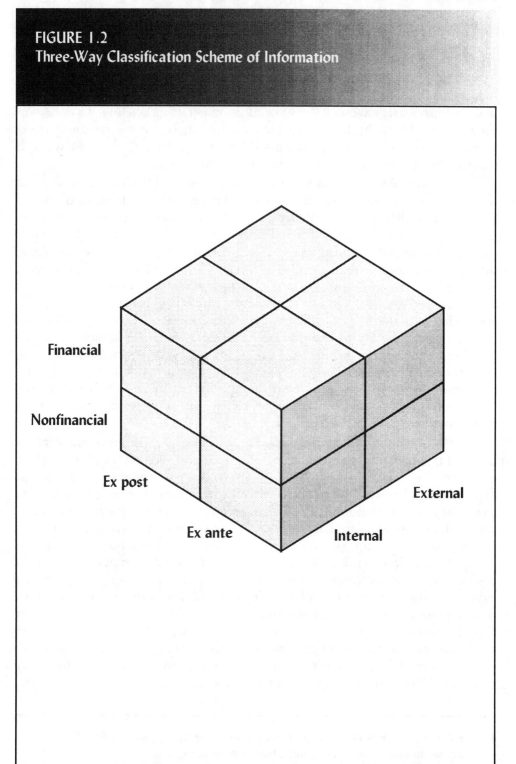

(3) financial, ex ante, internal (e.g., a firm's expected cost of producing a specific product); (4) financial, ex ante, external (e.g., a competitor's expected price for a specific product); (5) nonfinancial, ex post, internal (e.g., a firm's unit sales volume for a given product over the past year); (6) nonfinancial, ex post, external (e.g., an industry's unit sales volume for a given product over the past year); (7) nonfinancial, ex ante, internal (e.g., a firm's expected unit sales volume); (8) nonfinancial, ex ante, external (e.g., an industry's expected unit sales volume). An MAS, which contains information along all eight combinations, can be thought of as being "broad scope" in nature.

INFORMATION ECONOMICS

Information should be thought of as an economic good, which has certain costs and benefits associated with gathering, processing, and using it. When viewed in this light, managers wishing to improve the profits of their firms should continue to invest in information as long as they believe the benefits of the information exceed the costs. This view of information is often referred to as information economics. That is, **information economics** is the area of economics concerned with assessing the costs and benefits of gathering, processing, and using information. A formal analysis of information economics is usually based on Bayesian statistics. However, the essence of information economics is most easily understood via an example and the use of decision tree analysis as illustrated below.

Assume the MaLa Toy Corporation is contemplating the introduction of a new toy based on a recent big hit, action movie. Given the demand estimates, the company is fairly certain that the total revenues generated from the new product will be around $2,000,000. The total costs associated with the toy are less certain. The best estimates, however, place the total costs at either $1,000,000 or $2,500,000, with an equal probability of occurrence. Hence, without any additional information, the expected value of this new product line is a positive $250,000 [i.e., (.5)($2,000,000 - $1,000,000) + (.5)(2,000,000 - $2,500,000)] and the firm would go ahead with the project.[5] However, before initiating the project, the company has an opportunity to develop, at a cost of $40,000, a specialized information system which will assist in predicting the new product's costs. The specialized information system will predict whether costs are going to be $1,000,000 or $2,500,000 with 80% accuracy (i.e., the information system does not give a perfect signal as to the true costs). As the manager responsible for evaluating the desirability of the new toy, the initial decision confronting you is whether or not to develop the specialized information system. This decision is most easily considered based on the decision tree shown in Figure 1.3.

---

5.   This example assumes the firm is risk neutral with respect to gains or losses on the new product.

FIGURE 1.3
MaLa Toy Corporation
Information Economics

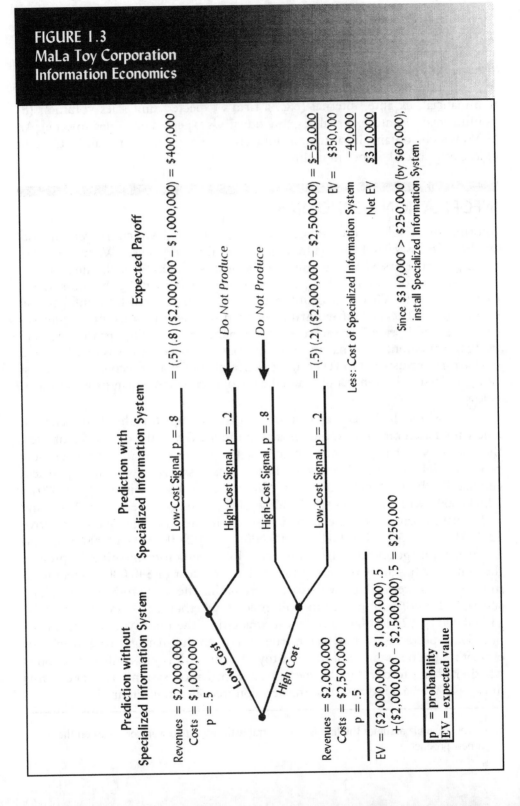

As shown in Figure 1.3, it is in the company's best interest to develop the new specialized information system. The reason being that with the specialized information system the net expected value (net of the cost of the specialized information system) of the new toy is $310,000, whereas without the specialized information system the expected value is $250,000. In other words, the company has a $60,000 increase in the expected value of the new toy with the specialized information system as compared to not having the system.

MANAGERIAL ACCOUNTING VS. FINANCIAL ACCOUNTING

The focus of managerial accounting is on the use of information by individuals inside the organization. That is, managerial accounting is primarily intended to facilitate planning and control by managers who are employed by the organization. In contrast, the main focus of financial accounting is on the use of financial reports by individuals outside the organization. Investors, creditors, tax authorities, and other individuals external to the organization are the primary users of financial accounting reports.

Another difference between managerial and financial accounting is that the preparation of accounting information for external purposes (i.e., financial accounting) is governed by generally accepted accounting principles (GAAP). These principles are promulgated by various regulatory accounting bodies. For example, the Securities and Exchange Commission (SEC), Financial Accounting Standards Board (FASB), and Internal Revenue Service (IRS), all play an important part in determining the type and form of financial accounting data reported in the United States. In contrast, the type and form of managerial accounting information reported are not governed by accounting regulatory bodies. Managers can request and utilize any information they believe will be helpful to the planning and control activities of their organization.

The distinction between management and financial accounting is not absolute. The same accounting data is often used by both the organization's internal and external stakeholders. Managers frequently utilize data which is considered to be prepared primarily for external reporting purposes. For example, most managers utilize information appearing on earnings statements, statements of financial position, and statements of cash flows. In the same vein, external users of accounting data are also interested in utilizing accounting data often thought to be prepared for managers. For example, forecasts of sales and expenditures are frequently requested by existing and potential creditors.

The use of accounting data by an organization's managers has roots which date back as far as the field of accounting itself, although the modern view of managerial accounting is linked to the developments of manufacturing in the late 19th and early 20th centuries. As manufacturing firms became involved in sophisticated production processes, the need for detailed cost accounting data became more obvious. Initially, this need was derived from financial reporting issues in that production costs had to be allocated to inventory values and cost of goods sold for purposes of preparing balance sheets and earnings statements. However, the focus of cost accounting ultimately shifted from financial reporting to cost management for managerial planning and control purposes. Issues surrounding cost allocations, cost planning, budgeting, standard costing, and costs for pricing decisions all played an important role in shifting this concern. Today, cost accounting is usually considered a subset of management accounting, although its important role in financial accounting remains.

MANAGEMENT ACCOUNTANT

A **management accountant** is an individual who helps develop, implement, and use the management accounting system. Management accountants are also involved in preparing financial reports for individuals outside the organization. In many organizations, the senior management accountant has the title of controller or chief financial officer, although the duties and title associated with this position vary from firm to firm. The management accountant's activities often include preparing budgets and forecasts, preparing financial statements, determining and evaluating control procedures, providing information for current decisions (e.g., capital budgeting and pricing decisions), evaluating past performance, and making various kinds of decisions based on the management accounting system.

It is difficult to draw a line as to exactly where the management accountant's activities end and the manager's activities begin. In fact, in many organizations, the tasks of management accountants and managers are so highly interrelated that to draw such a line is inappropriate. In this regard, the Institute of Management Accountants (formerly known as the National Association of Accountants) has argued that participating in the process of managing the firm is one of the two main objectives of the management accountant.[6] The other objective is to select and provide information to all levels of management. The Certified Management Accountant (CMA) certificate has helped solidify the importance of the role of a management accountant to organizations. Holders of this certificate have demonstrated, through a combination of education and examination, substantial evidence as to their ability to facilitate managerial planning and control via accounting systems.[7]

---

6. National Association of Accountants, *Objectives of Management Accounting*, (New York: NAA 1982).
7. The CMA certificate is awarded by the Institute of Management Accountants.

MANAGERIAL ECONOMICS VS. MANAGERIAL ACCOUNTING

Managerial economics is concerned with the application of economic theory, especially microeconomic theory, to managerial decision making (i.e., planning and control). The emphasis in managerial economics is on the efficient (optimal) allocation of scarce organizational resources via economic analysis. The use of management science techniques (e.g., math programming and probability theory) is an integral part of this allocation process. The information required for the economic analysis underlying managerial economics is usually assumed to be available, or obtainable at some cost, via the organization's internal information system (i.e., the management accounting system).

To the extent that management accounting systems focus on economic related events, it seems reasonable to think of an MAS as the measurement arm of managerial economics. At the same time, to the extent that managerial planning and control are to be grounded in microeconomic analysis, it seems reasonable to think of managerial economics as the analytical arm of managerial accounting. Viewed in these terms, there is little wonder why many scholars and managers view the fields of managerial accounting and managerial economics as being quite similar, if not inseparable. Textbooks and journal articles in both fields strongly reinforce this belief.

The traditional view of managerial economics is based on the assumption that managers behave in a fashion which is consistent with the best interest of the owners of firms. In recent years, this assumption has been challenged by a rapidly growing body of literature concerning principal-agent relationships, whereby it is assumed that the separation between managers (agents) and owners (principals) in modern organizations often brings about a **conflict of interest.** That is, certain actions which are in the best interest of managers may not be in the best interest of owners. (For example, a manager may reap more satisfaction out of consuming additional entertainment funds than by increasing firm profits by a corresponding amount from not spending such funds.) As a result, managers may have an incentive to take actions which are not in the best interest of the owners of a firm. The fact that managers have the incentive to operate in such a fashion is not, by itself, sufficient to allow such actions to occur. The opportunity for such actions to occur is premised on **asymmetric information** between managers and owners (i.e., agents have information not available to the principals).[8] The combination of conflict of interests and asymmetric information between

---

8. Principal-agent relationships (often called agency relationships) exist wherever there is a superior-subordinate relationship (e.g., owners versus senior level managers, senior level managers versus middle level managers). In essence, principals empower agents to operate on their behalf in return for some form of compensation. A brief summary of the mathematical aspects of agency theory is provided in Appendix 1.1.

principals and agents has important implications for managerial accounting, as will be noted in various places throughout this book.[9]

Managerial economics is only one part of the foundation of decision making. Nevertheless, given the importance of economic analysis to an organization's survival and the fact that accounting systems have always been concerned with measuring economic events, this book will draw heavily from the principles underlying managerial economics. This approach will facilitate developing the various topics of the book in a coherent and consistent fashion.

DECISION SUPPORT SYSTEMS[10]

As noted in the beginning of this chapter, managerial accounting is concerned with the design and use of information systems. A key aspect of modern information systems is their relationship with computers. Hence, in many organizations, if not most, the concept of a management accounting system automatically implies a computer based information system.

The field of managerial accounting, with its emphasis on the use of data for decision making, is experiencing many changes as a result of computer related developments. One development, in particular, has important implications for the field. This development concerns decision support systems (DSS). More specifically, the evolving work on decision support systems promises to greatly enhance our ability to design and use management accounting systems.

A **decision support system** is a computer based information system designed to support managerial decision making. As this definition suggests, computer based management accounting systems can actually be thought of as decision support systems. The conceptual framework underlying decision support systems is illustrated in Figure 1.4. The **user** shown in this figure represents the decision maker who interacts with the model base and the data base via an interactive query facility. An individual involved in pricing decisions would be a typical example of a user. The **model base** consists of subroutines which are utilized to carry out the firm's planning and control activities. For example, the portion of the model base which carries out pricing decisions, for our above noted user, could include subroutines for marginal analysis type pricing and target profit pricing (topics discussed in Chapter 6). The **model base management system (MBMS)** surrounding the model base includes the

---

9.   For excellent articles on the use of executive compensation plans as a mechanism
      for reducing agency conflicts between management and shareholders, see Larcker
      (1983), and Lambert and Larcker (1985a).

10.   The discussion contained in this section is based, in part, on the books by:
      Bonczek, Holsapple, and Whinston (1981), Sprague and Carlson (1982), and
      Gordon and Pinches (1984).

FIGURE 1.4
Decision Support System Overview

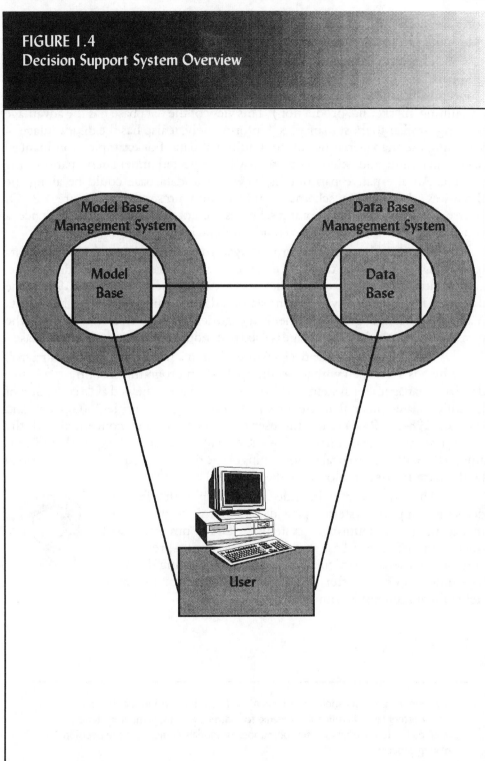

software necessary to update, retrieve, maintain, and interrelate the various subroutines in the model base.

The **data base** illustrated in Figure 1.4 consists of the various data (information) utilized in conducting the planning and control activities. Conceptually, the data base could be partitioned along functional lines (e.g., accounting, marketing, production). This view of the data base has the advantage of being familiar to most managers. Unfortunately, it also has the disadvantage of impeding the managerial use of nontraditional data. For example, nonfinancial data of an ex ante and external nature may be neglected under such a partitioning scheme. An alternative partitioning view of the data base could be along the three-way classification scheme of information presented in Figure 1.2. Of course, the above two partitioning schemes are not mutually exclusive; hence, a conceptual view of the data base could combine both schemes.

The **data base management system (DBMS)** surrounding the data base in Figure 1.4 can be thought of as the software necessary to update, retrieve, and maintain the information in the data base (Sprague and Carlson, 1982). The data base management system consists of a data definition language and a data manipulation language. The former language defines the physical structure of the data base, while the latter language is used to conduct operations on the data base.

Traditional data base design stores data in a particular file (e.g., a payroll file) which is associated with a specific application program. In contrast, where a data base management system is utilized, the data base is viewed as "a collection of logically related data that are grouped according to entities" (Gordon and Pinches, 1984, p. 23). Hence, the user does not have to be concerned with the physical storage of data, but can view the data in terms of the logical relationships among the data. The logical relationships of the data in the data base are described by the **data model** employed by the DBMS.[11]

This overview is intended to highlight the fact that decision support systems provide a useful way to view management accounting systems. Developments with microcomputers, data base management systems, spreadsheets, and the Internet are particularly relevant to facilitating this view. These developments offer exciting opportunities for the entire field of management accounting.

---

11.   The term **data model** should not be confused with the term **model base**. The former refers to a classification scheme for data base management systems, whereas the latter refers to the subroutines or models comprising the decision making process.

CONTINGENCY VIEW OF MANAGEMENT ACCOUNTING

The traditional approach to management accounting usually assumes that accounting systems are universally appropriate for all firms and situations. This assumption is, in part, the result of concern for consistency. However, since the mid-1970s this approach has been seriously challenged by the contingency view of management accounting (Gordon and Miller, 1976; Hayes, 1977; Otley, 1980; Macintosh, 1981; Gordon and Narayanan, 1984; Chenhall and Morris, 1986; Duncan and Moores, 1989; Mia, 1993; and Mia and Chenhall, 1994). **Contingency theory** applied to management accounting argues that the appropriateness of a management accounting system (and its component parts) depends on the specific organization and the circumstances under which the organization operates. Hence, according to this view, the goal is to find the proper match between the management accounting system and the factors (contingency variables) surrounding its use. The variables considered in this work on the contingency approach to management accounting include, but are not limited to, characteristics of the environment, organizational structure, organizational strategy, and production technology.[12]

One area of managerial accounting where the contingency view has made significant inroads concerns the association between the level of uncertainty confronting an organization and the perceived usefulness of a broad scope MAS. Gordon and Narayanan (1984), for example, provided empirical evidence that, for managers in successful firms, the perceived usefulness of a broad scope MAS (i.e., an MAS which includes nonfinancial, ex ante and external information, as well as the more traditional financial, ex post, and internal information) was positively associated with the level of environmental uncertainty confronting the organization. Chenhall and Morris (1986) had similar empirical findings regarding the association between a broad scope MAS and environmental uncertainty.[13] More recently, Mia and Chenhall (1994) extended these earlier findings by isolating organizational uncertainty within the particular functions of production (where task uncertainty for managers was assumed to be relatively low) and marketing (where task uncertainty for managers was assumed to be relatively high). Their basic argument, which has been empirically confirmed, is

---

12. The early work in management accounting utilizing the contingency approach was a direct outgrowth of contingency developments in the organization theory literature in the 1960s and 1970s (e.g., Burns and Stalker, 1961; Chandler, 1962; Cyert and March, 1963; Lawrence and Lorsch, 1967; Perrow, 1970; Pugh et al., 1963; Woodward, 1965).

13. The interaction between an organization's environment and its MAS is consistent with the open system view of organizations. An excellent discussion of how open systems help provide a framework for understanding accounting systems is given in a paper by Nowak and Jaruga (1998).

that the association between the use of a broad scope MAS and performance is stronger for managers of marketing activities than for managers of production activities.

The argument that the proper use of an MAS depends on the circumstances surrounding its use is hard to disagree with on a conceptual level. However, on a practical level, there are so many factors upon which the proper use depends that the combinations and permutations become mind-boggling. Hence, it is not surprising that many have criticized the practical usefulness of the contingency view. Otley (1980), for example, pointed out that: (1) much work was needed in developing the theoretical relationships among contingency variables and accounting systems, (2) organizational effectiveness and the contingency view needed to be more directly linked, and (3) the role of accounting systems could not be studied in isolation of other organizational control systems. Another concern often raised regarding the contingency view of management accounting is that the approach suggests the need for numerous management accounting systems within a given firm. As a result of these and related problems, the rise and fall of the use of the term **contingency theory** in management accounting occurred over a relatively short period of time following the Gordon and Miller (1976) paper. Nevertheless, as will be seen in various places throughout this book, the concepts underlying the contingency view are in widespread use in management accounting. In essence, without being labeled as such, the contingency approach toward management accounting is ubiquitous. The developments related to decision support systems have facilitated such an approach because the data base and model base can be accessed by numerous users in multiple ways (i.e., one management accounting system can meet the needs of a multitude of users).

CONCLUDING COMMENTS

Managerial accounting is concerned with the design and use of information systems for managerial planning and control. Hence, the two fundamental components of managerial accounting are to provide and use information for managerial decision making. The approach in this book will be to continually ask (either implicitly or explicitly) the following two questions: (1) What type of decisions are managers making? (2) What type of information do managers need to make their decisions? This approach is often referred to as a decision making or user oriented perspective of management accounting. In asking the above two questions, it will be assumed that the overriding objective is to improve the profits of firms.

The field of management accounting has been rapidly evolving over the past three decades. Nevertheless, there is still a long way to go before the field can be considered mature. This book, with its emphasis on conceptual and empirical aspects of management accounting, is intended to help in this maturing process.

APPENDIX 1.1:
Basic Agency Model

Agency theory is concerned with the delegation of decision making authority by a principal (e.g., an owner) to an agent (e.g., a manager). In addressing this concern, it recognizes the existence of asymmetric information[14] and the inherent conflict of interests between the principal and agent. The outcome (e.g., production, profit) of an agent's action is usually assumed to be observable to both the agent and the principal and can be expressed as:

$$x = f(a, \theta) \qquad\qquad\qquad\qquad \text{Eq. 1.1}$$

where,

x	$=$	outcome,
a	$=$	agent's action, which corresponds to different effort levels (i.e., for each action, a, from the set of actions, A, a different effort level is assumed),
θ	$=$	a random variable, representing different states of nature incorporating market conditions and technological factors over which the agent has no control.

Both the agent and principal are assumed to be motivated by self-interest and the agent is assumed to have a disutility for effort. Hence, the agent is interested in the incentive compensation (reward) received, y, which is a function of the outcome, x [i.e., $y = F(x)$] and the disutility derived from taking the action, a (where the disutility from exerting effort can be stated as $V(a)$). This can be expressed in terms of the agent's utility function, U_a. More formally, $U_a(x, a) = F(x) - V(a)$, assuming that the agent is risk-neutral. If the agent were risk-averse, $U_a(x,a) = G(F(x)) - V(a)$, where $G(F(x))$ represents the utility derived by the agent for the monetary reward $F(x)$. The principal is interested in the residual payoff, that is the outcome, x, less any incentive compensation, y, given to the agent. This can be expressed in terms of the principal's utility function, U_p. More formally, assuming risk neutrality, $U_p = (x-y)$. Accordingly, the principal's problem is to select an incentive compensation schedule which maximizes her (his) expected utility (i.e., residual payoff). Assuming the principal and agent have similar expectations regarding the set of states of nature, and their corresponding

---

14. Two types of asymmetric information commonly discussed are moral hazard and adverse selection. **Moral hazard** refers to the principal's inability to observe the agent's effort level and **adverse selection** refers to precontracting information available only to the agent.

probabilities, p, the principal's objective function can be expressed in terms of her (his) expected utility function as:

$$\max_{a \in A} \quad \sum_{\theta \in \Theta} (x-y)p(\theta) \qquad\qquad \text{Eq. 1.2}$$

Two basic constraints are usually associated with the above objective function. First, it is necessary for the agent to receive enough compensation so as to remain in the employment of the principal. This is referred to as the reservation wage constraint and can be expressed in terms of a minimal expected utility for the agent as:

$$\sum_{\theta \in \Theta} F(x)p(\theta) - V(a) \geq \overline{U} \qquad\qquad \text{Eq. 1.3}$$

where, $\overline{U}$ represents the agent's utility from the next best employment alternative (i.e., the reservation wage).

The second constraint is that the agent is assumed to select the action which maximizes her (his) utility, given the incentive compensation schedule in place. (It should be noted that the optimal action is not necessarily the greatest effort level.) Since the different incentive schemes imply different optimal actions on the part of the agent, this constraint is usually referred to as the self-selection constraint and can be expressed as:

$$a \in Argmax \sum_{\theta \in \Theta} F(x)p(\theta) - V(a) \qquad\qquad \text{Eq. 1.4}$$

The $a \in Argmax$ notation means that the agent's potential action is a member of the set of actions (arguments) that maximizes the expression to follow, which in Eq. 1.4 is the agent's expected utility function.[15]

---

15. For an excellent review of agency theory applied to managerial accounting, see the paper by Baiman (1982).

PROBLEMS

Problem 1.1

Discuss the relationships among managerial accounting, managerial economics, and decision support systems.

Problem 1.2

Explain the strengths and weaknesses associated with using contingency theory as the basic paradigm for the field of managerial accounting.

Problem 1.3

The *information economics* example provided in this chapter assumes that the specialized information system does not provide a perfect signal. If that assumption were changed (such that the specialized information system would provide a perfect signal), what is the maximum amount the firm should be willing to pay for such a system? (Show all work.)

Problem 1.4

The developments with the Internet (often referred to as the Net) over the last five years have been nothing short of phenomenal. Indeed, one way or the other, the Net has influenced the behavior of people, organizations, and the activities of organizations around the world. Since the field of managerial accounting is concerned with the use of information for managerial planning and control, the Net also has tremendous implications for developments in this field. For example, through the Net, a manager can gather information on competitors previously viewed as either unavailable or too costly to justify gathering from an information economics perspective.

Required:

A. Explain the generic claim stated above concerning the effect the Net has on the field of managerial accounting.

B. One database which is readily available to managers relates to companies' filings with the U.S. SEC (Securities Exchange Commission). This database is called Edgar and can be easily accessed at no cost via the SEC's World Wide Web address, www.sec.gov.com. Browse through Edgar and discuss how a manager may utilize this database in carrying out managerial accounting activities.

C.   Provide a list, including World Wide Web addresses, of at least three additional (i.e., in addition to Edgar) sources of data which can be accessed via the Net (at no cost) that could be helpful to managerial accounting related activities.

Problem 1.5 *(Adapted from CMA examination)*

The management at JEM Associates, Inc., a manufacturer of farm machinery, has begun the process of implementing a formal planning system incorporating strategic and operational planning. After three months of management discussions, JEM management has defined the following strategic goals for the next three years.

- Develop better integrated relations with Japan, Korea, and Mexico in order to minimize the cost of steel and parts used in manufacturing.

- Develop new marketing strategies in the agrarian economies of emerging nations.

- Procure additional funds from the public investment community to acquire and develop new products.

- Perform a human resource audit of JEM personnel to develop training programs in order to fill planned job vacancies with internal personnel.

- Procure and implement a computerized system to accommodate the global growth objectives.

After two months of submissions and revisions, JEM management has completed the operational and financial plans for the first year of operations under the newly established strategic goals. The managers are now concerned with being able to measure progress toward these goals and are considering various ways of controlling and evaluating performance. The managers are also concerned about how their employees will react to these performance measures.

Performance controls can be introduced at one or more of three general points—before, during, or after the goal attainment process. The figure on the following page shows how controls can focus on the inputs, attainment, and outputs of the goal attainment process.

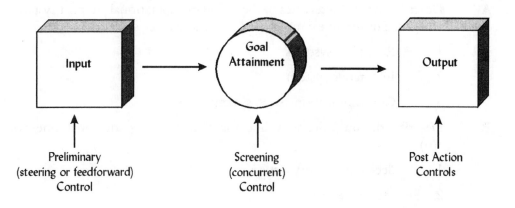

Required:

A.   Identify at least three reasons why JEM Associates Inc. needs an effective control system in order to realize their strategic goals for the next three years.

B.   Define preliminary, screening, and post-action controls and give an example of each.

C.   1.   Explain why employees frequently resist controls.

        2.   Identify those characteristics that make controls effective and acceptable.

Problem 1.6 *(Adapted from CMA examination)*

Advances in computer hardware technology and software design have enabled management information systems to evolve from systems that primarily process transaction data to systems that impart knowledge. One type of management information system, an operational support system, is used by managers and accountants to support the operational activities of organizations. These systems emerged in the late 1960s and supported short-range planning and control. Three examples of such systems are real-time, interactive, and communication-based systems. However, managers required more flexible systems that could respond to less well-defined questions. With advances in hardware technology and software engineering, higher level systems such as decision support systems and expert systems evolved.

Required:

A.   Describe the characteristics of the following operational support systems and give a different example of each of these three systems.

     1.   Real-time systems.

     2.   Interactive system.

     3.   Communication-based system.

B.   Describe the purpose, as well as the characteristics and capabilities, of a(n)

     1.   decision support system.

     2.   expert system.

PROFIT PLANNING: AN OVERVIEW

CHAPTER OUTLINE

- Basics of Profit Planning

- Contribution Margin and Incremental Analysis

- Operating Leverage

- Contribution Margin Paradox

- Relevant Costs vs. Sunk Costs

- Relevant Range of Operations

- Taxes

- Multiproduct Considerations

- Uncertainty Considerations

- Information Needs

INTRODUCTION

As discussed in Chapter 1, management accounting is concerned with the design and use of accounting information systems for managerial decision making (i.e., planning and control). This chapter will examine the process of short-run profit planning, with emphasis on the overall role of management accounting systems in such planning.

By the end of this chapter, the reader will be familiar with the generic components of profits and the relationships among these components to various levels of activity. Issues related to profit planning and uncertainty, as well as the basic role of taxes in profit planning, will also be discussed.

BASICS OF PROFIT PLANNING

Profit planning is the process by which firms go about trying to earn profits. In its simplest form, the management accounting view of profit planning (often called cost-volume-profit analysis) is short-run in focus and based largely on the following three related definitions.[1] First, **profits** are defined as the difference between revenues and costs.[2] Second, **total costs** are defined as being equal to variable plus fixed costs. **Variable costs** are those costs which go up or down with increases or decreases in the production level of a particular product.[3] Conversely, **fixed costs** are those costs that remain the same for a specified period of time, regardless of the changes in the level of production.[4] It should be noted, however, that when speaking of per unit variable or fixed costs, their behavior is the opposite of what is stated above. Per unit variable costs are assumed to remain the same as production level varies, while per unit fixed costs decrease (increase) as production level increases (decreases). Third, and finally, the difference between revenues and variable costs is defined as the **contribution margin**.

---

1. The short-run focus means that consideration is limited to a relatively short time period (such as one year or a firm's normal operating cycle).
2. No distinction between **costs** and **expenses** will be made in this chapter. Chapter 3 will address this issue.
3. The term **product** refers to a physical good or service which represents output of a firm.
4. It is common to discuss the dichotomy between variable and fixed costs in terms of production levels. More generically, this dichotomy can be related to any activity which has varying levels.

The above definitions lead to the following algebraic expression of profits:

$$\pi = TR - TC$$
$$\pi = TR - (TVC + FC)$$
$$\pi = P \bullet X - [(VC \bullet X) + FC] \qquad \text{Eq. 2.1}$$
$$\pi = (P - VC)X - FC$$
$$\pi = (CM \bullet X) - FC$$

where,

π	=	profits,
TR	=	total revenues,
TC	=	total costs,
P	=	sales price per unit of product,
VC	=	variable cost per unit of product,
X	=	number of units (of a product) produced and sold,[5]
TVC	=	total variable costs,
FC	=	total fixed costs, and
CM	=	contribution margin per unit.

To determine the number of units of a product needed to be sold to earn a target level of profits,[6] X_π, Equation (Eq.) 2.1 can be written as:

$$X_\pi = \frac{FC + \pi}{P - VC} \qquad \text{Eq. 2.2}$$

It should be noted that the denominator in Eq. 2.2, $P - VC$, represents the contribution margin per unit. Hence, if a firm wishes to determine the volume of unit sales required to earn a target level of profits, fixed costs plus the desired profits is divided by the contribution margin per unit.

---

5. It is assumed that production and sales levels are the same. Hence, issues concerning the optimal level of inventory are avoided.

6. The determination of the target profit amount is often derived from a firm's target return on investment (ROI), as discussed in Chapter 8. The notion of earning a target level of profits is not equivalent to the notion of maximizing profits. However, it is consistent with the objective of continually improving profits, which, as discussed in Chapter 1, is the overriding objective assumed to be pursued by firms and managers. In essence, a target profit level can be thought of as the starting point from which firms continually strive to improve profits.

A special case of the above formulation is where the firm wishes to determine its breakeven point in terms of units sold, X_{BE}. In this case, profits equal zero (i.e., breakeven occurs where total revenues equal total costs) and Eq. 2.2 becomes:

$$X_{BE} = \frac{FC}{P - VC}$$

Eq. 2.2a

The relationships presented above are illustrated in graphic form in Figures 2.1a and 2.1b.[7]

To illustrate the points made thus far, assume that a recent business school graduate forms a limousine service firm, Leta Inc., specializing in trips to and from the center of a small town and the nearest mid-size airport. The new firm estimates that each round trip to and from the airport will generate average revenues of $50. Estimates of the firm's costs indicate that some costs will vary with increases or decreases in the level of business activity and others will remain constant. More to the point, the firm estimates that variable costs will equal $30 per trip and fixed costs will be $57,600 per year. Hence, the firm estimates a contribution margin of $20 ($50 - $30) per round trip. The new firm is interested in determining the estimated number of round trips required over the course of the year in order to earn a profit of $15,000. The firm would also like to know the number of trips required in order to at least break even.

Based on Eq. 2.2, the number of trips required to produce a total profit of $15,000 can be computed as follows:

$$X_{\pi} = \frac{FC + \pi}{P - VC}$$

$$X_{\pi} = \frac{\$57,600 + \$15,000}{\$20}$$

$$X_{\pi} = \frac{\$72,600}{\$20} = 3,630 \text{ round trips per year.}$$

---

7. A similar type of analysis can be applied to governmental organizations. One variation, in this regard, is a scenario where a fee generating activity is supplemented with a lump-sum appropriation. In such a scenario, the total revenue curve in Figure 2.1a would be shifted upward (or, alternatively, the fixed cost and total cost curves shifted downward) by the lump-sum amount. For a further discussion of the application of cost-volume-profit analysis to governmental organizations, see Caldwell and Welch (1989).

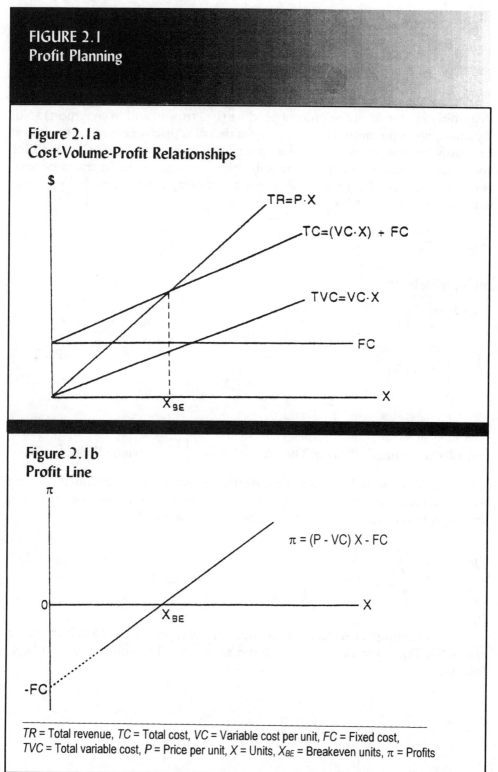

FIGURE 2.1
Profit Planning

Figure 2.1a
Cost-Volume-Profit Relationships

Figure 2.1b
Profit Line

$\pi = (P - VC) X - FC$

TR = Total revenue, TC = Total cost, VC = Variable cost per unit, FC = Fixed cost, TVC = Total variable cost, P = Price per unit, X = Units, X_{BE} = Breakeven units, π = Profits

The breakeven point can be computed with the aid of Equation 2.2a:

$$X_{BE} = \frac{\$57,600}{\$20} = 2,880 \text{ round trips per year.}$$

In the above analysis, the target profit and breakeven points were determined in terms of the units of product (i.e., trips to and from airport) sold. By multiplying the number of units times the sales price per unit, this solution can easily be transformed into sales dollars. An alternative approach, which for some cases is easier to apply, is to solve the initial problem in terms of total revenues required. To see how this alternative works, let us return to Eq. 2.2 and express it in a different form:

$$X_\pi = \frac{FC + \pi}{P - VC} \qquad\qquad \text{Eq. 2.2}$$

multiplying by P:
$$X_\pi \bullet P = \frac{FC + \pi}{P - VC} \bullet P$$

$$TR_\pi = \frac{FC + \pi}{\left(\dfrac{P - VC}{P}\right)} \qquad\qquad \text{Eq. 2.3}$$

where, TR_π equals total revenues required to earn the target profits and all other variables are defined as above. The expression $\dfrac{P - VC}{P}$ shown on the right side of Eq. 2.3 is often referred to as the **contribution margin ratio**. Of course, solving for a breakeven level of sales, TR_{BE}, is nothing more than a special case of Eq. 2.3, where profits are zero. This can be expressed as follows:

$$TR_{BE} = \frac{FC}{\left(\dfrac{P - VC}{P}\right)} \qquad\qquad \text{Eq. 2.3a}$$

Returning to Leta Inc., where the firm wishes to earn a $15,000 profit, we can utilize Eq. 2.3 to obtain the required sales level. The solution would be as follows:

$$TR = \frac{\$57,600 + \$15,000}{\left(\dfrac{\$50 - \$30}{\$50}\right)} = \frac{\$72,600}{.4}$$

$$TR = \$181,500$$

This solution is similar to the earlier solution where it was found that 3,630 round trips were required to earn $15,000 profits (i.e., 3,630 x $50 = $181,500).

CONTRIBUTION MARGIN AND INCREMENTAL ANALYSIS

The basic logic underlying the use of contribution margin is straightforward. If the additional revenues from selling additional units of a product (defined as **incremental revenues**) exceed the additional costs associated with those units (defined as **incremental costs**), profits (losses) of a firm will increase (decrease). In other words, where the incremental revenues exceed the incremental costs (which consist of only variable costs), there is a positive contribution to the profit margin. This logic has led many firms to provide managers with a contribution margin income analysis for individual subunits and product lines. This type of information facilitates the ability of managers to pursue the objective of improving profits.

To illustrate the contribution margin logic noted above, consider the Alb, Inc., retail store. Alb is divided into three departments: clothing, household goods, and toys. Each department occupies roughly 10,000 square feet of space. As a result, the $300,000 annual fixed costs (for the firm as a whole) are evenly divided among the three departments. The revenues and variable costs for each department vary substantially (see Exhibit 2.1). As shown in Exhibit 2.1, the clothing department has a substantial profit (taxes are not considered in this illustration). In contrast, the household goods and toys departments are both losing money. Nevertheless, there is a substantial difference between the latter two departments. The household goods department has a positive contribution margin, whereas the toys department has a negative contribution margin. Hence, assuming: (1) there are no better options for utilizing the floor space in the store, (2) the demand for the products sold in each department is independent of the demand for products sold in other departments, and (3) the fixed costs remain at $300,000 in total regardless of the number of departments, Alb will be best off to close the toys department and keep the household goods department open. If this were done, the firm's total profits would equal $350,000 rather than $330,000 (i.e., an increase of $20,000 due to the elimination of the negative contribution margin in the toys department).

EXHIBIT 2.1
Alb Inc.
Contribution Margin Analysis

	DEPARTMENTS			
	Clothing	Household Goods	Toys	TOTAL
Revenues	$900,000	$300,000	$50,000	$1,250,000
Total Variable Costs	300,000	250,000	70,000	620,000
Contribution Margin	600,000	50,000	(20,000)	630,000
Fixed Costs	100,000	100,000	100,000	300,000
Profits	$500,000	$(50,000)	$(120,000)	$330,000

OPERATING LEVERAGE

As discussed above, the total costs of producing a product (whether a physical good or service) are composed of both fixed and variable costs. The relationship between operating fixed costs and total operating costs is often referred to as **operating leverage**. The higher the proportion of total operating costs that are fixed, the higher the operating leverage. For example, assume that two firms each have total operating costs of $100,000. If one of these firms has $30,000 in fixed costs (i.e., 30% of total costs) and the second has $40,000 in fixed costs (i.e., 40% of total costs), the second firm is said to have a higher operating leverage.

Operating leverage is an important concept because it will affect operating profits. Generally speaking, high volume products will benefit more from high operating leverage than lower volume products. This is due to the fact that average fixed costs decrease as production or volume increase. Accordingly, it is important for managers to select the operating leverage in light of the planned level of production.

CONTRIBUTION MARGIN PARADOX

The above discussion of contribution margin may, at first glance, lead one to conclude that the pursuit of a positive contribution margin is a sufficient condition to guarantee overall profits. Of course, this is not the case because a firm's total fixed costs also need to be covered. In other words, a positive contribution margin is a necessary, but not sufficient, condition for overall profits. In the Alb illustration provided above, the positive contribution margins provided in the clothing and household goods departments were large enough to cover the firm's $300,000 fixed costs. However, even if each one of the three departments had a positive contribution margin, the sum of these positive contribution margins would have to equal or exceed the firm's total fixed costs if an overall loss were not to be incurred. To the extent that a firm's fixed costs are not covered, a loss will ultimately result (i.e., all costs, including those classified as fixed costs, need to be covered if profits are to be earned). Hence, a positive contribution margin is no guarantee that a firm will not lose money. This situation is referred to as the **contribution margin paradox**.

An alternative way of viewing the concern noted above is to recognize that, by definition, fixed costs are only fixed with respect to the number of units produced over a given time period. In the long-run (in terms of time periods), all costs are variable. Any firm that does not recognize this fact may well find itself in the awkward position of selling a product that has a positive contribution margin, but at an overall loss after considering the fixed costs. The financially troubled U.S. airline firms in the 1970s and 1980s, with their various forms of discounted travel tickets that were priced above variable costs but apparently not high enough to cover a fair share of fixed costs, seem to have been entangled in the contribution margin paradox.

RELEVANT COSTS VS. SUNK COSTS

Contribution margin and incremental analysis are two important profit planning concepts. Two other concepts which are also important to discussions of profit planning are relevant costs and sunk costs.

Relevant costs are costs that affect the decision under consideration. In making a particular decision, only relevant costs need to be considered. That does not mean that there are no other costs associated with the decision, but rather these other costs can be ignored (i.e., they are irrelevant) for the decision at hand. The following simple example should help make this concept clear.

Assume you are considering two job offers, both of which require a commute into a major city approximately 60 miles from your home. The commute will be exactly the same under either job and cost $3,000 per year (i.e., $250 per month). The **opportunity costs** (which are implicit costs of not using a resource in the best alternative) from commuting-downtime is also assumed to be the same from both job offers. Other aspects of the two jobs, such as salary, learning and advancement opportunities, wardrobe costs, and physical job surroundings do vary. In making your decision as to which job to choose, the commuting and opportunity costs are not relevant and should not affect your decision as to the choice of jobs. It should be noted, however, that the commuting costs of $3,000 per year are certainly real and, although not relevant to the decision at hand, will have to be paid. Although not involving an out-of-pocket payment, the opportunity costs associated with commuting-downtime are also real costs. Alternatively, if the decision at hand were to accept either, or neither, job, than the commuting and opportunity costs become relevant costs to the new decision at hand. In contrast, the varying wardrobe costs are relevant costs in terms of which job to accept. The other varying aspects of the two jobs (i.e., salary, learning and advancement opportunities, and physical surroundings) also need to be considered (i.e., they are relevant to the decision at hand).

A cost concept closely related to relevant costs is that of sunk costs. **Sunk costs** are costs that have been incurred, but are not relevant (i.e., they are irrelevant) to the decision under consideration. To illustrate this point, let us return to the above example. Assume the two job offers were the direct result of your recently completing a Master's degree at total "out-of-pocket" costs of $30,000. In terms of which job to accept, the $30,000 costs of your education are both irrelevant and sunk costs. Further, in terms of the decision to accept either, or neither, job, the costs of the graduate education are still irrelevant and sunk costs. However, the expected commuting costs from accepting either job are irrelevant, but not sunk costs. Hence, we see that all sunk costs are irrelevant, but not all irrelevant costs (e.g., the expected commuting costs in the above example) are sunk costs.[8]

Before leaving the discussion of sunk costs, the following point needs to be noted. The fact that certain costs are sunk, and thus irrelevant to a decision at hand, does not mean that the costs represent a poor investment. Indeed, the graduate education referred to above may well prove to be the best investment of your life!

Economics Approach to Profit Planning

The above discussion has assumed that variable costs and revenues behave in a linear fashion. In other words, it has been assumed that the average unit variable costs remain constant and, in turn, the total variable costs increase in direct proportion to the number of units produced. In terms of revenues, it has been assumed that the sales price per unit also remains constant and, in turn, the total sales increase in direct proportion to the number of units sold. As noted earlier, this approach to short-run profit planning is often referred to as the management accounting view of profit planning. In contrast, the economics view of short-run profit planning assumes that variable costs and revenues behave in a nonlinear fashion. More to the point, in economics it is assumed that total variable costs initially increase at a decreasing rate, and eventually increase at an increasing rate. This means that the average variable cost per unit (of good or service) initially declines, but eventually increases.[9] Total revenues, based on the economics view, are assumed to initially increase at a decreasing rate and eventually decrease. These points are illustrated in Figure 2.2.

---

8.   To the extent sunk costs are associated with items that have a recapture value
      (e.g., salvage or tax savings value), the sunk costs are reduced by the
      corresponding amount.

9.   For a more detailed discussion of the microeconomic aspects of cost analysis, see
      Appendix 2.1.

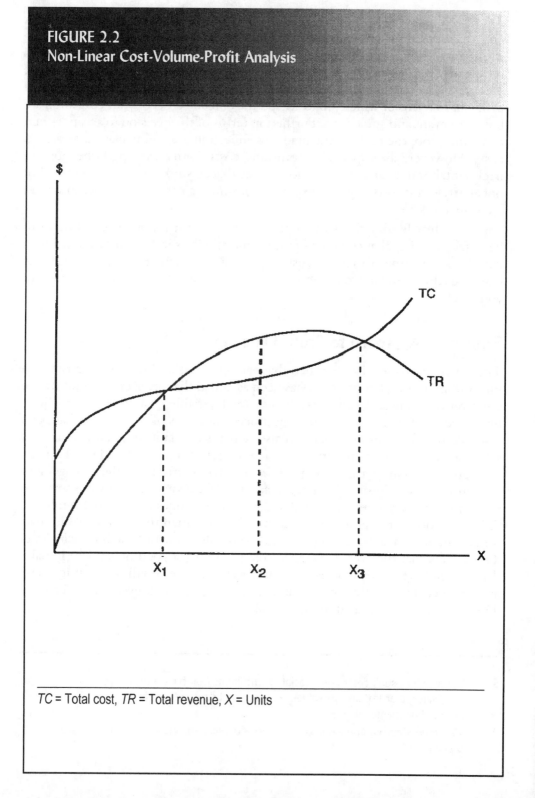

FIGURE 2.2
Non-Linear Cost-Volume-Profit Analysis

TC = Total cost, TR = Total revenue, X = Units

As can be seen from Figure 2.2, there are two breakeven points, X_1 and X_3, under the economics view of profit planning. Further, profits are maximized at point X_2. Hence, the economics approach to profit planning assumes that there is a specific point at which profits are maximized and the primary objective of the firm is to find that point. In essence, X_2 is the point where marginal revenue (MR) equals marginal cost (MC) as derived in the following:

$$\pi = TR - TC$$

$$\frac{d\pi}{dx} = \frac{dTR}{dx} - \frac{dTC}{dx} = 0$$

$$\frac{dTR}{dx} = \frac{dTC}{dx}$$

$$MR = MC^{10} \hspace{4cm} \text{Eq. 2.4}$$

The economics view to profit planning is theoretically sound, but extremely difficult to implement in most practical situations. In order to utilize this approach it is necessary to be able to estimate the total revenue and total cost functions of the organization. Unfortunately, estimating these functions is next to impossible in most organizations. In contrast, the management accounting view of profit planning is theoretically troublesome due to its assumption of linear costs and revenues, but easy to implement in most practical situations. That is, the approach relies on readily available accounting data. Thus, the validity of its use relies on whether the assumption of linear costs and revenues is realistic. Management accounting usually responds to this concern in terms of the relevant range of operations, as discussed below.

---

10. Technically speaking MR and MC are first derivatives of TR and TC, respectively (i.e., rate of change as $\Delta X \Rightarrow 0$). This concept is operationalized in economics in terms of the changes in revenues and costs associated with one extra unit.

RELEVANT RANGE OF OPERATIONS

For most organizations, it is quite reasonable to assume that the range of operations will not vary from zero to infinity. That is, in most firms it is probably reasonable to assume that the likely range of production is quite narrow. The lower bound of the production range is denoted X_L and the upper bound is denoted as X_U. Within this range (which is usually called the **relevant range**), it is assumed that the linearity of costs and revenues, as derived from accounting data, is realistic. Hence, the use of the management accounting view of profit planning seems appropriate in many real world situations. It should be emphasized, however, that this view does not attempt to maximize a firm's profit. Instead, it aims for a target level of profits as a satisfying mechanism. Accordingly, many firms use this approach as a means for identifying an initial target level of output and utilize the marginal concepts of economics for making incremental decisions. As a result, to the outside observer it may appear that firms are trying to maximize their profits when in fact they are trying to improve profits based on an existing satisfactory position. This relevant range concept is illustrated in Figure 2.3.

TAXES

The analysis thus far has not considered taxes. However, it is a straightforward matter to extend the analysis to include taxes. To begin, we note that a firm's profits after taxes are equal to its profits before taxes multiplied by one minus the tax rate (tr). Therefore, profits before taxes are equal to the profits after taxes divided by one minus the tax rate. To illustrate this point, let us return to Leta Inc. which wished to earn a $15,000 profit per year. This time, however, we assume the firm wants to earn this $15,000 after taxes. Further, the firm estimates that it will be in the 25% tax bracket. Equation 2.2 can be rewritten as follows:

$$X_\pi = \frac{FC + [\pi / (1 - tr)]}{P - VC} \qquad \text{Eq. 2.5}$$

$$\text{Hence, } X_\pi = \frac{\$57{,}600 + [\$15{,}000 / .75]}{\$20}$$

$$X_\pi = \frac{\$77{,}600}{\$20} = 3{,}880 \text{ units.}$$

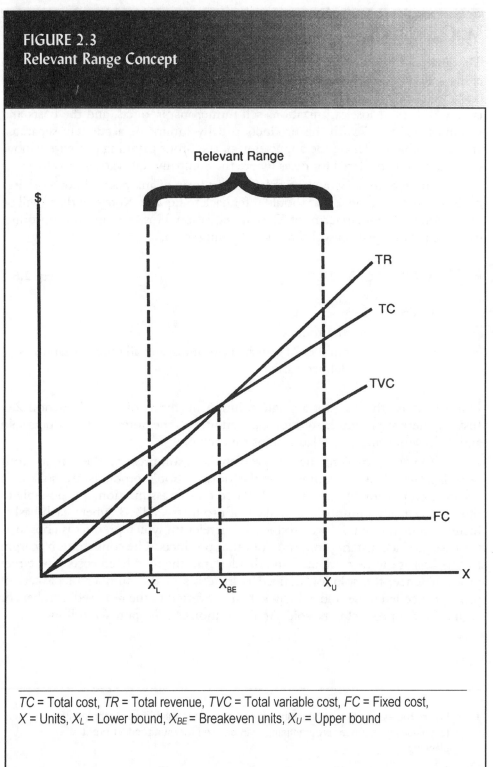

FIGURE 2.3
Relevant Range Concept

TC = Total cost, TR = Total revenue, TVC = Total variable cost, FC = Fixed cost, X = Units, X_L = Lower bound, X_{BE} = Breakeven units, X_U = Upper bound

MULTIPRODUCT CONSIDERATIONS

The analysis presented thus far has implicitly assumed that the organization either sells a single product or, if several products are sold, that each one can be considered independent of one another. Of course, neither of these assumptions is very realistic. Most organizations sell numerous products, and the costs and revenues associated with the products usually cannot be accurately separated among products. Hence, the application of the profit planning presented above needs to be reconsidered for cases where the company sells various products.

In order to see why the single product form of analysis will not work in a multiproduct case, the reader should refer back to Eq. 2.1. Note that there will be one unique solution, in terms of X, to this equation. However, in a multiproduct case, the profit equation will take the following form:

$$\pi = \sum_{i=1}^{n} X_i \left(P_i - VC_i \right) - FC \qquad\qquad \text{Eq. 2.6}$$

where,

i	=	ith product,
n	=	number of different products, and all other variables as defined earlier.

Unfortunately, there is not a single solution, in terms of X, to Equation 2.6. Instead, there are multiple solutions, depending on the number of products sold and the revenue and cost relationships for each one.

One way to overcome this problem, and still preserve the simple profit planning model, is to assume that the organization's products are sold in a constant proportion to one another.[11] Based on this assumption, it is possible to think in terms of a number of "baskets of products sold", B, where each basket includes one unit of the base product (it is irrelevant which product is chosen as the base) and a constant proportion of other products. The contribution margin for the basket can be computed and divided into the total fixed costs plus target profits. Hence, the solution derived is in terms of the number of baskets of products needed to be sold, which is then converted to the required number for each different product to be sold. An illustration of this approach follows.

---

11. Where the assumption of constant proportions is not valid, math programming techniques (e.g., linear programming) can be used for multiproduct profit planning.

   Maac Inc. is a manufacturing firm which produces two products. It is determined that for every unit of the first product sold three units of the second product are sold. In the relevant range, the sales price for the first product is $25 per unit and for the second product the sales price is $15 per unit. The variable costs per unit are $15 and $10 per unit for the first and second products, respectively. Total combined annual fixed costs are estimated at $100,000. The firm is in the 30% tax bracket and wishes to earn a $140,000 profit after taxes. The solution to this problem would be as follows:

$$B = \frac{FC + \left[\pi / (1-tr)\right]}{CM_B} \qquad\qquad \text{Eq. 2.7}$$

$$B = \frac{\$100,000 + \left[\$140,000 / .7\right]}{1(\$25 - \$15) + 3(\$15 - \$10)}$$

$$B = \frac{\$300,000}{\$25} = 12,000$$

   where,
   CM_B =   contribution margin per basket of goods, and all other variables as defined earlier.

Thus, in order to earn its target profit, Maac would have to sell 12,000 units of the first product and 36,000 units of the second product.

UNCERTAINTY CONSIDERATIONS

The analysis presented thus far has assumed a level of certainty, in terms of costs and revenues, not found in most real world situations (Clarke, 1986). For example, even if the sales price per unit, variable cost per unit, and fixed costs associated with a single product firm were known within the relevant range, a firm's ability to achieve a particular level of sales at a given price is uncertain. Hence, the likelihood that the firm will be able to sell enough units to earn a target level of profits or break even is uncertain.

   One way to consider the above problem is to view the firm's unit sales level as a random variable. The expected profits of the firm, under this approach, could be stated in probabilistic terms. Figure 2.4, which extends Figure 2.1b, illustrates this point under the assumption that the sales level is a normally distributed random variable.

FIGURE 2.4
Profit Line and Uncertainty

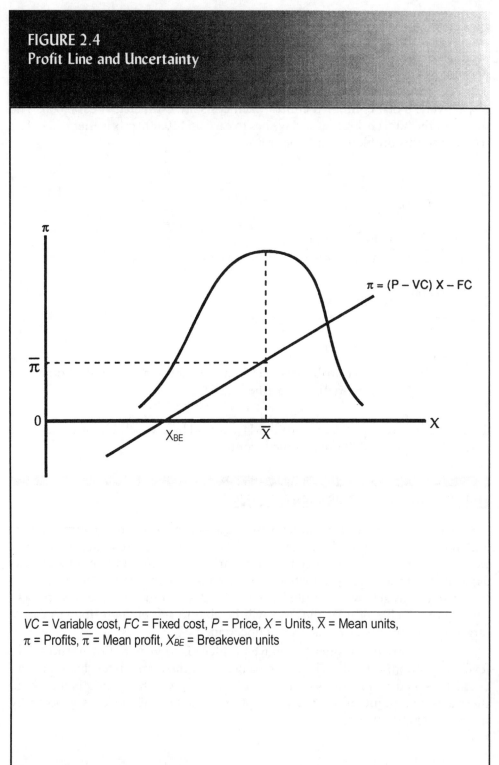

VC = Variable cost, FC = Fixed cost, P = Price, X = Units, $\overline{X}$ = Mean units,
π = Profits, $\overline{\pi}$ = Mean profit, X_{BE} = Breakeven units

In Figure 2.4, $\overline{X}$ represents the expected sales based on the assumption that X is a normally distributed random variable. The expected profits at this level are represented by $\overline{\pi}$. Given information concerning the cost and revenue structure and the sales level distribution, questions such as the following can easily be addressed.

- What is the probability that the firm will at least earn a particular target profit?

- What is the probability that the firm will at least break even?

- What is the probability that the firm will incur a loss equal to or greater than some specified level?

An illustration should help demonstrate how questions like these would be answered.

The H.G. Werp Co. is a small consulting firm which specializes in financial planning services. The firm charges an average of $100 per hour for its services. The variable costs incurred per chargeable hour are $60 and the fixed costs are $400,000 per year. The number of chargeable hours for the Werp Co.'s. consulting can be viewed as a random variable which is normally distributed. Based on past performance, the expected chargeable hours are 13,000, which results in before-tax profits of $120,000. The standard deviation, σ, is estimated (again, based on past performance) at 2,000 hours. As the new company controller, you are asked to determine the number of hours that must be billed to break even and the probability that the company will at least break even.

Given the assumptions, the number of hours that must be billed for Werp Co. to break even, X_{BE}, can be computed as follows:

$$X_{BE} = \frac{\$400,000}{\$40}$$

$X_{BE} = 10,000$ hours.

Hence, the probability, P, that Werp will at least break even can be derived as follows:

$$Z = \frac{X_{BE} - \overline{X}}{\sigma},$$

where

Z   =   the number of standard deviations that the breakeven
point is away from the mean.

$$Z = \frac{10,000 - 13,000}{2,000} = -1.5$$

$P (Z > -1.5) = .9332.$[12]

Of course, the complexities associated with addressing uncertainty in profit planning analysis would not be limited to treating the sales level as a random variable. For example, variable and/or fixed costs may also be treated as random variables. Where more than one of these variables are randomly distributed, the solution becomes extremely complex because joint probability functions need to be derived. Further, in a multiproduct firm, these complexities grow at an exponential rate.

INFORMATION NEEDS

Management accounting systems have traditionally emphasized information which is of a financial, ex post, and internal nature. This emphasis has been largely the result of financial accounting's influence on management accounting. However, as noted in the first chapter, effective utilization of accounting systems to support managerial planning and control requires a broader view of information. As is obvious from this chapter, the design of management accounting systems to support profit planning should take this fact into consideration.

Information on projected production levels is one example of the type of management accounting information required to successfully carry out profit planning. Information on external labor markets, such as industry labor cost trends, and customer profiles may also be very useful to conducting profit planning. Further, this information should be of a probabilistic nature. Of course, information of a broader scope should be viewed as a complement to, and not as a substitute for, more traditional management accounting information. For example, information on past product costs and revenues are also of fundamental importance to profit planning.

---

12.   The probability of a Z > -1.5 can be obtained from any standard table for the normal probability distribution.

CONCLUDING COMMENTS

Profit planning provides one meaningful perspective by which to view the use of a management accounting system. This perspective is based on three fundamental concepts.

- First, profits are equal to the difference between revenues and costs.

- Second, total costs can be divided between variable and fixed portions. In such a division, variable costs increase (decrease) with increases (decreases) in output, while fixed costs remain constant over different levels of output.

- Third, the difference between revenues and variable costs is the contribution margin.

Management accounting systems help provide the data related to all of these concepts.

Deriving cost and revenue data which is useful for profit planning, as well as other management decision making needs, is a nontrivial task. Nevertheless, a sound understanding of how this data is derived is essential if one is to be in a position to properly design and/or utilize a management accounting system. Hence, the next four chapters are devoted to explaining issues surrounding the gathering and processing of cost data which is useful for managerial planning and control. In Chapter 7, we will turn our attention to the issues surrounding the derivation of data related to revenues.

APPENDIX 2.1:
Cost Analysis

The conceptual underpinnings of cost analysis are largely derived from the part of the microeconomics literature which addresses issues concerned with production theory. According to this literature, a firm's outputs (i.e., its products) are viewed as a function of its inputs. This input-output relationship is referred to as a production function. In the short-run, some inputs are fixed and others are variable. The costs of a firm's fixed inputs represent its fixed costs. Total fixed costs are constant; hence, average unit fixed costs decrease (increase) as output increases (decreases). This view of fixed costs underlies our discussion of such costs in this chapter. The average fixed cost concept is illustrated in Figure 2.5.

The costs associated with a firm's variable inputs represent its variable costs. The economic concept of variable costs is based directly on the input-output relationship underlying a firm's production function, with particular focus on the concept of **returns to scale**. When outputs increase in equal proportion to increases in inputs (e.g., double inputs and outputs double), this situation is known as **constant returns to scale**. When outputs increase more rapidly than corresponding increases in inputs, this situation is known as **increasing returns to scale**. Conversely, when outputs increase less rapidly than corresponding increases in inputs, this situation is known as **decreasing returns to scale**. Assuming constant input prices, the relationship between the total costs of variable inputs and a firm's outputs is determined by whether the firm is operating in the region of constant, increasing, or decreasing returns to scale. In the region of increasing returns to scale, total variable costs are increasing at a decreasing rate. In the region of decreasing returns to scale, total variable costs are increasing at an increasing rate. In the region of constant returns to scale, total variable costs are increasing at a constant rate.

It should be recalled that accountants view variable costs as being linear (at least within the relevant range). In essence, the assumption underlying the linear variable cost approach is that of **constant returns to scale**. This explains why accountants usually view average variable costs as being constant. In contrast, the economic (nonlinear) view of average variable costs is directly related to the different regions of returns to scale in which a firm is operating. If a firm is operating in the increasing returns to scale region, then average variable costs are decreasing. In the constant returns to scale region, average variable costs are constant. In the decreasing returns to scale region, average variable costs are increasing. Marginal costs, therefore, initially decrease, level off, and then increase. These notions of average variable costs and marginal costs are illustrated in Figure 2.6. Average total costs are a combination of average variable costs and average fixed costs.

FIGURE 2.5
Average Fixed Costs

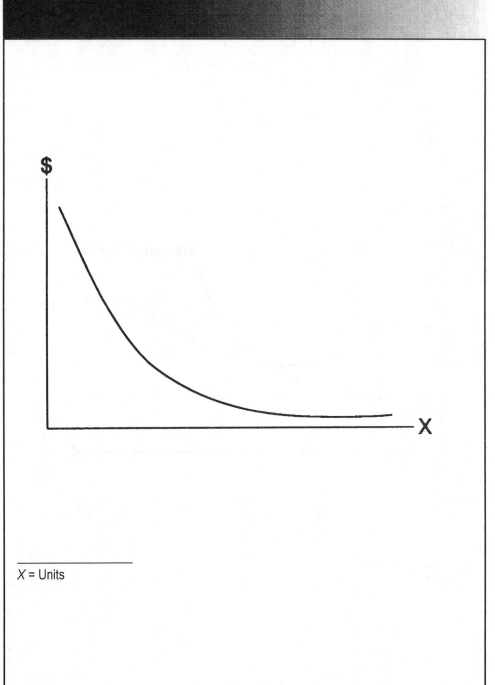

X = Units

FIGURE 2.6
Average Variable Costs and Marginal Costs

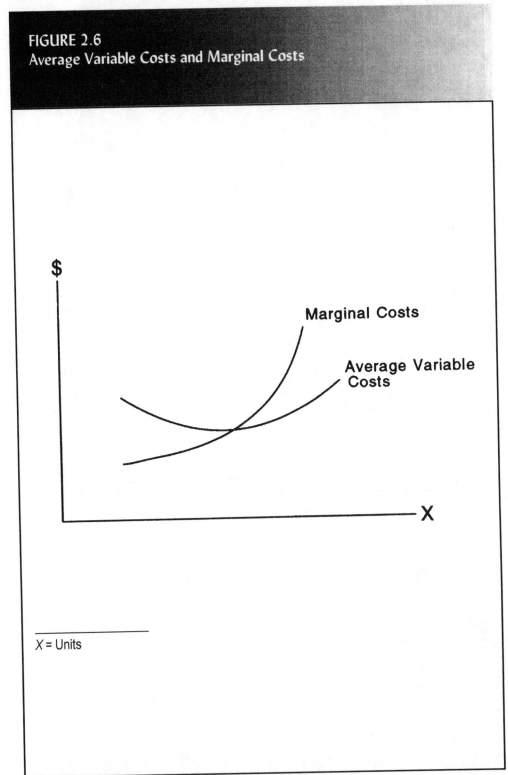

X = Units

PROBLEMS

Problem 2.1

BAT, Inc. is a new manufacturing company which sells men's ties for $18 per tie. The company presently has $1,600 per month in fixed costs and variable costs of $14 per unit. The company has an opportunity to buy new, high technology equipment which will add an additional $1,100 per month in fixed costs, but reduce direct labor costs by $2 per unit. The end result for an average sales month, if the new equipment is purchased, is that profits would increase by $400.

Required (Show all work):

A. Explain how the $400 increase in profits noted above was derived.

B. Assuming the $18 sales price is unchanged, at what average monthly sales level would the company be indifferent to having or not having the new equipment?

C. Provide a graph to demonstrate the cost-volume-profit relationships for having and not having the new equipment. (Label your graph(s), so that the relationships are clear.)

D. A key issue underlying the first three requirements of this problem concerns the trade-off between fixed and variable costs. Explain this issue in the context of the problem.

Problem 2.2

Ladg Company produces the following three different lines of personal computers: State of the Art, Professional, and Standard. The forecasts for the next year are:

	State of the Art	Professional	Standard
Sales (per unit)	$4,000	$2,000	$1,000
Variable Manufacturing Costs (per unit)	$2,000	$1,200	$700
Fixed Manufacturing Costs	$1,200,000	$2,000,000	$3,000,000
Units of Sales	1,000	5,000	10,000

In addition to the above, there are fixed costs of $1,000,000 to cover general and administrative expenses for the company as a whole.

Required (Show all work):

A.   Assuming the computers are sold in the above forecasted ratio of 1:5:10, how many units of each line of computers must be sold to break even?

B.   A market study shows that if the company reduces the selling price of the State of the Art line by $500, the sales of that line would be doubled. However, such a move would also cause a decline in sales of the Professional and Standard lines by 500 units and 1,000 units respectively. Should the price cut be undertaken?

C.   Instead of the information given in (b) above, assume the market study shows that if the company increases its advertising expenditures by $5,000,000, the sales of State of the Art, Professional and Standard will increase by 500 units, 2,000 units, and 3,000 units respectively. Should the advertising campaign be undertaken?

Problem 2.3

Kim and Jim are graduating from TOPS University at the end of this semester. Although they each have an offer (at $60,000 per year to start) from a large corporation, they are considering the possibility of starting up their own consulting firm. The plan, if they start up the consulting firm, would be to concentrate their efforts for the first year on marketing and implementing a decision support cost management software package they jointly developed. After the first year, they would expand into other consulting services.

Kim and Jim estimate that their new cost management software package could be sold for $15,000 per client, with variable costs of $5,000 per client. Fixed costs, apart from Kim and Jim's salaries, are expected to be $80,000 per year. In addition, Kim and Jim would like to draw a fixed salary of $40,000 each for the first year.

Before making a final decision on the consulting firm option, Kim and Jim decide to do some basic analysis along the lines required below (treat each part separately).

Required Analyses (Show all work):

A.   How many clients for the software package would Kim and Jim need in the first year to cover their fixed costs (including their own fixed salaries)?

B.   What salary, and how many clients, would Kim and Jim need in the first year to earn $40,000 each, after paying taxes at a personal tax rate of 20%?

C.   Assuming Kim and Jim share company profits equally, how many clients for the software package must Kim and Jim secure for them to earn, in the first year, the same level of total personal earnings (i.e., fixed salary plus a share of profits) in their consulting firm as they would have earned had they accepted the positions in the large corporations?

D.   It is possible for Kim and Jim to lower their first year's fixed costs by $48,000. If they do this, however, their variable costs will increase by $2,000 per client. If they do go with the consulting firm, should they make this trade-off between fixed and variable costs? (Explain your decision, with numbers to back up your position.)

Problem 2.4

Circle the answer which best describes the following concepts:

A.   Contribution margin paradox refers to:

(1)   the difference between revenues and variable costs;

(2)   the argument to close a department (or subunit) that does not have a positive contribution margin;

(3)   the notion that a positive contribution margin will not guarantee that a firm will not lose money;

(4)   the paradox that in the long run, all costs are variable.

B.   Sunk costs are:

(1)   costs that are relevant to the decision at hand, but not yet incurred;

(2)   costs which have been incurred, but are not relevant to the decision at hand;

(3)   costs which are both relevant to the decision at hand and have been incurred;

(4)   none of the above.

C.   The relevant range of operations is:

(1)   the firm's likely range of operations;

(2)   the range between the firm's breakeven sales level and its current operations;

(3)   the firm's range of operations that includes the point where marginal revenues equal marginal costs;

(4)   none of the above.

D.   The relationship between production levels and average per unit costs is:

(1)   effected by total variable and total fixed costs;

(2)   effected by total variable costs, but not total fixed costs;

(3)   effected by total fixed costs, but not total variable costs;

(4)   none of the above.

Problem 2.5 *(Adapted from CMA examination)*

Kipmar Company produces a molded briefcase which is distributed to luggage specialty stores. The following operating data from the current year has been accumulated in order to make plans for the coming year. Kipmar's physical plant has a practical capacity of 1,500,000 cases annually. The projected net income (after-tax profit) for the coming year is expected to be $1,800,000. Kipmar has no interest expense and is subject to an effective income tax rate of 40 percent.

Current Year Data	Molded Case
Selling price per case	$40.00
Variable costs per case	
Direct material	12.00
Direct labor	5.80
Manufacturing overhead	4.80
Selling expenses	3.00
Annual fixed costs	
Manufacturing overhead	$7,800,000
Selling expenses	1,550,000
Administrative expenses	3,250,000

Required:

A.   Kipmar Company has been reviewing its costs and expenses, and estimates that the cost of direct materials used in its molded briefcase will increase 15 percent in the coming year. Fixed administrative expenses are also estimated to increase by $150,000. All other costs and expenses are expected to remain at the same rates or levels experienced in the current year.

   1.   What dollar sales volume will Kipmar have to achieve in the coming year to earn the projected net income, $1,800,000?

   2.   How much would Kipmar have to charge for its molded briefcase in the coming year in order to maintain the same contribution margin ratio as that experienced in the current year?

B.   Kipmar Company is considering expanding its product line by introducing a leather briefcase in the coming year. Operating data for this proposed case follows.

Projected Data	Leather Case
Selling price per case	$90.00
Variable costs per case	
Direct material	18.50
Direct labor	7.50
Manufacturing overhead	6.00
Selling expenses	4.00

If Kipmar decides to introduce the leather briefcase, no additional manufacturing facilities would be required. Fixed advertising costs would be increased by $300,000 to promote both briefcases. Kipmar's Marketing Department has estimated that one new leather briefcase would be sold for every four molded briefcases. If Kipmar does introduce the leather briefcase in the coming year, maintains the current price on the molded briefcase, and experiences the cost changes detailed in Requirement A, how many units of each briefcase (molded and leather) would be required to break even in the coming year?

Problem 2.6 (Adapted from CMA examination)

GEAR-UP Co. produces gears and other machine parts. In 1994, the firm sold 704,000 gears. In recent years demand has accelerated, and the firm is approaching its full-production manufacturing capacity, which is estimated to be 900,000 gears. GEAR-UP's sales prices are in line with those of its competitors.

There are 345 non-unionized employees in the Production Department who worked 690,000 hours in 1994, and whose average wage per hour, including employee benefits, was $40 per hour.

In 1994, raw materials used in production cost $64 per unit, and the gear sold for an average sales price of $205. GEAR-UP's income statement for the year ended September 30, 1994, is shown below.

GEAR-UP Co.
Income Statement
For the Year Ended September 30, 1994

Sales		$144,320,000
Costs		
Labor	$27,600,000	
Raw materials	45,056,000	
Other manufacturing expenses	27,918,000	100,574,000
Gross margin		43,746,000
General & admin. expenses	36,185,000	
Marketing expenses	3,204,000	39,389,000
Income before taxes		4,357,000
Income taxes at 40%		1,742,800
Net income		$ 2,614,200
Fixed portion of 1994 costs:		
Other manufacturing costs	$14,518,000	
General & admin. expenses	36,185,000	
Marketing expenses	2,428,000	
Total fixed costs	$53,131,000	

At the annual shareholders' meeting, the owners expressed disappointment with these results. The economy is booming and demand for machine parts, particularly gears, is unprecedented. A new chief executive officer, John Henrich, was recently hired. In 1995, Henrich promises to deliver an increase in revenues exceeding 25 percent and a net income figure of at least 10 percent of revenue. To do this, he plans to increase fixed marketing expenses by 10 percent and increase sales to the level of full capacity. In addition, he plans to decrease all other fixed costs by 25 percent through a reengineering effort that will improve the efficiency of the company's processes.

Required:

A.   For GEAR-UP Co. for the year ended September 30, 1994, and the year ending September 30, 1995, as projected by John Henrich, calculate the

   1.   contribution margin.

   2.   before-tax breakeven point in gears.

   Assume that the selling price and variable cost rates remain the same. Round all numbers to two decimal places.

B.   If John Henrich succeeds in increasing sales and decreasing fixed costs as planned, will he be able to deliver on his promise for 1995 revenue and net income? Assume that the selling price and variable cost rates remain the same.

Problem 2.7 *(Adapted from the CMA examination)*

Garner Strategy Institute (GSI) presents executive-level training seminars nationally. They have been approached by Eastern University to present 40 one-week seminars during 1998. This activity level represents the maximum number of seminars that GSI is capable of presenting during a year. The week-long seminars would be presented by GSI staff in various cities throughout the United States and Canada.

   Terrie Garner, GSI's president, is evaluating three financial options for the revenues from Eastern.

   • Accept a flat fee for each seminar.
   • Receive a percentage of Eastern's "profit before tax" from the seminars.
   • Form a joint venture to share costs and profits.

   Estimated costs for the 1998 seminar schedule are given below.

	Garner Strategy Institute	Eastern University
Fixed costs		
Salaries and benefits	$200,000	N/A [1]
Facilities	48,000	N/A [1]
Travel & hotel	0	$210,000
Other	70,000	N/A [1]
Total fixed costs	$318,000	$210,000

Variable costs		Per Participant
Supplies & materials	$0	$47
Marketing	0	18
Other site costs	0	35

[1] Eastern's fixed costs are excluded because the amounts are not considered relevant for this decision (i.e., they would be incurred whether or not the seminars were presented). Eastern would not include these costs when calculating the "profit before tax" from the seminars.

Eastern plans to charge $1,200 per participant for each one-week seminar. All of the variable promotion, site costs, and materials costs will be paid by Eastern.

Required:

A.   Assume that the seminars are handled as a joint venture by Garner Strategy Institute (GSI) and Eastern University in order to pool costs and revenues.

    1.   Determine the total number of seminar participants needed to break even on the total costs for this joint venture. Show supporting computations.

    2.   Assume that the joint venture has an effective income tax rate of 30 percent. How many seminar participants would the joint venture need in order to earn a net income of $169,400? Show the supporting computations.

B.   Assume that no joint venture is formed by Garner Strategy Institute (GSI) and Eastern University, and GSI is an independent contractor for Eastern. The two payment options offered by Eastern to GSI are a

- flat fee of $9,500 for each seminar.
- fee of 40 percent of Eastern's "profit before tax" from the seminars.

Compute the minimum number of participants needed for GSI to prefer the 40 percent fee option rather than the flat fee. Show supporting computations.

3

COST ACCUMULATION AND MEASUREMENT

CHAPTER OUTLINE

■ Direct vs. Indirect Costs

■ Inventoriable vs. Period Costs

■ Cost/Product Flow

■ Applied vs. Actual Indirect Manufacturing Costs

■ Job Order vs. Process Costing

■ Absorption vs. Variable Costing

■ Just-in-Time Production System

■ Backflush Costing

■ Cost Accumulation and Measurement in Nonmanufacturing Firms

INTRODUCTION

As discussed in Chapter 2, costs play a critical role in deriving and planning for profits. Although the conceptual underpinnings of cost analysis seem straightforward, the practical aspects of accumulating and measuring costs are often anything but straightforward. These practical difficulties have led accountants to devote much effort to developing elaborate cost accounting systems for accumulating and measuring costs. In fact, the subfield of managerial accounting referred to as cost accounting (or cost management) is in large part devoted to measuring and accumulating costs. It is to these issues that we now turn. The approach will be to first consider cost accounting systems for manufacturing firms, followed by a discussion of such systems in nonmanufacturing firms.

DIRECT VS. INDIRECT COSTS

Costs are measured for various purposes. For example, manufacturing firms are interested in measuring the cost of a product, the cost of a particular activity, and the cost of a given department. The purpose for which a cost is being measured is referred to as the **cost objective**. **Direct costs** are those costs which can be directly related (traced) to the cost objective. In contrast, **indirect costs** (often called overhead costs, especially in a manufacturing setting) are those costs which cannot be directly related to the cost objective. Since a specific cost can be measured for multiple purposes, it is quite possible, even likely, for a specific cost to be direct with respect to one cost objective but indirect with respect to another. Further, whereas some direct costs are variable, others are fixed. In a similar fashion, some indirect costs are variable, whereas others are fixed. Figure 3.1 highlights this 2 x 2 dichotomy. In addition, the best way to measure a cost is dependent upon the purpose for which it is being measured. Hence, there is no one right way to measure a cost for all purposes.[1] To better understand these points, let us consider the following illustration of the Ren Corporation.

---

1.   Discussions relating to the fact that the appropriate way to measure a cost is dependent on the context in which the cost is being used, date back at least as far as Clark's (1923) seminal book.

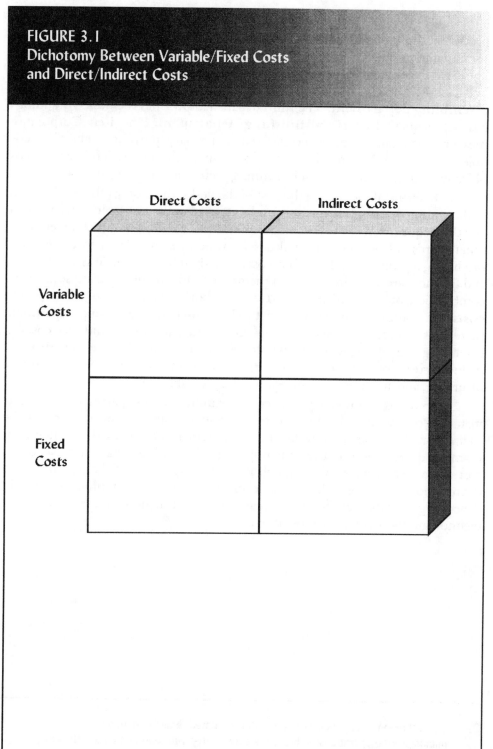

FIGURE 3.1
Dichotomy Between Variable/Fixed Costs
and Direct/Indirect Costs

The Ren Corporation manufactures wooden desks. This manufacturing process is accomplished in three sequential departments. The first department uses a lathe to cut desk tops and legs out of bulk lumber. This department is known as the **cutting department**. The second department assembles the desks by attaching the legs to the tops with a set of steel bolts and nuts. This is the **assembling department**. The third department finishes the desks by adding a coat of lacquer. This is the **finishing department.** The Ren Corporation measures its manufacturing costs for two primary purposes. The first cost objective is to determine the cost of producing the desks. The second cost objective is to measure the cost of running each of its three departments.

In terms of measuring the cost of the desks, the costs of the lumber used in the cutting department, the bolts and nuts used in the assembling department, and the lacquer used in the finishing department all represent direct materials. In other words, all of these material costs can be directly related to the costs of producing a given desk. The labor costs directly related to cutting, assembling, and finishing are also direct costs of the product. In a manufacturing setting, the combination of direct material and direct labor costs are often called **prime costs**.[2] In contrast, depreciation on the lathe used in the cutting department represents indirect costs with respect to the product. Other indirect costs of producing the product, which would be incurred in all three departments, include costs of utilities, depreciation on manufacturing plant facilities, insurance, and supervisors' salaries (i.e., indirect labor).

In terms of measuring the cost of running each department, the direct materials cost would also be direct department costs. However, some of the indirect product costs will now be direct costs with respect to the department. For example, depreciation on the lathe utilized in the cutting department is a direct cost of the department, even though it is an indirect cost of the product. This depreciation could be either variable or fixed (in terms of units produced), depending on whether the lathe wears out as a function of use or becomes technologically obsolete as a function of time.

---

2.   This definition of prime costs is somewhat outdated. Indeed, in many manufacturing operations, indirect costs associated with automation are the key (i.e., prime) costs.

INVENTORIABLE VS. PERIOD COSTS

Whereas retail firms have only finished goods inventory, manufacturing firms have several types of inventories. More specifically, they have raw materials, work-in-process, and finished goods inventories. (See the note to the Statement of Financial Position for International Business Machines (IBM) Corporation in Appendix 3.1.) The manufacturing costs, which are incurred as a result of producing these inventories, do not become an expense <u>until the inventory is sold</u>. Instead, these costs are initially treated as part of the firm's current assets (i.e., inventory) and are referred to as **inventoriable costs**. Both direct and indirect manufacturing costs of producing a product are treated as inventoriable costs. In contrast, the nonmanufacturing costs are treated as **period costs** and charged as operating expenses of the period.[3] These latter costs include selling expenses, nonmanufacturing administrative type expenses, and research and development expenses (see IBM's Statement of Operations in Appendix 3.1). The relationship between manufacturing costs (i.e., inventoriable costs) and nonmanufacturing costs (i.e., period costs) is shown in Figure 3.2.

COST/PRODUCT FLOW

Direct and indirect manufacturing costs, which are inventoriable costs, can be thought of in terms of a cost/product flowchart. Figure 3.3 provides such a chart for the Ren Corporation example discussed above. As shown in the figure, both direct and indirect manufacturing costs are incorporated into the value of the desks produced and do not become part of the period's expenses until the goods are sold.

An expanded view of Figure 3.3 is provided in Figure 3.4. In Figure 3.4 the direct materials costs, direct labor costs, and several possible indirect manufacturing costs (commonly referred to as manufacturing overhead costs) are listed. Figure 3.4 also highlights the fact that the manufacturing of a product does not involve one work-in-process department. For Ren Corporation there are three departments (i.e., Cutting, Assembling, and Finishing) involved in producing the desks. The partially completed desks in all three departments make up Ren's work-in-process.

---

3. Technically speaking, expenses can be thought of as expired costs. Hence, period costs are actually period expenses. Unfortunately, the accounting literature is not consistent in keeping the dichotomy between **costs** and **expenses**. If it were, cost of goods sold would be referred to as expenses of goods sold.

FIGURE 3.2
Manufacturing (Inventoriable) vs.
Nonmanufacturing (Period) Costs

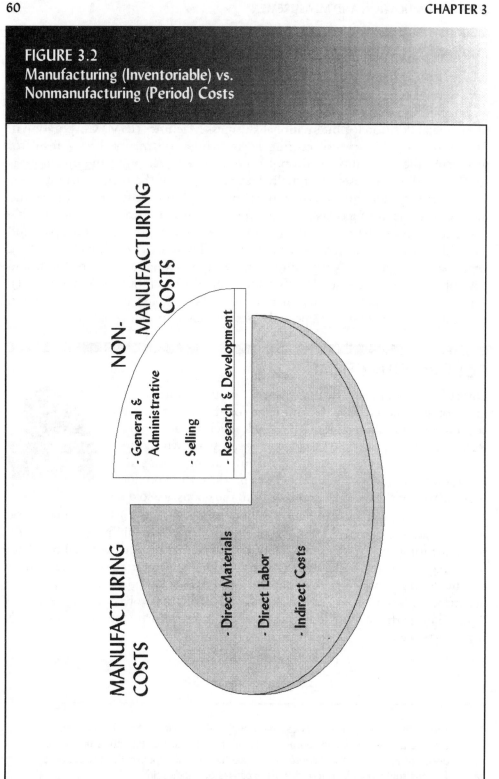

FIGURE 3.3
Ren Corporation
Basic Cost / Product Flow Chart for Manufacturing Firm

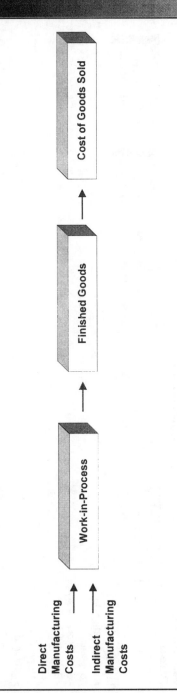

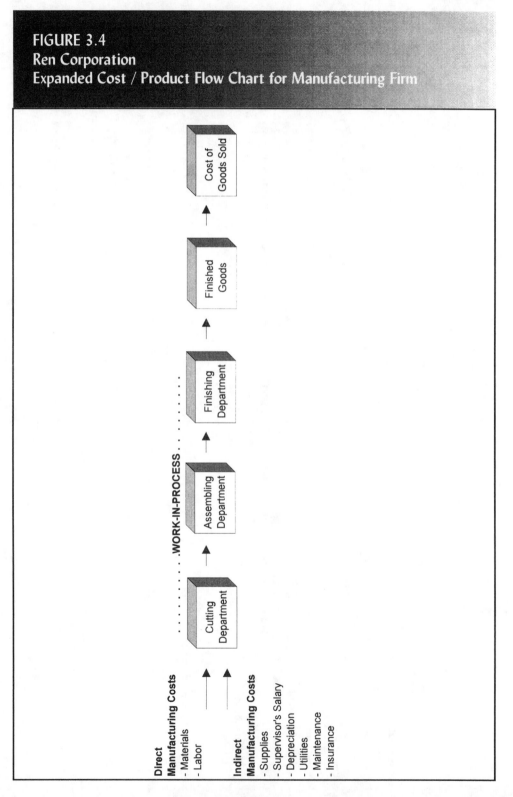

FIGURE 3.4
Ren Corporation
Expanded Cost / Product Flow Chart for Manufacturing Firm

As desks are completed, they are transferred to Ren's finished goods. Once desks are sold, their cost is transferred to cost of goods sold. Cost of goods sold, which is deducted from the firm's revenues to arrive at gross profit (see IBM's Statement of Operations in Appendix 3.1), can be computed as shown in the generic Cost of Goods Schedule illustrated in Exhibit 3.1.

APPLIED VS. ACTUAL INDIRECT MANUFACTURING COSTS

When cost accounting systems were first developed, it was normal for manufacturing firms to compute the actual cost of producing a product.[4] Over time, it became common for manufacturing firms to use cost accounting systems that charge the product with the actual direct costs of materials and labor, but charge the product for an estimate of the indirect manufacturing costs (i.e., manufacturing overhead costs). Today, such systems are often referred to as conventional costing systems. The actual procedure for estimating indirect costs is to derive an applied overhead rate based on some cost driver. More to the point, the indirect costs for the next time period (usually one year) are estimated and divided by the factor which presumably drives those costs. Then, as production takes place, the indirect costs are applied based on the overhead rate resulting from this division.

Let us return to the Ren Corporation which manufactures wooden desks to illustrate the idea underlying applied overhead costs. Assume that Ren estimates its next year's total indirect manufacturing costs for the plant as a whole to be $2,000,000. Further, assume that the firm has decided that the one factor most closely associated with driving these costs is the 1,000,000 direct labor hours estimated to be worked in the plant next year. (This single cost driver assumption will be modified in Chapter 5.) Given these estimations and the assumption that the firm uses a plant-wide overhead rate,[5] the firm would apply $2 of indirect costs (i.e., $2,000,000 /1,000,000 direct labor hours) for every direct labor hour worked on the product (i.e., the overhead rate is $2 per direct labor hour).

The use of an applied manufacturing overhead charge, in lieu of an actual charge, has several advantages. First, it averages out periodic aberrations in indirect costs, thereby giving a more realistic charge to a company's product(s). For example, assume a major piece of equipment breaks down and is repaired in a given month at a large cost. Further, assume the repair will benefit production for at least the next year. In this case, it would be inappropriate to charge units produced in the month for the entire repair cost. Instead, it would make more sense to spread these costs over the units produced during the entire time period

---

4.   For an excellent discussion on the history of cost accounting, see Johnson and Kaplan (1987).

5.   Some firms use a plant-wide overhead rate, whereas other firms derive an individual rate for each department.

EXHIBIT 3.1
Ren Corporation
Cost of Goods Sold Schedule

Direct materials used		X
Direct labor		X
Indirect Manufacturing Costs		X
Total Manufacturing Costs		XXX
+Work-in-Process at Beginning of Period	XX	
-Work-in-Process at End of Period	X	X
Cost of Goods Manufactured (Finished) this Period		XXXX
+Finished Goods at Beginning of Period		XX
Cost of Goods Available for Sale		XXXXXX
-Finished Goods at End of Period		XXXX
Cost of Goods Sold		XX

benefited. Second, the use of an applied overhead rate also averages out periodic aberrations in the level of activity associated with indirect costs. For example, assume in a given month production levels drop drastically relative to normal activity due to a labor strike which lasted for two weeks. It would be inappropriate to charge units produced in that month with an extraordinarily large share of indirect costs resulting from fixed supervisory salaries. Here again, it would make more sense to spread these costs over the entire period benefited from the newly agreed upon labor contract (e.g., the next year). Third, an applied overhead rate is helpful in situations where the determination of actual costs (e.g., utility charges) lags behind the production of products.

The three advantages presented above for using an applied overhead rate are based on the need to avoid aberrations in costs allocated to products produced during a particular period of time and the lag factor associated with accumulating actual costs. A fourth, and more generic, advantage is that an applied overhead rate facilitates organizational planning and control. Planning is facilitated via the need to identify and estimate the various indirect costs in advance of their actual occurrence. Such planning should be of major benefit to firms in terms of budgeting, pricing decisions, and financing decisions. An automatic outgrowth of this planning is control. That is, the ex ante activity of planning costs automatically permits the ex post control activity of comparing actual costs with planned costs. A careful analysis of the difference between actual and planned costs should be beneficial to firms in terms of decisions relating to future activities, as well as improving upon activities in progress.

JOB ORDER VS. PROCESS COSTING

The cost accumulation for a particular product can be accomplished in one of several ways. One such way is job order costing. Under **job order costing**, costs are accumulated by jobs. As a particular job is completed with respect to a given stage of production, the costs associated with that job are accumulated and moved to the next stage of production. This procedure is continued until the job is completed and placed in finished goods.

The accumulation of a job's cost is accomplished via a job cost sheet,[6] which contains the various direct costs and indirect manufacturing costs (i.e., overhead charged to the units in the job by the various production departments). Hence, direct and indirect manufacturing costs are assigned to the product on a job-by-job basis as the units in a particular job move through the various stages of production. The unit cost associated with a job is determined by dividing the total

---

6. In the pre-computer days, job cost sheets were manually maintained. Today, these documents are easily derived from a firm's computer-based cost accounting system.

costs by the number of units in the job. Job order costing is most appropriate for accumulating the costs associated with custom made products. In such situations, the product being produced presumably varies from customer to customer (e.g., high performance, military air planes for the U.S. Air Force).

At the other end of the spectrum, some products are mass produced by firms because no distinction exists between the product being purchased by one customer and that being purchased by another customer (e.g., gallons of regular milk). In these cases, a process costing system is most appropriate for accumulating the costs of a product. Under **process costing**, costs are accumulated by production processes rather than by jobs. As units of the product are completed with respect to one stage of the production process, a cost is assigned to those units and transferred to the next stage of the production process. A key aspect of process costing is that, at any given point in time, some units are completed with respect to a given stage of production whereas other units are not completed. Hence, in order to compute the cost of producing a product, there is a need to find a common denominator for finished and partially finished units in a given stage of production. This common denominator is referred to as the **equivalent units of production**.

The accumulation of a product's cost under a process costing system is accomplished via a cost-of-production report,[7] which contains the various direct and indirect manufacturing costs charged to the units in a given stage of the production process. Hence, direct and indirect manufacturing costs are assigned to the product based on the various stages of production for a given time period. The unit cost associated with a process costing system is determined by dividing the total costs of a production process by the equivalent units of production for the time period being considered. For example, assume that during a given time period 200 units of a product have been completed in the first stage of production and moved to the second stage. Further, assume that another 100 units have been half-completed (with respect to both direct and indirect costs) in the first stage of production during the time period under consideration. In determining how much of the costs to assign to the 200 units transferred to the second stage of production and how much to assign to the 100 half-completed units remaining in the first stage of production, the equivalent units of production would be 250 [i.e., 200 + (.5)(100)]. Thus, in this example, 80% (i.e., 200 completed units divided by 250) of the costs would be assigned to the units completed and transferred to the second stage of production and 20% (i.e., the equivalent of 50 completed units divided by 250) to the first stage of production.

As with job order costing, process costing involves an averaging notion in terms of computing a product's unit cost. In job order costing, the averaging takes place in terms of a particular job. In process costing, the averaging takes place in

---

7.   As with job cost sheets, cost-of-production reports are easily derived from a firm's computer-based cost accounting system.

terms of a particular process for a particular time period. Due to the need for utilizing the notion of equivalent units of production, the averaging under process costing usually involves more computational complexities than the averaging under job order costing.

Job order costing and process costing represent the opposite ends of the same continuum. In the middle of this continuum are various hybrid costing systems. For example, in some production processes, costs are accumulated based on batches. Under a **batch costing** system, the cost of a batch of mass produced units is accumulated and moved from one stage of production to the next. Batch costing is often used in situations where a firm mass produces variations of a given product (e.g., shoes). In such cases, the **conversion costs** (i.e., direct labor and indirect costs) may be the same for the various products, but direct material costs vary. An interesting example of a hybrid costing system is provided by Lee and Jacobs (1993) in their discussion of the Kunde Estate Winery.

It should be noted that for many firms it is not a case of using one costing system for all products. Instead, it is quite common for a given manufacturing firm to use one costing system for some products and other systems for other products. Hence, a given firm may be using job order costing, process costing, and hybrid costing systems in a parallel fashion.

Job Order Costing Illustration

In order to illustrate some of the key points noted above, consider the following job order costing example. This example is based on the earlier noted Ren Corporation, which manufactures wooden desks and uses a conventional cost accounting system (i.e., direct manufacturing costs are based on actual amounts, whereas indirect manufacturing costs are based on an applied overhead rate).

Assume Ren receives an order, call it job #22, for 100 desks. It takes two hours of direct labor to cut and shape each desk, one half hour to assemble, and one hour to finish a desk. The cost per hour for direct labor in each department is assumed to be: $15 for cutting, $5 for assembling, and $12 for finishing. With this information and that previously given regarding Ren's applied indirect manufacturing costs (i.e., application of indirect costs of $2 per direct labor hour, derived by dividing $2,000,000 by 1,000,000 direct labor hours), the direct labor costs and the application of indirect costs to each department can be derived. The direct labor costs for the cutting, assembling, and finishing departments are $3,000, $250, and $1,200, respectively, for 100 desks related to the job in question. Using the application rate of $2 per direct labor hour, the indirect costs applied are $400, $100, and $200, respectively.

Now consider the cost of direct materials. Assume the cost of bulk lumber required to cut the legs and desk tops is $20 per desk. The steel bolts and nuts used in the assembling department cost $1 per desk. The cost of lacquer used in the finishing department is $5 per desk. As a result, the direct material costs for each of the three departments are $2,000, $100, and $500, respectively.

Combining the direct materials, direct labor, and overhead costs, the amount of the work-in-process leaving the cutting department for job #22 as a whole is $5,400. This equals $54 per desk for 100 desks. (For simplicity, it is assumed there is no need to either rework or scrap any desks.) After completing the assembly of the desks, an additional $450 (or $4.50 per desk) has been added to the job with a resulting job cost of $5,850, or $58.50 per desk. Finally, the finishing department adds an additional $1,900 (or $19.00 per desk) to the cost of the job. Thus job #22 would ultimately have $7,750 of incurred and applied costs for a total of $77.50 per desk. This amount per unit is what will be added to finished goods inventory and charged to cost of goods sold as units are sold. The job cost sheet shown in Exhibit 3.2 summarizes the data presented in the example.

As summarized in Exhibit 3.2, the cost of producing the 100 desks is based on actual direct manufacturing costs and applied manufacturing indirect costs. Given that the applied overhead rate is based on estimates, it is quite likely that the actual overhead will differ from the applied amount. This difference is usually handled by keeping two overhead accounts—one to accumulate actual indirect manufacturing costs and one to accumulate the applied indirect manufacturing costs. At the end of some time period (e.g., a month or year) the charges to the applied overhead account (for all jobs) are transferred to the actual (sometimes called control) overhead account. The difference is usually charged to cost of goods sold.[8] If the actual overhead costs exceed the applied amount (i.e., overhead has been underapplied), cost of goods sold would be increased by the difference. If the actual overhead costs were less than the amount applied (i.e., overhead has been overapplied), cost of goods sold would be decreased by the difference. (Journal entries to record the information in the above example, including the actual sale of job #22, but excluding the transfer of applied overhead to the actual overhead account, are provided in Appendix 3.2.)

---

8.   Conceptually, the difference between actual and applied manufacturing overhead costs should be proportionately charged to cost of goods sold, finished goods, and work-in-process, depending on where the goods worked on are located. As a practical matter, most firms charge the difference to cost of goods sold. Where the amounts involved are relatively minor, this practical approach is usually justified on a cost/benefit basis.

EXHIBIT 3.2
Ren Corporation Job Cost Sheet

JOB STARTED: 4/15/94
JOB #: 22

COMPLETION DATE: 5/15/94
JOB DESCRIPTION: Wooden Desks
QUANTITY: 100

		CUTTING	ASSEMBLING	FINISHING
DIRECT MATERIALS	Quantity	100	100	100
	Unit Cost	$20.00	$1.00	$5.00
	Cost for 100 Desks	$2,000.00	$100.00	$500.00
DIRECT LABOR	Hours	200	50	100
	Rate	$15.00	$5.00	$12.00
	Cost for 100 Desk	$3,000.00	$250.00	$1,200.00
APPLIED OVERHEAD	$2 Per Direct Labor Hour	$400.00	$100.00	$200.00
DEPARTMENTAL COST		$5,400.00	$450.00	$1,900.00
CUMULATIVE TOTAL		$5,400.00	$5,850.00	$7,750.00
CUMULATIVE UNIT COST		$54.00	$58.50	$77.50

ABSORPTION VS. VARIABLE COSTING

Thus far it has been assumed that products will be charged with fixed as well as variable manufacturing costs. This means that the value of work-in-process and finished goods inventories will include charges for the fixed portion of manufacturing overhead (indirect) costs. In turn, cost of goods sold charges also will include fixed manufacturing overhead costs. Such an approach is referred to as an **absorption costing** system. In contrast, a **variable costing** system is one whereby only the variable manufacturing costs (i.e., direct materials, direct labor, and variable overhead) are considered inventoriable costs. Under a variable costing system, the fixed portion of manufacturing overhead is treated as period costs and charged to the income for the period incurred. The cost flow shown in Figure 3.4 would change accordingly.

To see how variable costing would differ from absorption costing, let us return to the Ren Corporation example illustrated in Exhibit 3.2. We begin by assuming that the total indirect manufacturing costs of $2,000,000 are evenly split between variable and fixed costs. Thus, under a variable costing system, applied overhead for job #22 would be $200, $50, and $100 for the cutting, assembling, and finishing departments. The total departmental costs for the 100 units would also change accordingly (i.e., $5,200 in cutting, $400 in assembling, and $1,800 in finishing) and the total cumulative unit cost would be reduced by $3.50 (i.e., $350/100) to yield a new cumulative cost of $74.00. As for the fixed portion of indirect manufacturing costs, under a variable costing system these costs would be charged to the period's operating expense as they are incurred.

There are several arguments in favor of using a variable versus an absorption costing system and vice-versa. For example, advocates for variable costing point out that variable costs are the only incremental costs and as such are the only **relevant costs** (i.e., costs which affect a decision) for contribution margin and profit maximization purposes.[9],[10] Advocates of variable costing also often point out that inventory values should not include fixed costs, since these fixed costs will be incurred regardless of the production level.

---

9. The reader should recall the discussion in Chapter 2, where it was shown that profit maximization takes place where marginal revenues equal marginal costs. The best, if not only, proxy for marginal costs in most firms is the accounting based variable costs.

10. For an excellent example of how variable costing can facilitate the contribution margin approach to performance analysis, see the article by Briner, Akers, Truitt, and Wilson (1989) concerning Martin Industries.

In contrast, absorption costing advocates usually note that in the long-run all costs are variable. Hence, they argue that managers need to consider fixed, as well as variable, costs associated with manufacturing. These advocates usually point out that a key reason managers fall into the contribution margin paradox (discussed in Chapter 2) is their haste in ignoring fixed manufacturing costs. Absorption costing advocates also argue that inventory values should include fixed as well as variable manufacturing costs. The argument in this latter regard is premised on the belief that fixed manufacturing costs are as essential to the production of inventory as are variable manufacturing costs.

For external reporting purposes, the absorption costing method is required by various accounting regulatory bodies in most countries. Nevertheless, the conceptual arguments on both sides of the variable/absorption costing controversy seem compelling. Hence, managers often find it useful to have access to both methods of costing for making various decisions. Empirical studies relating to pricing decisions show this to be the case (e.g., Gordon et al., 1981). (More will be said about this point in Chapter 7.) Given the current technological capabilities of computer based decision support cost accounting systems, such an approach is easily implemented in most firms.

JUST-IN-TIME PRODUCTION SYSTEM

There are several costs associated with stockpiling inventories, such as inventory storage and financing costs. There is also the possibility that inventories may become obsolete and, in turn, scrapped or sold for nominal amounts. In addition, the building up of inventory may slow down the efficiency of production and thus increase the **throughput time** (i.e., the time required to move a product through the entire production cycle, from start to final sale). Increased throughput time will in turn lead to increased production costs. As a result of the costs associated with inventory, many companies have pursued the goal of achieving a just-in-time production system.

A **just-in-time (JIT)** production system is one in which the goods in one stage of the production-sales cycle are completed just prior to being needed at the next stage. Hence, a JIT system strives to eliminate, or at least greatly reduce, inventories. In addition to saving the inventory costs noted above, a JIT system tends to push companies toward more efficient production processes. Hence, another benefit of JIT inventory systems is the elimination of non-value added activities.

The MAS can play an important role in facilitating a JIT production system. Since the JIT system is intended to eliminate, or at least greatly reduce, inventories, it is important for the MAS to include measures which signal inconsistencies with this goal. For example, by tracking throughput times, inventory levels, and delivery times, the MAS can alert the appropriate managers as to JIT inconsistencies.

A JIT system is not, however, problem-free. One potential problem is the increased dependency on suppliers created by the lack of inventory. This dependency is especially prevalent where suppliers provide intermediary products, rather than merely raw materials. Another potential problem with a JIT production system is that a sudden, unexpected demand for a final product may be very difficult, if not impossible, to meet. A JIT system also makes it more difficult for firms to take advantage of the economies of scale associated with inventory production and raw material purchases. One more potential problem with a JIT system is the fact that a temporary shutdown at one stage of production will necessarily stop production at further sequential stages. These problems can be thought of as the costs of a JIT system. In other words, there are costs associated with having, as well as not having, a JIT production system. The key is for a firm to minimize the sum of both these costs. Figure 3.5 illustrates the relationship between the costs of having, and not having, a JIT system.

In designing a JIT system, it is important for firms to consider, on an ex ante basis, a contingency plan for the potential problems noted above. A key aspect of this plan is to make sure that suppliers and the firm's production processes take a **total quality control** approach (i.e., an approach which assures continuous, high quality production) toward activities. Another aspect of such a contingency plan may be to develop a **flexible manufacturing system (FMS)**, whereby production facilities and activities are capable of quickly and easily being reconfigured.

BACKFLUSH COSTING

Backflush costing is a delayed costing system where the cost of producing a product is computed (i.e., flushed out) after the product is sold. That is, backflush costing focuses on the outputs (e.g., sales) and works backward to consider the input costs of production. Cost of goods sold and any remaining inventories are charged at a standard cost under such a system. Hence, backflush costing is a form of standard costing and is most appropriate when there is zero (or very little) inventory. Accordingly, backflush costing often is discussed in connection with JIT production systems.

Where work-in-process and/or finished goods exist, the appropriateness of backflush costing is directly related to the stability of input prices and inventory levels. The more stable the input prices, and the lower the level of inventories, the more appropriate is the use of backflush accounting. Where inventories do exist, the charging of standard cost variances to cost of goods sold would still occur, since to do otherwise would cause a firm to undo the backflush approach.

A key limitation of backflush costing, even where inventories are zero, is its lack of focus on cost management at the production level. In other words, since the actual costs are not tracked through the production process, planning and control of such costs are difficult, at best.

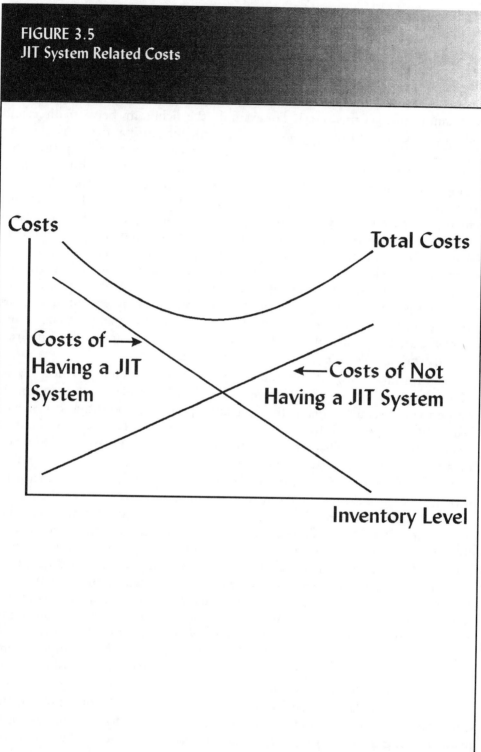

FIGURE 3.5
JIT System Related Costs

COST ACCUMULATION AND MEASUREMENT IN NONMANUFACTURING FIRMS

The concepts presented in this chapter have thus far focused on manufacturing firms. However, many of these concepts may also be applied to nonmanufacturing firms as well. For example, the dichotomy between direct and indirect costs is equally important to nonmanufacturing firms as it is to manufacturing firms. To illustrate this point, consider a consulting firm that receives its revenues from specific consulting contracts. These contracts can be thought of as the equivalent of a job order in a manufacturing firm. The direct labor costs to a contract would be the wages paid to the staff consultants, supervisors, partners, and secretarial support for their time spent directly related to that contract. Direct materials costs of a contract would typically be minimal. Nevertheless, some direct materials costs may be incurred, including the cost of specialized supplies used for the specific contract. Indirect costs of a particular contract would include a portion of office rent, utilities, national and local office administration, and the use of computers and other equipment. Indirect costs would also include a portion of the wages paid to partners and secretaries not directly related to a particular contract. Not surprisingly, some of these indirect costs may be variable whereas others may be fixed in nature.

Consulting firms do not build up an inventory of their products. Thus, whereas manufacturing firms emphasize the distinction between inventoriable and period costs, such a distinction is inappropriate for consulting firms. As a result, the emphasis shifts from accumulating the costs of inventory to estimating the costs of contracts. This estimation process provides the basis for bidding on consulting contracts (as discussed in Chapter 7).

As indicated above, consulting firms are different from manufacturing firms in that they do not, nor can they, build up an inventory of their basic product because their product is essentially a service rather than a tangible physical unit. Retail firms fall somewhere between manufacturing and consulting firms. Retail firms usually have a large amount of inventory, but only in the form of finished goods. In other words, unlike manufacturing firms, they do not have work-in-process or raw materials inventory. Nevertheless, most of the cost concepts discussed in the earlier sections of this chapter are relevant to retail firms as well. For example, consider Amb, Inc., which is a retail store specializing in three lines of women's clothing: dresses, sweaters, and pants. For purposes of assessing performance, the firm collects revenue and cost data on a product line basis. More specifically, the product line contribution margin and profits (before taxes) are key concerns to this firm.

In accumulating the required cost data, it should be obvious that the distinction between direct and indirect costs is as important to Amb, Inc. as it is to manufacturing and consulting firms. The same would be true for the distinction between variable and fixed costs. More to the point, a key concern in accumulating costs for Amb is the identification of the direct and indirect costs associated with each product line. In this regard, product line becomes a key cost objective. The cost of the merchandise for each product line and the labor costs directly associated with each product line would be direct costs. On the other hand, those costs not directly related to specific product lines (e.g., indirect labor, depreciation on the building, utilities) would represent indirect costs and some mechanism for allocating such costs would have to be derived. The issues associated with allocating these indirect costs are, in many ways, similar to those associated with allocating indirect costs in a manufacturing firm. In determining the contribution margin for each product line, Amb would need to separate fixed from variable costs.

CONCLUDING COMMENTS

The focus of this chapter has been on describing cost concepts and the basic accounting procedures used in accumulating costs. An important argument presented in this chapter, as well as the previous chapter, is that cost accounting techniques and concepts should be considered in terms of facilitating managerial planning and control. Indeed, the use of cost accounting for managerial planning and control purposes is seen by many as the cornerstone of management accounting. In recent years, this aspect of management accounting has been thought of in terms of managing costs and is sometimes referred to as **cost management**.

The importance of cost management cannot be overstated and Chief Executive Officers (CEOs) have clearly recognized this fact. Indeed, the letter to stockholders by the CEO of many corporations make reference to this very point. For example, in his letter to shareholders for the year ending 1995, the highly regarded CEO of Polaroid Corporation specifically noted the importance of reducing corporate overhead costs in meeting competitive cost targets (DiCamillo, 1996). In Hewlett-Packard's 1995 Annual Report, the CEO's letter to stockholders specifically noted that managing costs was an important contributing factor to the firm's profitability (Platt, 1995). The CEO of General Motors Corporation, in his annual letter to shareholders for the year ending 1996, also specifically noted the importance of managing costs, especially in a highly competitive industry (Smith, 1997).

There are many ways in which the basic concepts discussed in this chapter can be extended. One such extension concerns the use of standard costing techniques. Another such extension is in terms of more elaborate cost allocation techniques. Standard costing will be the focus of the next chapter, whereas Chapters 5 and 6 will concentrate on issues related to cost allocations.

APPENDIX 3.1:
Consolidated Statement of Earnings, IBM Corporation and Subsidiary Companies

(Dollars in millions except per share amounts) For the year ended December 31:	1997	1996	1995
Revenue:			
Hardware sales	$ 36,229	$ 36,316	$ 35,600
Services	19,302	15,873	12,714
Software	12,844	13,052	12,657
Maintenance	6,402	6,981	7,409
Rentals and financing	3,731	3,725	3,560
Total revenue	78,508	75,947	71,940
Cost:			
Hardware sales	23,538	23,396	21,862
Services	15,281	12,647	10,042
Software	3,784	4,082	4,428
Maintenance	3,394	3,659	3,651
Rentals and financing	1,902	1,624	1,590
Total cost	47,899	45,408	41,573
Gross profit	30,609	30,539	30,367
Operating expenses:			
Selling, general and administrative	16,634	16,854	16,766
Research, development and engineering	4,877	4,654	4,170
Purchased in-process research and development	–	435	1,840
Total operating expenses	21,511	21,943	22,776
Operating income	9,098	8,596	7,591
Other income, principally interest	657	707	947
Interest expense	728	716	725
Earnings before income taxes	9,027	8,587	7,813
Provision for income taxes	2,934	3,158	3,635
Net earnings	6,093	5,429	4,178
Preferred stock dividends and transaction costs	20	20	62
Net earnings applicable to common shareholders	$ 6,073	$ 5,409	$ 4,116
Net earnings per share of common stock	$ 6.18	$ 5.12*	$ 3.61*
Net earnings per share of common stock – assuming dilution	$ 6.01	$ 5.01*	$ 3.53*

Average number of common shares outstanding:
1997 – 983,286,361; 1996 – 1,056,704,188*; 1995 – 1,138,768,058*

* Adjusted to reflect a two-for-one stock split on May 9, 1997.

The notes of the 1997 IBM Annual Report are an integral part of this statement.

The financial statements in this Appendix are from IBM's 1997 Annual Report.

APPENDIX 3.1 (continued): Consolidated Statement of Financial Position, IBM Corporation and Subsidiary Companies

Assets

Current assets:		
Cash and cash equivalents	$ 7,106	$ 7,687
Marketable securities	447	450
Notes and accounts receivable – trade, net of allowances	16,850	16,515
Sales-type leases receivable	5,720	5,721
Other accounts receivable	1,256	931
Inventories	5,139	5,870
Prepaid expenses and other current assets	3,900	3,521
Total current assets	40,418	40,695
Plant, rental machines and other property	42,133	41,893
Less: Accumulated depreciation	23,786	24,486
Plant, rental machines and other property – net	18,347	17,407
Software, less accumulated amortization		
(1997, $12,610; 1996, $12,199)	819	1,435
Investments and sundry assets	21,915	21,595
Total assets	$ 81,499	$ 81,132
Liabilities and Stockholders' Equity		
Current liabilities:		
Taxes	$ 2,381	$ 3,029
Short-term debt	13,230	12,957
Accounts payable	5,215	4,767
Compensation and benefits	3,043	2,950
Deferred income	3,445	3,640
Other accrued expenses and liabilities	6,193	6,657
Total current liabilities	33,507	34,000
Long-term debt	13,696	9,872
Other liabilities	12,993	14,005
Deferred income taxes	1,487	1,627
Total liabilities	61,683	59,504
Contingencies		
Stockholders' equity:		
Preferred stock, par value $.01 per share –		
shares authorized: 150,000,000		
shares issued: 1997 – 2,597,261; 1996 – 2,610,711	252	253
Common stock, par value $.50* per share –		
shares authorized: 1,875,000,000*		
shares issued: 1997 – 969,015,351; 1996 – 1,018,141,084*	8,601	7,752
Retained earnings	11,010	11,189
Translation adjustments	791	2,401
Treasury stock, at cost (shares: 1997 – 923,955;		
1996 – 2,179,066*)	(86)	(135)
Employee benefits trust, at cost (10,000,000 shares)	(860)	–
Net unrealized gain on marketable securities	108	168
Total stockholders' equity	19,816	21,628
Total liabilities and stockholders' equity	$ 81,499	$ 81,132

Note D. Inventories (in Millions) at Dec. 31	1997	1996
Finished Goods	$1,090	$1,413
Work-in-Process	4,026	4,377
Raw Materials	23	80
Total	$5,139	$5,870

The notes of the 1997 IBM Annual Report are an integral part of this statement.
The financial statements in this Appendix are from IBM's 1997 Annual Report.

APPENDIX 3.2:
Ren Corporation—Journal Entries for Job Order Costing Illustration

	Debit	Credit
Work-in-process (Cutting)	$5,400.00	
Lumber inventory		$2,000.00
Wages payable		3,000.00
Applied overhead		400.00
Work-in-process (Assembling)	5,400.00	
Work-in-process (Cutting)		5,400.00
Work-in-process (Assembling)	450.00	
Bolts and nuts inventory		100.00
Wages payable		250.00
Applied overhead		100.00
Work-in-process (Finishing)	5,850.00	
Work-in-process (Assembling)		5,850.00
Work-in-process (Finishing)	1,900.00	
Lacquer inventory		500.00
Wages payable		1,200.00
Applied overhead		200.00
Finished Goods Inventory	7,750.00	
Work-in-process (Finishing)		7,750.00
Cost of Goods Sold	7,750.00	
Finished Goods Inventory		7,750.00

PROBLEMS

Problem 3.1

Explain why some operations are best suited for a job order costing system, while others are best suited for a process costing system. When would a hybrid costing system (i.e., something between a job order and process costing system) be most appropriate?

Problem 3.2

Elite, Inc., a small manufacturer of men's shirts, uses a job order costing system. Unfortunately, on May 1,1997, there was a major fire in the company's plant that destroyed the entire finished goods and all "hard copy" records relating to such inventory. Fortunately, other inventories (i.e., raw materials and work-in-process) are handled in a different part of the plant which was not affected by the fire. The company is now in the process of filing a claim with its insurance company. In order to confirm computer records concerning the value of the inventory lost due to the fire, the following information was gathered:

Balance Sheet—December 31, 1996

Direct Materials Inventory—$10,000
Work-in-Process Inventory—$40,000
Finished Goods Inventory—$30,000

Inventory—May 1, 1997

Direct Materials Inventory—$15,000
Work-in-Process Inventory—$18,000

The January 1 through April 30, 1997 sales were determined to be $90,000. Also, over the past couple of years, gross profits have been averaging 40% of the company's sales. Purchase orders show that direct materials purchased during the first four months of 1996 were equal to $22,000. Payroll records show that direct labor costs for the same period were $30,000 and overhead (i.e., indirect costs) were applied at 50% of direct labor costs.

Required (Show all work):

A.   Determine the value of the finished goods inventory lost due to the fire based on the above.

B.   Would your answer to (A) above be different if Elite, Inc. used a process costing system rather than a job order costing system? Explain your answer.

Problem 3.3

As a manager not involved in the actual calculations related to your products' costs, why is it important for you to understand how such costs are derived?

Problem 3.4

The costs associated with stockpiling inventories have led many firms to pursue a JIT (just-in-time) production system. However, a JIT system is not without problems. These problems result in the "costs of having a JIT system."

Required:

Discuss the potential costs associated with having, and not having, a JIT production system.

Problem 3.5 *(Adapted from CMA examination)*

ErgoFurn Inc. manufactures ergonomically designed furniture for computer stations. ErgoFurn uses a job order cost system and employs the full absorption accounting method for cost accumulation. ErgoFurn's work-in-process inventory at April 30, 1993, consisted of the following jobs.

Job No.	Item	Units	Accumulated Cost
CC723	Computer caddy	20,000	$ 900,000
CH291	Chair	15,000	431,000
PS812	Printer stand	25,000	250,000
			$1,581,000

At April 30, 1993, the company's finished goods inventory, which is evaluated using the first-in, first-out (FIFO) method, consisted of four items.

Item	Quantity & Unit Cost	Accumulated Cost
Computer caddy	7,500 units @ $64 each	$ 480,000
Chair	19,400 units @ $35 each	679,000
Printer stand	21,000 units @ $55 each	1,155,000
Desk	11,200 units @ $102 each	1,142,400
		$3,456,400

At the end of April, the balance in ErgoFurn's Materials inventory account, which includes both raw materials and purchased parts, was $668,000. Additions to, and requisitions from, the materials inventory during the month of May included the following.

	Raw Materials $242,000	Purchased Parts $396,000
Requisitions:		
Job CC723	51,000	104,000
Job CH291	3,000	10,800
Job PS812	124,000	87,000
Job DS444 (5,000 desks)	65,000	187,000

ErgoFurn applies factory overhead on the basis of machine hours. The company's factory overhead budget for the fiscal year ending May 31, 1993, totals $4,500,000, and the company plans to expend 900,000 machine hours during this period. Through the first eleven months of the year, a total of 830,000 machine hours were used, and total factory overhead amounted to $4,274,500.

During the month of May, machine hours and labor hours consisted of the following:

Account	Machine Hours	Labor Hours	Labor Cost
CC723	12,000	11,600	$122,400
CH291	4,400	3,600	43,200
PS812	19,500	14,300	200,500
DS444	14,000	12,500	138,000
Indirect labor		3,000	29,400
Supervision			57,600
			$591,100

Listed below are the jobs that were completed and the unit sales for the month of May.

Job No.	Item	Quantity Completed
CC723	Computer caddy	20,000
CH291	Chair	15,000
DS444	Desk	5,000

Item	Quantity Shipped
Computer caddy	17,500
Chair	21,000
Printer stand	18,000
Desk	6,000

Required:

A. Describe when it is appropriate for a company to use a job order cost system.

B. Calculate the dollar balance in ErgoFurn Inc.'s work-in-process inventory account as of May 31, 1993.

C. Calculate the dollar value of the chairs in ErgoFurn Inc.'s finished goods inventory as of May 31, 1993.

D. Explain the proper accounting treatment for overapplied or underapplied overhead balances when using a job order cost system.

Problem 3.6 *(Adapted from CMA examination)*

Kristina Company, which manufactures quality paint sold at premium prices, uses a single production department. Production begins with the blending of various chemicals, which are added at the beginning of the process, and ends with the canning of the paint. Canning occurs when the mixture reaches the 90 percent stage of completion. The gallon cans are then transferred to the Shipping Department for crating and shipment. Labor and overhead are added continuously throughout the process. Factory overhead is applied on the basis of direct labor hours at the rate of $3.00 per hour.

Prior to May, when a change in the process was implemented, work-in-process inventories were insignificant. The change in the process enables greater production but results in material amounts of work-in-process for the first time. The company has always used the weighted average method to determine equivalent production and unit costs. Now, production management is considering changing from the weighted average method to the first-in, first-out method.

The following data related to actual production during the month of May.

Costs for May	
Work-in-process inventory, May 1	
(4,000 gallons 25% complete)	
Direct materials—chemicals	$45,600
Direct labor—($10 per hour)	6,250
Factory overhead	1,875
May costs added	
Direct materials—chemicals	228,400
Direct materials—cans	7,000
Direct labor ($10 per hour)	35,000
Factory overhead	10,500

Units for May	
	Gallons
Work-in-process inventory, May 1 (25% complete)	4,000
Sent to Shipping Department	20,000
Started in May	21,000
Work-in-process inventory, May 31 (80% complete)	5,000

Required:

A.   Prepare a schedule of equivalent units for each cost element for the
      month of May using the

      1.   weighted average method.

      2.   first-in, first-out method.

B.   Calculate the cost (to the nearest cent) per equivalent unit for each cost
      element for the month of May using the

      1.   weighted average method.

      2.   first-in, first-out method.

Problem 3.7 (Adapted from CMA examination)

Byrd Company is a manufacturer of small appliances for both residential and
commercial use. The company's accounting and financial reporting system is
primarily designed to meet external reporting requirements in accordance with
generally accepted accounting principles. For inventory costing purposes, Byrd
uses the absorption costing method in conjunction with a standard costing system.
Relevant information on one of Byrd's product lines is provided below for the last
two years. The standard costs for this product have not changed since 1990.

Unit Information	1992	1993
Beginning inventory	900	1,400
Production	2,000	400
Sales	1,500	1,700
Normal activity	2,000	2,000
Other Data		
Sales price per unit	$100.00	$100.00
Standard prime costs per unit	40.00	40.00
Standard variable overhead cost per unit	15.00	15.00
Variable marketing and administrative costs per unit sold	1.00	1.00
Total budgeted (and actual) fixed manufacturing costs	10,000	10,000
Total fixed marketing and administrative costs	3,000	3,000
Net unfavorable variance* pertaining to variable manufacturing costs	1,000	1,000

*All variances are expenses in the period incurred.

Currently, Byrd evaluates the performance of its product line managers and calculates bonuses on the basis of operating income computed on an absorption costing basis. It has been suggested that the use of variable costing for internal reporting purposes would more accurately reflect the performance of the product line managers.

Required:

Using the data provided above, calculate Byrd Company's operating income for 1992 and 1993 using

A.   absorption costing

B.   variable costing

4

STANDARD COST SYSTEM

CHAPTER OUTLINE

- Standard Cost Concept

- The Demise of Standard Costing Myth

- Standard Costs and Nonmanufacturing Activities

INTRODUCTION

This chapter builds upon the cost accumulation and measurement concepts covered in Chapter 3. The particular topic covered is a standard cost system. The key advantage of a standard cost system is its ability to facilitate planning and control. Hence, the discussion will focus on this aspect of standard costing.

STANDARD COST CONCEPT

The generic rationale discussed in Chapter 3 for using an applied manufacturing overhead rate, in lieu of actual overhead costs, is the fact that it facilitates planning and control. This argument is not limited to indirect manufacturing costs. Planning and control for the direct costs of manufacturing also would be facilitated if these costs were initially estimated prior to deriving the actual costs. For example, the ex ante estimates of direct (as well as indirect) manufacturing costs should be of major benefit to firms in terms of budgeting and bidding decisions related to competitive jobs. At the same time, an automatic outgrowth of planning for direct manufacturing costs (e.g., direct materials and direct labor) is the ex post control activity of comparing actual costs with planned costs. This control activity is beneficial to firms in terms of decisions related to future activities, as well as improving upon activities in progress. In addition, the control activity can be used as a performance evaluation device.

The importance of planning and control for direct and indirect costs has been well recognized by large manufacturing firms. This recognition has led a large number of manufacturing firms to use a standard cost accounting system. Under a **standard cost system**, both direct and indirect manufacturing costs are initially estimated. Further, the quantity aspects of production are also estimated. These estimates are referred to as *standards* and are used as the basis for product costing. This means that inventories and cost of goods sold are valued at standard, rather than actual, costs. At the end of a given period, a reconciliation of the differences between standard and actual costs takes place.

The appropriateness of using a standard costing system is contingent upon the type of product being produced. Products which are mass produced are strong candidates for a standard costing system because the costs and quantity aspects of producing the product are often relatively stable over a large number of units and several time periods. In contrast, products produced on a one time, special order basis usually do not lend themselves to a standard costing system.[1]

---

1.   If a one time, special order (e.g., construction of a building) were composed of regularly used subcomponents, a standard costing system could be appropriate in such a situation.

The empirical evidence indicates that a large percentage of manufacturing firms use a standard cost system. For example, in a study of 104 of the Fortune 1000 largest industrial companies, Landeman and Schaeberle (1983) found that 50 of the firms used only standard costs for product costing purposes, and another 32 used standard costs in conjunction with actual costs. Hence, 79% (i.e., 82/104) of the firms participating in the study used standard costs, in one form or another, to derive the cost of manufacturing a product. A more recent study by Gaumnitz and Kollaritsch (1991) found that 87% of large U.S. manufacturing firms are using standard costing systems. An illustration of a standard cost system follows.

Standard Cost Illustration

Returning to our manufacturer of wooden desks discussed in Chapter 3, Ren Corporation, assume that for every desk produced it is estimated that one sheet of plywood, at a cost of $20, will be used in the cutting department. Each sheet is large enough to produce the top and legs for one desk. It is also estimated that it takes two hours of direct labor, at a cost of $15 per hour, to cut the wood for each desk produced in this department. It is also estimated that under normal conditions, 5,000 desks per month, and thus 60,000 desks per year, will be produced. Further, next year's indirect costs for the cutting department are estimated to be $240,000, evenly divided over the 12 months. (For this example, it is assumed that each department derives its own overhead rate.) Of the $240,000, $180,000 are variable costs and $60,000 are fixed costs. Hence, on a monthly basis, $15,000 are indirect variable costs and $5,000 are indirect fixed costs. Both the variable and fixed portions of indirect costs are allocated based on direct labor hours. Given these assumptions, the cutting department's standard (i.e., planned) cost of producing one desk is $54 per desk, determined as follows: direct materials of $20 per desk; direct labor of $30 (i.e., $15 x 2) per desk; indirect (overhead) costs of $4 per desk (i.e., $240,000/60,000 desks). Exhibit 4.1, part A, summarizes the above information. In other words, the cutting department's costs used in the illustration in Chapter 3 are now considered the standard costs for the next year. Hence, for every desk completed in the cutting department, a total standard cost charge of $54 is added to inventory costs.

EXHIBIT 4.1
Data for Standard Cost Illustration
Ren Corporation, Cutting Department

MONTH OF JANUARY

A. STANDARDS

Normal level of production (per month)
is 5,000 desks

1 sheet of plywood per desk, at $20 per sheet	=	$20.00 per desk
2 direct labor hours per desk at $15 per hour	=	$30.00 per desk
Indirect costs (2 hours per desk)		
Variable: $15,000 / 10,000 hours $= \$1.50 \times 2hrs/desk \; DL \, hr.$ =		$3.00 per desk
Fixed: $5,000 / 10,000 hours	=	1.00 per desk
Total Standard Cost	=	$54.00 per desk

B. ACTUALS

Number of desks produced	4,800
Sheets of plywood purchased	5,200
Sheets of plywood put into production	4,824
Direct labor hours worked	9,500
Plywood cost per sheet	$21
Labor cost per hour	$16
Indirect costs	
Variable	$17,100
Fixed	$4,900

Under a standard costing system, the cost flow illustrated in Figure 3.3 is based on standard costs. Hence, as Ren Corporation's units move from the cutting to the assembling department, $54 per desk would be transferred from work-in-process (cutting) to work-in-process (assembling). Once the actual costs associated with cutting the desks are derived, they are compared to the standard costs and any difference, usually called variance, is analyzed. A management report containing an analysis of standard cost variances can be prepared for Ren's cutting department at regular intervals (e.g., once a month).[2] This comparison of actual with standard costs is the control activity referred to earlier.

The process taking place in the cutting department would also take place in Ren's assembling and finishing departments. Only now, both the transferred costs and the individual department's costs would be part of the accumulation and processing charges. As desks are sold, the charge to cost of goods sold would be at the accumulated standard costs for all three (i.e., cutting, assembling, and finishing) of Ren's producing departments. At the end of the year, an adjustment to cost of goods sold would be made for differences between actual and standard costs.[3]

To demonstrate how the variances between actual and standard costs are computed, let us continue with the above example concerning Ren Corporation's cutting department. At the end of January, the actual level of production and actual costs are determined to be as summarized in part B of Exhibit 4.1. Based on the data in Exhibit 4.1, the differences between actual and standard costs are derived as shown in Exhibit 4.2.[4] The analysis of standard cost variances shown in Exhibit 4.2 derives a total of eight separate variances, as illustrated in Figure 4.1.

The material price variance shown in Exhibit 4.2 is based on the units of material purchased, rather than the units of material put into production. The reason for isolating this variance at the time of purchase is based on the argument that variances should be determined at the earliest possible time.

---

2. As noted by Gaumnitz and Kollaritsch (1991), standard cost variance reports are most frequently prepared on a monthly basis, although some firms prepare weekly or daily reports.

3. Conceptually, the entire adjustment for differences between standard and actual costs should be charged to cost of goods sold only if all of the goods associated with the differences were sold. If a portion of the goods were not sold, then inventories should be charged with a share of the adjustment. On a practical level, most firms charge cost of goods sold for the entire adjustment.

4. Other methods of analyzing standard cost variances exist which either combine or expand upon these eight variances.

EXHIBIT 4.2
Analysis of Differences (Variances) between Actuals and Standards, Ren Corporation, Cutting Department

MATERIALS *vs used*	
(1) Actual Quantity Purchased (5,200) • Actual Price ($21)	$109,200
(2) Actual Quantity Purchased (5,200) • Standard Price ($20)	104,000
Price Variance (1-2), Unfavorable	**5,200**
(3) Actual Quantity Placed in Production (4,824) *used* • Standard Price ($20)	96,480
(4) Standard Quantity for Level of Production Achieved (4800) • Standard Price ($20)	96,000
Quantity Variance (3-4), Unfavorable	**480**
LABOR	
(1) Actual Hours Worked (9,500) • Actual Labor Rate ($16)	152,000
(2) Actual Hours Worked (9,500) • Standard Labor Rate ($15)	142,500
Rate Variance (1-2), Unfavorable	**9,500**
(3) Standard Hours for Level of Production Achieved (9,600) • Standard Labor Rate ($15) *└ 4800 desks × 2 D6H*	144,000
Efficiency Variance (2-3), Favorable	**(1,500)**
VARIABLE OVERHEAD *$17,100 / 9,500 DL hrs*	
(1) Actual Hours Worked (9,500) • Actual Variable Overhead Rate ($1.80)	17,100
(2) Actual Hours Worked (9,500) • Standard Variable Overhead Rate ($1.50)	14,250
Spending Variance (1-2), Unfavorable	**2,850**
(3) Standard Hours for Level of Production Achieved (9,600) • Standard Variable Overhead Rate ($1.50)	14,400
Efficiency Variance (2-3), Favorable	**(150)**
FIXED OVERHEAD	
(1) Actual Fixed Overhead	4,900
(2) Budgeted Fixed Overhead	5,000
Budget Variance (1-2), Favorable	**(100)**
(3) Standard Fixed Overhead for Level of Production Achieved ($.50 • 9,600)	4,800
Volume Variance (2-3), Unfavorable	**200**

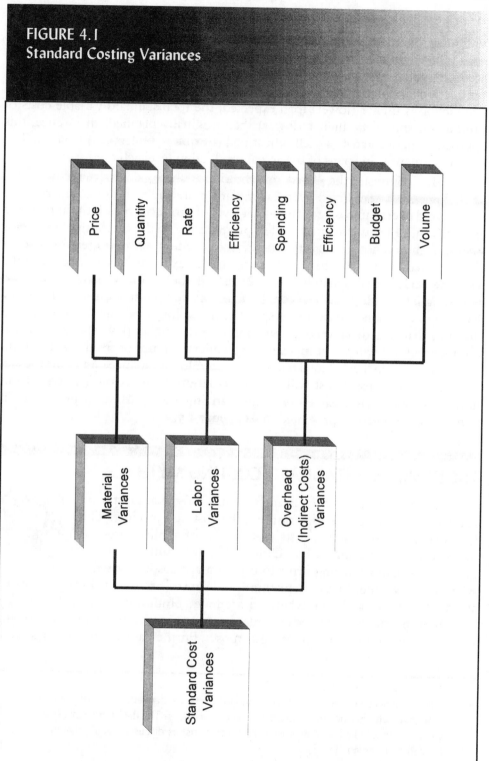

FIGURE 4.1
Standard Costing Variances

It should be emphasized, however, that the analysis in Exhibit 4.2 of the differences (variances) between actual and standard production related to variable costs is based on the actual (not standard) level of production. This is based on the argument that it makes the most sense to compare the actual costs for a production level with the standard costs for the same level of activity. If the actual production is higher (lower) than expected, the total standard variable costs of production should be higher (lower) than originally planned. In essence, this approach incorporates a self-adjusting (flexible) budgeting device. The self-adjustment is in terms of the actual production level achieved.

In contrast, the fixed overhead variances do not include this self-adjusting device. Fixed overhead variances are the result of comparing the actual fixed overhead costs for the actual level of production with the anticipated fixed overhead for the normal level of production. To the extent that total fixed overhead should not vary at different levels of production, a **budget variance** is not expected. However, there is no such similar expectation with regard to the **volume variance** shown in Exhibit 4.2. Instead, the volume variance is intended to highlight the difference between the actual level of production and the normal level of production. To be more specific, the volume variance is intended to illustrate that an actual level of production which is higher (lower) than a normal production level will result in a smaller (higher) amount of fixed cost per unit. Hence, for a given level of total fixed costs, the volume variance highlights the fact that the per unit fixed cost will vary as actual production volume varies from normal activity.[5] (Journal entries summarizing the illustration presented in Exhibits 4.1 and 4.2 are presented in Appendix 4.1).

THE DEMISE OF STANDARD COSTING MYTH

In the early years of cost accounting systems, most manufacturing firms used actual costs in determining the cost of a product. The first step away from actual costs was the use of applied rates for indirect manufacturing costs. Ultimately, it became common practice for manufacturing firms to use standard costing systems. As noted above, there are both planning and control arguments in favor of using standard costs. In addition, where an accurate compilation of actual costs lags behind the production of goods, standard costing permits timely product costing for inventory and financial reporting purposes. Further, a standard costing system

---

5.   Once variances between actual and standard costs are derived, it is important to
      determine whether or not to investigate such variances. The decision to investigate
      variances should be based on cost/benefit concerns, as discussed by Dyckman
      (1969) and Kaplan (1975).

averages out aberrations in various production costs due to periodic increases (decreases) in input prices and/or activity levels.

Most firms using a standard costing system assume that some changes in business conditions, and in turn product costs, will occur. Indeed, through an analysis of standard cost variances, these changes are identified and utilized for learning, correcting (e.g., the revision of standards), and evaluating purposes. This fact notwithstanding, a standard cost system does assume that future costs are stable enough to make the use of standard costs meaningful. The validity of these assumptions will of course vary from product to product, firm to firm, industry to industry, country to country, and time period to time period. However, a growing number of researchers and practitioners argue that the global business environment is changing too rapidly for an effective application of standard costs. Further, the fact that many operations have become less labor and more machine intense has led many to argue that the benefits derived from computing labor cost variances are greatly reduced. These arguments, coupled with the technological ability to quickly and accurately collect and process data, have led many to call for the demise of standard cost accounting systems in favor of using actual costs (sometimes called running actual, or real time, costs).

Recent evidence suggests that some firms are listening to the call in favor of actual costs. For example, Tyson et al. (1989) found that several firms are switching from using standard costs to using actual costs, especially in connection with products best suited for job order costing systems. Despite the move by some firms toward actual costs, the planning and control aspects of a standard cost accounting system continue to provide key benefits for many firms. More to the point, the use of standard costs forces a firm to develop a detailed ex ante plan related to the product's costs and production level. It is less likely that such a detailed plan would result under a system using actual costs. Further, the presence of such a plan permits a more detailed and accurate level of control, which in turn should assist future planning. In addition, for many products it is still difficult to assess actual costs in a timely manner. Hence, a large percentage of firms still find it advantageous to use standard costs for many of their products—especially those that are mass produced under a process costing system. In fact, the study referred to earlier by Gaumnitz and Kollaritsch (1991) not only found that 87% of large manufacturing firms are using standard costing systems, but also found that such use is on the rise, not decline. In recent discussions between the author of this book and five major U.S. manufacturing firms, all five firms indicated that they are using (in one form or another), and have no intention of abandoning, a standard costing system. Studies of companies based in countries other than the U.S. (e.g., Sweden and Ireland) also indicate that standard costing systems are commonly used (Ask and Ax, 1992; Clark, 1992). Thus, it would appear that reports of the demise of standard costing systems are greatly exaggerated.

STANDARD COSTS AND NONMANUFACTURING ACTIVITIES

Standard costs are actually a special case of planned (or budgeted) costs. The special case when the use of standard costs is considered most appropriate is where a detailed, specifiable relationship (sometimes called engineering relationship) exists between inputs and outputs. (The reader should recall from Chapter 2 that the mapping of inputs to outputs is often referred to as a production function.) Such a relationship is common for manufacturing activities. Accordingly, the use of standard costs usually has been associated with manufacturing costs. However, nonmanufacturing activities can also be represented by the production function concept of showing detailed relationships between inputs and outputs. Hence, the notion of computing standard costs can be, and often is, meaningfully applied to nonmanufacturing costs within manufacturing firms, as well as to entire nonmanufacturing firms.

To understand the use of standard costing systems for nonmanufacturing activities, consider selling expenses of a firm. If the selling activities of the firm in question could be broken down to a cost per sales unit, then a standard cost per unit of selling could be derived. By way of an example, consider the McG Corporation. This firm purchases various brands of watches, which it then sells through a distribution system of retailers. On average, the firm normally sells 100,000 watches per year and it estimates that its total distribution (selling) expenses (including both variable and fixed costs) for next year will be $300,000. Given these facts, the McG Corporation estimates its standard distribution expenses to be $3 (i.e., $300,000/100,000 watches) per watch.[6]

CONCLUDING COMMENTS

Standard costs facilitate planning by forcing firms to anticipate or forecast their costs prior to their actual occurrence. The comparison of these planned or anticipated costs to the actual costs is the control side of standard costs. The planning and control benefits of a standard costing system are recognized by managers, as evidenced by the fact that a large percentage of manufacturing firms currently use such systems. Where a standard costing system is used, it is common for managers to receive periodic (e.g., monthly) reports summarizing the cost variances.

---

6.   Some firms have a **distribution cost accounting** system, which in effect derives a standard selling cost per unit of product. A distribution cost accounting system is extremely beneficial for firms wishing to use the **cost defense**, under the U.S. Robinson Patman Act, in defending against a price discrimination charge.

The planning and control benefits of a standard cost system are not limited to manufacturing activities. Nonmanufacturing activities within manufacturing firms, as well as nonmanufacturing firms, may benefit from the use of standard costs. This claim notwithstanding, there are circumstances where it may be preferable to use actual costs rather than standard costs (e.g., for a special order, in a highly uncertain business environment). Hence, it seems best to view the appropriateness of using a standard cost system as being contingent upon the characteristics of the firm's product(s) and environment.

APPENDIX 4.1:
Ren Corporation
Journal Entries for Standard Cost Illustration

	Debit	Credit
Materials Inventory	$104,000	
Materials Price Variance	5,200	
Accounts Payable		$109,200
Work-in-process (Cutting)—Materials	96,000	
Materials Quantity Variance	480	
Materials Inventory		96,480
Work-in-process (Cutting)—Labor	144,000	
Labor Rate Variance	9,500	
Labor Efficiency Variance		1,500
Salaries Payable		152,000
Variable Overhead—Control	17,100	
Accounts Payable		17,100
Work-in-process (Cutting)—Overhead	14,400	
Variable Overhead—Applied		14,400
Variable Overhead—Applied	14,400	
Variable Overhead Spending Variance	2,850	
Variable Overhead—Control		17,100
Variable Overhead Efficiency Variance		150
Fixed Overhead—Control	4,900	
Accounts Payable		4,900

(continued on next page)

APPENDIX 4.1 *(continued)*

	Debit	Credit
Work-in-process (Cutting)—Overhead	$4,800	
Fixed Overhead—Applied		$4,800
Fixed Overhead—Applied	4,800	
Fixed Overhead Volume Variance	200	
Fixed Overhead—Control		4,900
Fixed Overhead Budget Variance		100
Cost of Goods Sold[a]	16,480	
Labor Efficiency Variance	1,500	
Variable Overhead Efficiency Variance	150	
Fixed Overhead Budget Variance	100	
Materials Price Variance		5,200
Materials Quantity Variance		480
Labor Rate Variance		9,500
Variable Overhead Spending Variance		2,850
Fixed Overhead Volume Variance		200

[a] For illustrative purposes it is assumed that standard cost variances are transferred to cost of goods sold on a monthly basis. The usual approach is for such variances to be transferred at the end of the year.

PROBLEMS

Problem 4.1

Assume you are a new Assistant Controller in a major manufacturing firm which uses a standard cost system. The Controller of the firm, Ms. Baker, has recently read several articles that argue against standard costing systems and in favor of using actual costs. As a result of these articles, Ms. Baker asks you to prepare a memo outlining the strengths and weaknesses of using a standard costing system versus an actual costing system.

Problem 4.2

One objective of global competitiveness is being able to produce products at, or below, the costs incurred by competitors with similar products. Explain how a standard costing system can help a firm meet this objective.

Problem 4.3

At a recent senior management meeting, the Controller of your company stated the following: "When periodic (e.g., annual) standard cost variances are charged to cost of goods sold, profits vary as a result of variations in production levels even if sales for the period were zero." As you left the meeting, one of your colleagues asked you to explain the Controller's statement.

Required:

A.   Explain the Controller's statement.

B.   What, if anything, is wrong with having a firm's profits vary as a function of production levels irrespective of sales levels?

C.   If standard cost variances were charged to the goods produced, rather than the cost of goods sold, would the Controller's statement still be true? Explain.

D.   Why is it so common for firms to charge standard cost variances to cost of goods sold?

Problem 4.4

As the Assistant Administrator of a large hospital, you believe it is time for your hospital to consider initiating a standard costing system. Upon mentioning this idea to your boss, the hospital's Administrator (i.e., senior administrative officer), your idea is quickly rebuffed. In fact, in a rather stern tone, the Administrator says the following: "This is a hospital, not some manufacturing firm. Our doctors and nurses are trying to save lives, not produce a cheaper mouse trap." You reply by saying that "of course we are concerned with saving lives. However, the health care environment has gone through significant changes over the past 10 years and it is time for the accounting system to help facilitate those changes." After hearing your response, the Administrator says to you: "Okay, prepare a brief memo outlining why you believe a standard costing system may be appropriate for a hospital."

Required:

Prepare the memo requested by the Administrator.

Problem 4.5 *(Contributed by Raghavan Iyengar)*

Rita, a client, requested your assistance in analyzing the operations of her firm which uses a standard costing system. "I am completely lost here. I received the income statements for the past two quarters from the divisional manager (see Exhibit A). The sales have declined in the second quarter, but the net income has shot up! I think something strange is going on here. It appears as if the divisional manager is hiding his losses somewhere. Could you look into this for me?"

Exhibit A

	1st Quarter	2nd Quarter
Sales Revenue ($200 per unit)	$1,000,000	$900,000
Less: Standard Cost of Materials (2 pounds of material for each unit at a standard cost of $60 per pound)	600,000	540,000
Other Cost of Sales	100,000	90,000
Standard Gross Profit	$300,000	$270,000
Material Price Variance	194,000U	---
Material Usage Variance	30,000F	54,000U
General and Administrative Costs	50,000	50,000
Net Income	$86,000	$166,000

(U = Unfavorable Variance, F = Favorable Variance)

Rita confirms that material price variances are isolated at the time of purchase and that all materials were bought in the first quarter. Rita also affirms that she had no inventory at the beginning of the first quarter or at the end of the second quarter.

Required:

A.   How many pounds of material were bought in the first quarter?

B.   At what price per pound was the material purchased?

C.   Do you agree that the manager has manipulated the income statement in the second quarter to reflect an increase in net income despite the fall in sales? Explain.

Problem 4.6 (Adapted from CMA examination)

Leather Works is a family-owned maker of leather travel bags and briefcases located in the northeastern part of the United States. Foreign competition has forced its owner, Heather Dimesdale, to explore new ways to meet the competition. One of her cousins, Wallace Harding, who recently graduated from college with a major in accounting, told her about the use of cost variance analysis to learn about efficiencies of production.

In May 1994, Dimesdale asked Neil Jones, chief accountant, and Alfred Prudest, production manager, to implement a standard cost system. Jones and Prudest, in turn, retained Cecilia Pangloss, an accounting professor at Harding's college, to set up a standard cost system by using information supplied to her by Jones' and Prudest's staff. To verify that the information was accurate, Pangloss visited the plant and measured workers' output using time and motion studies. During those visits to the plant, she was not accompanied by either Jones or Prudest, and the workers knew about Pangloss' schedule in advance. The cost system was implemented in June 1994.

Recently, Dimesdale asked Jones and Prudest how the business was performing. Prudest was the first to respond, "You know, we are producing a lot more than we used to, thanks to the contract you helped obtain from B.B. Lean for Laptop Covers." B.B. Lean is a national supplier of computer accessories. Jones then said, "Thank goodness for that new product. It has kept us from sinking even more due to the inroads into our business made by those foreign suppliers of leather goods." Dimesdale then asked about the standard cost system and was told that the variances are mostly favorable, except for the first three months, when the supplier of leather started charging more. "How did the union take to the standards?" Dimesdale then asked. Prudest responded, "Not bad. They grumbled a bit at first, but they've taken it in stride. We've consistently shown favorable efficiency labor variances as well as positive material quantity variances. The labor rate variance has been flat." Jones added, "It should be since labor rates are negotiated by the union representative at the start of the year and they remain the same for the entire year." Before moving on, Dimesdale asked Jones to send her the variance report for Laptop Covers immediately.

In the chart below are summaries of the material and labor variances from November 1994 through April 1995 for the Laptop Covers. Standards for each Laptop Cover are

- three feet of material at $7.50 per foot.

- 45 minutes of labor at $14 per hour.

In addition, the data for May 1995, but not the variances for the month, are given below.

Laptop Covers made in May	2,900 units
Total actual material costs incurred	$68,850
Actual quantity of material used	8,500 feet
Total actual labor cost incurred	$25,910
Total actual labor hours	1,837.6 hours

Actual labor cost per hour exceeded the budgeted labor rate by $.10 per hour.

			Laptop Covers		
Month	Actual Expense*	Material Price Variance	Material Efficiency Variance	Labor Rate Variance	Labor Efficiency Variance
November	$150,000	$10,000U	$5,000F	$100U	$5,000F
December	155,000	11,000U	5,100F	110U	6,500F
January	152,000	10,100U	4,900F	105U	7,750F
February	151,000	9,900U	4,500F	95U	6,950F
March	125,000	9,000U	3,000F	90U	8,200F
April	115,000	8,000U	2,000F	90U	8,500F

*Represents actual money spent on both material and labor.

Required:

A.   For Leather Works, calculate the following variances for the month of May 1995.

- material price variance.
- material efficiency variance.
- labor rate variance.
- labor efficiency variance.

B.   Discuss the resulting trend of the material and labor variances.

Problem 4.7 *(Adapted from CMA examination)*

Smylan Company employs a standard costing system using absorption costing. The standards for manufacturing overhead are established at the beginning of each year by estimating the total variable and fixed manufacturing costs for the year and then dividing the costs by the estimated activity base. Smylan has a fairly automated manufacturing operation, and the variable overhead closely follows machine hour usage. Thus, machine hours are used to apply both variable and fixed manufacturing overhead.

The standard manufacturing overhead application rates shown below were based on an estimated manufacturing overhead for the coming year of $4,080,000 of which $1,440,000 is variable and $2,640,000 is fixed. These costs were expected to be incurred uniformly throughout the year. The total machine hours (MH) for the expected annual output, also expected to be uniform throughout the year, were estimated at 120,000 MH.

Standard Manufacturing Overhead Application Rates	
Variable	$12 per MH
Fixed	22 per MH
Total	$34 per MH

Smylan has reduced production in the past three months because orders have been down. In fact, manufacturing activity for the current month was 80 percent of what was expected. This reduced level of demand for Smylan's products is expected to continue for at least the next three months.

Sara Edwards, cost accountant, has prepared some preliminary figures on manufacturing overhead for the current month at the request of Frank Paige, vice president-production, and these amounts are presented below.

Manufacturing Overhead Preliminary Figures for the Month		
Actual machine hours for the month		<u>8,050</u>
Standard machine hours allowed for actual output produced		<u>8,000</u>
Total applied manufacturing overhead		$272,000
Actual manufacturing overhead:		
Variable	$95,800	
Fixed	<u>211,200</u>	<u>307,000</u>
Total manufacturing overhead variance		<u>$35,000U</u>

Edwards and Paige had the following conversation about this analysis.

Paige: "I just don't understand these numbers. I have tried to control my costs with the production cut back. I figured that my budget for one month should be about $340,000, which would give me a $33,000 favorable variance, yet you show that I have a $35,000 unfavorable variance."

Edwards: "Well, you may have done a pretty good job in controlling your costs. You really cannot take one-twelfth of your annual estimated costs to get the monthly budget for comparing to your actual costs. A detailed variance analysis of manufacturing overhead would shed more light on your performance. The largest component is probably your fixed manufacturing overhead volume variance."

Paige: "Can you do that detailed variance analysis for me? What do I have to do to reduce or eliminate that fixed manufacturing overhead volume variance?"

Edwards: "Sure, we can do the detailed variance analysis. I would have done it for you, but we just got these figures together now. The fixed manufacturing overhead volume variance is not that important. I'm not sure that you really can or want to reduce it under our present economic situation."

Required:

A.   Sara Edwards indicated that Frank Paige should not take one-twelfth of the annual estimated costs to get a monthly budget figure for comparing to the actual costs for the month. Explain what Edwards meant by this comment.

B.   Prepare a detailed variance analysis of the manufacturing overhead for Smylan Company for the current month by calculating the following variances.

　　　1.   Overhead spending variance.

　　　2.   Variable overhead efficiency variance.

　　　3.   Fixed overhead budget variance.

　　　4.   Fixed overhead volume variance.

C.   Sara Edwards also commented that the fixed manufacturing overhead volume variance is not that important and Frank Paige might not really be able to or want to reduce the fixed overhead volume variance for the month.

　　　1.   Explain what the fixed overhead volume variance measures.

　　　2.   Explain how Paige could eliminate the fixed overhead volume variance.

　　　3.   Under the present economic conditions, would it be to Paige's *best* interest to eliminate the fixed overhead volume variance? Explain your answer.

5

COST ALLOCATION ISSUES

CHAPTER OUTLINE

- Single Base vs. Multiple Base Approach to Allocating Indirect Costs

- Service Departments' Costs

- Joint Costs

INTRODUCTION

As discussed in Chapter 3, direct costs can be directly related to the cost objective under consideration. Hence, the allocation of direct costs to a given cost objective is, by definition, rather straightforward. For example, the cost of direct materials with respect to a given product can be directly related to the product in question. In the same fashion, the direct costs of a given department can be allocated to the department in a straightforward manner. Thus, while direct costs are allocated, they do not present an allocation problem. Unfortunately, the same statement cannot be made with respect to indirect costs.[1]

Indirect costs, by definition, cannot be directly related to the cost objective in question. Hence, these costs cannot be allocated to the cost objective in a straightforward manner. It is this inability to unambiguously allocate indirect costs that creates a cost allocation problem. The severity of this problem can be thought of in terms of a continuum. At one end of the continuum there are indirect costs for which an allocation scheme can be derived with a high degree of accuracy and reliability. (Of course, if the scheme were perfectly accurate and reliable, it could be argued that these costs are direct rather than indirect costs.) At the other end of the continuum are indirect costs for which any allocation scheme seems arbitrary, although not necessarily capricious. Joint costs, which represent a special class of indirect costs, are at this latter end of the continuum.

Cost allocation problems permeate nearly all aspects of cost analysis and accumulation. In fact, it would be impossible to cover the variety and depth of issues involved in an entire book devoted to the subject, let alone a couple of chapters of a book. Hence, our approach will be to discuss in this and the next chapter a few specific issues that are especially prevalent in the context of management accounting. The issues chosen for discussion in this chapter are: (1) single base versus a multiple base approach to allocating indirect costs, (2) allocation of service departments' costs, and (3) joint costs. A fourth issue, activity based costing, is the subject of Chapter 6. These four issues cover a large portion of the fundamental problems associated with allocating indirect costs and, as such, provide a basis for understanding a broad spectrum of allocation issues.[2]

---

1.   It should be recalled from the discussion in Chapter 3 that a given cost can be direct with respect to one cost objective, but indirect with respect to an alternative cost objective.

2.   Although beyond the scope of this book, there is a growing body of literature which addresses cost allocation issues from an agency theory perspective (e.g., Zimmerman, 1979; Demski, 1981; Cohen and Loeb, 1988).

Before proceeding to discuss these issues, it should be emphasized that cost allocation problems are not limited to manufacturing firms. In fact, cost allocation problems are pervasive in all types of private and public sector organizations. A final point that also bears noting before proceeding with a discussion of specific cost allocation issues concerns the fact that, while it is probably fair to say that fixed indirect costs are generally very difficult to allocate, it is by no means the case that variable indirect costs involve a straightforward allocation. This latter point will become especially clear in our discussion of joint costs.

SINGLE BASE VS. MULTIPLE BASE APPROACH TO ALLOCATING INDIRECT COSTS

In Chapters 3 and 4, indirect (overhead) costs were assumed to be allocated via a single base (sometimes called single cost driver) approach, with direct labor hours being the one base (driver). Of course, the varied nature of indirect costs makes it unlikely that any one cost driver, let alone direct labor hours, will provide an accurate and reliable allocation scheme. Thus many firms use a multiple base (driver) approach to the allocation of overhead costs.

The key point to keep in mind when considering procedures for allocating indirect costs is that the goal is to identify those factors which drive the costs.[3] One way to look at this goal is in terms of cost functions. In other words, indirect costs can be thought of as a cost function denoted as follows:

$$IC = f(X_1, X_2, \ldots . X_n), \qquad \text{Eq. 5.1}$$

where IC equals indirect costs, and X_1 to X_n equal independent variables driving the indirect costs. Once viewed in the above form, the notion of cost drivers can be specified in terms of a model of the form:

$$Y = B_0 + B_1 X_1 + B_2 X_2 + \ldots . + B_n X_n + \varepsilon \qquad \text{Eq. 5.2}$$

---

3.   In some circumstances, other goals may be the primary basis for allocating costs. In government contracting, for example, costs are often allocated based on the benefits received from costs (Bedingfield and Rosen, 1985). The net realizable sales value method of allocating joint costs (as discussed later in this chapter) is another example of allocating costs based on benefits.

where Y equals the indirect cost observation, B_0 equals the intercept, B_1 to B_n equal the parameters for the X_1 to X_n independent variables driving the indirect costs, and ε equals the error term related to the indirect cost observation. Estimating the parameter values shown in Eq. 5.2 (i.e., $B_0, \ldots, B_n$) via the statistical technique of multiple regression analysis (Appendix 5.1 provides a brief discussion of this technique) results in:

$$\hat{Y} = b_0 + b_1X_1 + b_2X_2 + \ldots + b_nX_n, \qquad\qquad \textbf{Eq. 5.3}$$

where $\hat{Y}$ the represents the estimated value of Y and the lower case parameter notation (i.e., $b_0, \ldots, b_n$) in Eq. 5.3 represents the estimated parameter values.

In essence, the independent variables considered in the above model represent the cost drivers related to the variable portion of indirect costs. The intercept can be thought of as the fixed portion of the indirect costs, assuming the model can be extended back to the origin. The importance of each one of these factors in driving costs can be assessed via statistical tests of significance.

An example at this point should be helpful to show: (1) how the allocation of indirect costs via a multiple regression analysis model would take place, and (2) the way the allocation based on the regression model differs from the single base approach used in Chapters 3 and 4. This example is based on the Vad Corporation, which utilizes a job order costing system.

The Vad Corporation has been working hard to improve upon the planning and control of indirect costs. One aspect of this concern involves an effort to more fully understand the factors driving these costs. In the past, the Vad Corporation has been applying its indirect manufacturing costs based on direct labor hours. This basis for allocating indirect costs was decided upon over two decades ago. However, in recent years the production process has become much more automated than was previously the case. As a result, the firm has decided to examine the production process, with a focus on determining those factors that drive indirect costs. After several months of close examination, it has been decided that the manufacturing indirect costs are largely driven by the number of direct labor hours worked, the number of machine hours worked, and the number of machine setups required. In addition, there are several indirect costs which are considered fixed in nature and really cannot be thought of as being related to any measure of volume (or quantity). Data summarizing these costs and the potential factors driving such costs for the past 20 months are provided in part A of Exhibit 5.1.

EXHIBIT 5.1
Vad Corporation
Regression Analysis

A. Data Summary

Month	Indirect Cost ($) Y	Labor Hours (X_1)	Machine Hours (X_2)	Machine Setups (X_3)
1	16,764	1,287	1,000	7
2	19,440	1,530	1,010	10
3	15,018	1,104	986	7
4	18,960	1,446	1,154	9
5	20,148	1,494	1,024	11
6	16,902	1,235	950	9
7	16,286	1,167	1,077	8
8	19,492	1,388	922	12
9	13,276	885	991	7
10	14,694	1,000	892	7
11	19,752	1,415	1,110	1
12	14,446	964	986	18
13	17,664	1,257	880	11
14	20,432	1,523	981	11
15	13,638	953	1,023	7
16	15,448	1,113	1,103	7
17	13,148	958	1,041	5
18	17,616	1,319	1,045	9
19	13,826	1,056	955	6
20	17,284	1,260	1,053	7

B. Estimated Model

$$\hat{Y} = 1{,}446.22 + 8.38X_1 + 1.68X_2 + 398.56X_3$$

Based on the data provided in part A of Exhibit 5.1, the firm has decided to use a multiple base approach to allocate its indirect costs. The estimated model for allocating such costs will be of the form:

$$\hat{Y} = b_0 + b_1X_1 + b_2X_2 + b_3X_3, \qquad \text{Eq. 5.4}$$

where X_1 represents direct labor hours, X_2 represents machine hours, and X_3 represents the number of machine setups. The parameter estimates for Eq. 5.4 are provided in part B of Exhibit 5.1. Hence, each job would be charged for indirect costs as follows: $8.38 per direct labor hour, $1.68 per machine hour, and $398.56 per machine setup. In addition, each job would be expected to pick up a $180.78 share of the total fixed costs of $1,446.22 because, for illustration purposes, it is assumed that these costs are to be allocated evenly to the average of 8 jobs per month.

For contrasting purposes, it is interesting to note that had the firm allocated its indirect costs based on direct labor hours alone, each job would receive an estimated $14.00 per direct labor hour. To illustrate the differing amounts allocated under the two procedures, let us assume that job #33, which consists of 100 units of a particular product, is just being completed. The data related to the job are derived from part A of Exhibit 5.2. As shown in parts B and C of Exhibit 5.2, the indirect costs allocated to job #33 under the multiple base procedures are substantially different than the amount allocated under the single base approach.[4]

The use of a multiple regression model is the most generic and statistically sound method for dealing with multiple cost drivers. Nevertheless, allocating indirect costs based on multiple cost drivers is not restricted to the use of regression analysis. Indeed, many firms group at least part of their indirect costs according to homogeneous cost pools (some firms call them cost buckets), and allocate each cost pool on a distinctive allocation base. Although each cost pool is allocated via a single base (i.e., single cost driver), the sum of indirect costs are allocated via a multiple cost drivers mechanism. One approach for accomplishing this goal, which has a long history of use in manufacturing firms, is to accumulate and allocate at least part of the indirect costs by service departments. Hence, our discussion will now shift to the topic of allocating service departments' costs.

---

4. An added feature of using a regression model for allocating indirect costs has to do with control. For control purposes, the regression approach can be used to test the statistical significance of the differences between actual and estimated costs.

EXHIBIT 5.2
Vad Corporation
Single Base vs. Multiple Base Cost Allocation

A.	Data Summary of Job #33	
	Direct Material Cost	$2,000
	Direct Labor Cost	1,700
	Machine Hours	1,000
	Machine Setups	4
	Direct Labor Hours	150
	Units Produced	100

B.	Cost Allocation to Job #33	
	Single Base	
	Direct Material Cost	$2,000.00
	Direct Labor Cost	1,700.00
	Indirect Cost Allocated ($14.00 x 150)	2,100.00
	Total Costs	$5,800.00
	Unit Cost	$58.00

C.	Cost Allocation to Job #33	
	Multiple Base	
	Direct Material Cost	$2,000
	Direct Labor Cost	1,700
	Indirect Cost Allocated [180.78 + 8.38(150) + 1.68(1,000) + 398.56(4)]	4,712.02
	Total Costs	$8,412.02
	Unit Cost	$84.12

SERVICE DEPARTMENTS' COSTS

Departments in a manufacturing firm are often distinguished in terms of whether they are producing or service departments. **Producing departments** are usually thought of as those departments through which the firm's products actually flow during the production process. In contrast, **service departments** are those departments which assist the producing departments in a fashion which can only be described as indirectly related to the actual production of the products. Hence, the costs of service departments are indirect with respect to determining the costs of the products. Examples of manufacturing service departments include maintenance and cafeteria departments. In essence, the costs of running the service departments are part of the manufacturing indirect costs. However, since these costs can be logically grouped into homogeneous cost pools, both planning and control should be facilitated by such a grouping.

Once costs are assigned to various service departments, drivers for allocating these costs to the various producing departments are determined. However, an additional fact which must be considered is whether the service departments service one another as well as the producing departments. If a reciprocal relationship among service departments exists, allocations among service departments also are required. The remaining indirect costs that could not be assigned to a service department, are allocated to the various producing departments based on a separate driver (e.g., direct labor dollars). Figure 5.1 illustrates the generic cost flow for a manufacturing firm where there are two producing departments and a portion of indirect costs can be pooled into two service departments. As shown in that figure, the two service departments are assumed to perform reciprocal services to each other.

FIGURE 5.1
Cost Flow with Reciprocal Service Departments

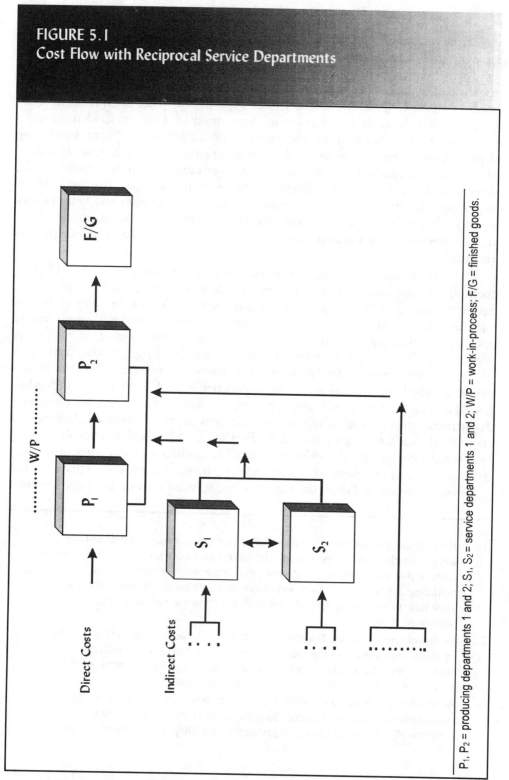

P_1, P_2 = producing departments 1 and 2; S_1, S_2 = service departments 1 and 2; W/P = work-in-process; F/G = finished goods.

There are three basic approaches to allocating the reciprocal service departments' costs. The first approach is to ignore the reciprocal relationship between the service departments and just allocate the costs directly to the producing departments. This approach is usually referred to as the **direct method**. The second approach, which is usually referred to as the **step method**, would first allocate the cost of the service department which spends more effort (in terms of dollars) on the other service departments.[5] This service department's costs would be allocated to the other service department and producing departments. Next, the costs in the remaining service department would be allocated to the producing departments. Although the step method moves in the direction of considering the reciprocal relationship between the two service departments, a more accurate approach would be to consider the simultaneity associated with the reciprocal service department's costs. This can be done via the use of simultaneous equations and is usually referred to as the **reciprocal method**.

The following example will be used to illustrate the three different methods of allocating service departments' costs. The example is based on the Spring Company, which is a small company specializing in the sales of several varieties of bottled spring water. The spring water is purified, and, where appropriate, flavored in a mixing department and then bottled in a bottling department. These two departments, mixing and bottling, are the company's producing departments. The company also has a maintenance department and cafeteria, which are treated as service departments.[6,7] The firm uses individual overhead rates for its producing departments; hence, the allocation of service departments' costs to producing departments may affect the ultimate allocation of costs to the different final products. Further, a reciprocal relationship exists between the two service departments in that the maintenance department services the machinery in the cafeteria and the cafeteria is the primary eating place for the maintenance workers. Given the nature of the services provided, it is determined

---

5.   The rationale for this allocation approach is that the more a service department services another service department, the more appropriate it is to transfer these costs to that other service department prior to transferring such costs to producing departments. If there were more than two service departments, the same rationale would guide a sequential allocation of the various service departments' costs.

6.   As the number of service departments and producing departments increases, the computational aspects of the reciprocal service departments costs increase. However, with the assistance of basic matrix algebra and microcomputers, the solution of more complicated problems is easily and quickly derived.

7.   Although not considered in this example, it is common for firms to have indirect manufacturing costs which cannot be grouped into service departments. These costs are allocated to producing departments separately, as illustrated in Figure 5.1.

that the primary cost driver for the maintenance department is machine hours and the primary cost driver for the cafeteria is direct labor hours.[8] Data relating to the service departments' annual costs and the bases for allocation are provided in part A of Exhibit 5.3. The actual allocation under the direct, step, and reciprocal methods of handling service departments' costs is provided in parts B, C and D of Exhibit 5.3. Not surprisingly, the different procedures result in different allocations.

As indicated above, the grouping of indirect costs into homogeneous cost pools and using a multiple cost drivers approach to allocating such costs is not new. However, in recent years a new slant on this idea has become quite popular under the name of activity based costing. In fact, the popularity of activity based costing and the related notion of activity based management, has given new life, if not new meaning, to the concept of allocating indirect costs via a multiple base (driver) approach. As such, Chapter 6 is devoted to these notions.

JOINT COSTS

The production of some products is inseparable from the production of other products. When this happens, the combined products are referred to as **joint products**. The costs associated with the inseparable production process of two or more products are referred to as **joint costs**. As an example, consider the case of meat production via the slaughtering of a steer. As a result of slaughtering a steer, several grades of meat, as well as saleable bones, automatically come about. In fact, you cannot produce one product without the other. That is, the production of one product is inseparable from the other products. Further, the costs which are common to the several products, in this case the cost of the steer, are joint costs.

In thinking about joint production processes, and hence joint costs, it is helpful to distinguish between the stage of production prior to the point of separating the various joint products and the stage of production beyond the separation of the joint products. The joint costs are those costs incurred prior to the separation (usually called split-off point), whereas beyond that point there may be separable direct costs associated with the individual joint products. Figure 5.2 illustrates the flow of costs to joint products. In terms of the allocation problem, the task is to figure out how to allocate the joint costs.

---

8.   Although this example is based on the assumption that each service department has a single cost driver, an individual service department can be associated with more than one cost driver. In fact, a separate cost function for each service department could be developed based on the multiple regression analysis approach discussed earlier in this chapter (Gordon 1974b).

EXHIBIT 5.3
Spring Company
Allocation of Service Departments' Costs

	Mainten-ance	Cafeteria	Mixing	Bottling
A. Data Summary				
Costs (Prior to Allocating Service Departments' Costs)	$100,000	$50,000	$1,000,000	$1,200,000
Services Provided in terms of Cost Driver				
Machine Hours		1,000	9,000	10,000
Direct Labor Hours	2,500		4,000	1,500
B. Direct Method				
Cost of Departments	$100,000	$50,000	$1,000,000	$1,200,000
Maintenance (9/19, 10/19)	(100,000)		47,368	52,632
Cafeteria (40/55, 15/55)		(50,000)	36,364	13,636
Cost (after allocation)	---	---	$1,083,732	$1,266, 268
C. Step Method				
Cost of Departments	$100,000	$50,000	$1,000,000	$1,200,000
Cafeteria (25/80, 40/80, 15/80)	15,625	(50,000)	25,000	9,375
Maintenance (9/19, 10/19)	(115,625)		54,770	60,855
Cost (after allocation)	---	---	$1,079,770	$1,270,230
D. Reciprocal Method				
Cost of Departments	$100,000	$50,000	$1,000,000	$1,200,000
Maintenance (1/20, 9/20, 10/20)	(117,460)*	5,873	52,857	58,730
Cafeteria (25/80, 40/80, 15/80)	17,460	(55,873)	27,937	10,476
Cost (after allocation)	---	---	$1,080,794	$1,269,206

* **Reciprocal Equations:**
Cost of Maintenance Department = $100,000 + (25/80 x Cost of Cafeteria)
Cost of Cafeteria = $50,000 + (1/20 x Cost of Maintenance Department)
Cost of Maintenance Dept. = $100,000 + (25/80 x ($50,000 + 1/20 x Cost of
        Maintenance Dept.)) = $117,460
Cost of Cafeteria = $50,000 + (1/20 x $117,460) = $55,873

FIGURE 5.2
Joint Costs and Joint Products

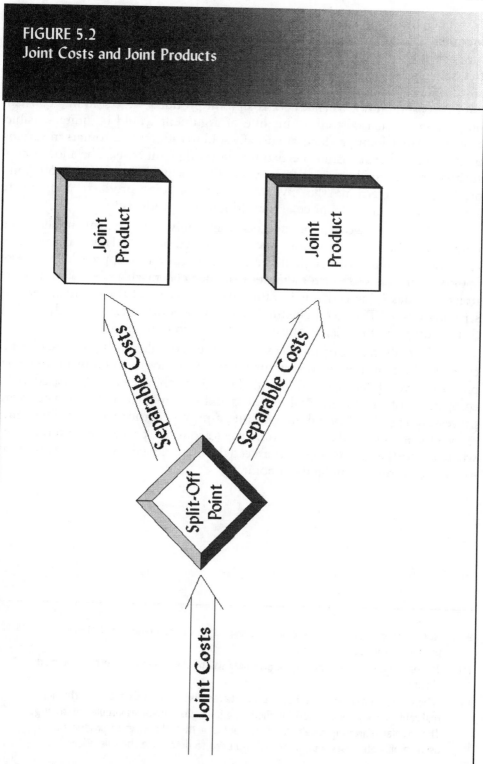

Generally speaking, there is no right way to allocate joint costs to joint products. By definition, these costs are inseparable with respect to the joint products involved. To the extent that they are separable, they are not joint costs. In essence, joint costs epitomize the problems associated with allocating indirect costs.[9] Hence, from a planning and control point of view, it is often argued that joint costs should not be allocated. If all joint products were sold in a constant proportion to each customer, this line of argument would be quite sensible. However, since joint products are usually sold to different customers in varying proportions, a mechanism is needed for allocating joint costs. The allocation of such costs is needed to assist in assessing the profitability of the various joint products, to determine the inventory value of joint products and, where appropriate, to derive the price of the various joint products.[10]

There are two generic methods commonly used by firms in allocating joint costs. The first is to allocate such costs based on the relative sales value of each joint product. Although different versions of this approach exist, one popular approach is to base the allocation on the net realizable sales value. The net realizable sales value is defined as the final sales value of the product, less any separable costs.[11] The second method of allocating joint costs commonly used by firms is based on the relative physical units of each joint product.

The allocation of joint costs is further complicated by two additional concerns. First, it must be determined whether or not to continue producing a product beyond the split-off point. This decision needs to be based on a comparison of the incremental revenues and incremental costs associated with processing a product beyond the split-off point. Where the incremental revenues exceed the incremental costs, it would pay to continue processing. Alternatively, where the further processing costs exceed the incremental revenues, it would pay to sell the product at the split-off point.

---

9.   Note that joint costs are variable with respect to the combined level of joint products produced.

10. The use of costs in the pricing of products will be discussed at length in the next chapter.

11. Where pricing decisions are based on costs (as discussed in Chapter 7), the net realizable sales value method for allocating joint costs involves circular reasoning. The circular reasoning results from the fact that the sale prices of products are used to allocate costs, but costs are also used to determine the sale prices.

The second additional concern regarding the allocation of joint costs is determining whether or not a joint product is a main product or a by-product. Joint costs are allocated to main products, but not to by-products. Hence, it is necessary to differentiate between these two types of joint products. From a conceptual perspective, **main products** are the products that a firm made an intentional decision to produce. In contrast, **by-products** are not intentionally produced, but rather result from the decision to produce main products. Unfortunately, it is difficult to translate the conceptual distinction between main products and by-products into a simple decision rule for practical use. As a practical matter, firms often designate a joint product as a by-product when, based on some rule of thumb, its net realizable sales value is quite low relative to other products. Where a product is designated as a by-product, the net sales value of the by-product is most often treated as a reduction of the joint costs prior to the allocation of such costs to the main products.[12]

The logical sequence in considering joint products is to determine which product(s) to complete beyond the split-off point, and then to assess the desirability of the entire joint production process. While there is no right way to allocate joint costs, the method chosen will affect the profitability picture of individual products but not the overall firm's profitability.[13] An illustration showing how to allocate joint costs, in terms of the West Company, follows.

The West Company is a meat packing firm which purchases steer from cattle ranchers. The average steer costs $415 and yields 400 pounds of grade A meat and 600 pounds of grade B meat. These two grades of meat represent the company's main products, called A and B. In addition, each steer yields an average of 50 pounds of bones as a by-product. There is no opportunity to sell either main product without some additional processing beyond the split-off point. The separable costs for the two products are $.10 per lb. for product A and $.05 for product B. The final sales value for A is $1.50 per lb. and for B is $.45 per lb.[14] The by-product sells for $.10 per lb., but has no separable costs (i.e., the bones are sold at the split-off point without further processing).

---

12. An alternative approach would be to treat the net realizable value of the by-product as "other income" to the firm.

13. To the extent that firms devote their resources to products as a result of their profitability, over time the total profitability of the firm could also be affected.

14. If there were a market to sell either one or both of the main products at the split-off point, then the incremental revenues between the final sales price and the split-off point price would be compared to the separable (incremental) costs of further processing. If the incremental revenues exceed the incremental costs then further processing should take place. If the incremental revenues were lower than the incremental costs, then further processing should not take place.

The West Company is considering the following two different procedures for allocating its joint costs: (1) net realizable value (NRV), and (2) physical units (PU). Under either method, the revenues generated from the by-product will be treated as a reduction of the joint costs. As illustrated in Exhibit 5.4, the profitability of the individual products is dependent on the method used. Under the NRV method, product A generates a profit of $273 per steer and product B generates a profit of $117 per steer. Under the PU method, the respective amounts are $396 profits for product A and a $6 loss for product B. Exhibit 5.4 also illustrates that the total profits of $390 remains the same regardless of the allocation method used. Hence, the joint production process as a whole is profitable to the firm. A final point worth noting concerning Exhibit 5.4 is that the NRV method, which essentially allocates the joint costs on an "ability to bear the costs" basis, results in a common profit-to-NRV ratio for each product [i.e., ($273/$560) = .4875 = ($117/$240)].

As noted elsewhere in this chapter, the problems associated with allocating indirect costs are not limited to manufacturing firms. Joint costs are no exception in this regard. For example, consider the case of a consulting firm which recently was awarded two new contracts, A and B, dealing with the installation of a highly specialized data base management system. Upon securing the contracts, the partner in charge has decided that three of the firm's senior consultants need to attend a two-week seminar. The seminar covers highly technical computer engineering aspects of data base design, which will facilitate the carrying out of the two new contracts. The total costs associated with the seminar are estimated to be $40,000, which include seminar fees, lodging, traveling, and the two weeks of salaries for the three senior consultants attending the seminar. These costs are, in essence, joint costs in that the knowledge gained from the seminar is an inseparable input to the carrying out of both consulting contracts. To the extent the knowledge gained from the seminar can only be applied to the two newly acquired contracts, the problem of allocating the joint costs would be similar in nature to joint costs found in a manufacturing firm. To the extent that this knowledge can be transferred to potential future contracts, the problem becomes even more complicated.[15]

---

15. An interesting twist to this problem concerns the procedure for allocating potential joint costs for contract bidding purposes. In such a case, the probabilities associated with securing contracts, as well as the usual problems associated with allocating joint costs, would need to be considered. For a further discussion of this point, the reader is referred to the paper by Cohen and Loeb (1990).

EXHIBIT 5.4
West Company
Joint Costs Illustration

A. Net Realizable Value Method	Product A	Product B	Total
Revenues (1)	$600	$270	$870
Separable Costs (2)	40	30	70
Net Realizable Value	560	240	800
Joint Costs $415 - $5 (By-Product Revenue) (3)	287 (4)	123 (5)	410
Profits (Per Steer)	$273	$117	$390

(1) Product A: 400 x $1.50 = $600
     Product B: 600 x $.45 = $270
(2) Product A: 400 x $.10 = $40
     Product B: 600 x $.05 = $30
(3) $.10 x 50 lbs. = $5.00
(4) 70% (i.e., 560 ÷ 800) of
     Joint Costs = $287
(5) 30% (i.e., 240 ÷ 800) of
     Joint Costs = $123

B. Physical Units	Product A	Product B	Total
Revenues (1)	$600	$270	$870
Separable Costs (2)	40	30	70
Net Realizable Value	560	240	800
Joint Costs $415 - $5 (By-Product Revenue) (3)	164 (4)	246 (5)	410
Profits (Per Steer)	$396	($6)	$390

(1) Product A: 400 x $1.50 = $600
     Product B: 600 x $.45 = $270
(2) Product A: 400 x $.10 = $40
     Product B: 600 x $.05 = $30
(3) $.10 x 50 lbs. = $5.00
(4) 40% (i.e., 400 ÷ 1,000) of Joint Costs = $164
(5) 60% (i.e., 600 ÷ 1,000) of Joint Costs = $246

CONCLUDING COMMENTS

This chapter has discussed several techniques for allocating indirect costs. It must be emphasized, however, that no procedure for allocating indirect costs will be free of problems. In fact, by definition, indirect costs cannot be directly related to the cost objective in question and thus create an allocation problem. Hence, in choosing one method over another method for allocating indirect costs, it is important for a firm to keep in mind the overall purpose for allocating such costs.

In some circumstances, the primary concern in allocating costs may be to derive an accurate cost of a product. In other situations, the primary concern may be to motivate behavior. In this latter regard, one reason many firms seem to prefer using direct labor hours as the single base for allocating indirect costs is because such a procedure encourages managers to move away from a labor intensive operation. In other words, the focus is on reducing direct labor costs and not on accurately allocating indirect costs. Of course, there is no reason why a firm could not strive for accuracy in terms of cost allocation procedures and simultaneously establish incentives for controlling labor costs.

Costs are a critical component of a firm's profits. Indeed, the distinguishing feature between successful and unsuccessful firms is often the ability to plan and control costs. One idea which has taken on a particular significance in allocating costs is activity based costing. It is to this topic, and the related idea of activity based management, that we now turn.

APPENDIX 5.1:
Regression Analysis[16]

Regression analysis is a statistical technique used for examining the relationship between a dependent variable and one or more independent variables.[17] In its simplest form, one dependent variable (Y) is related to one independent variable (X). This is known as simple regression analysis. If the dependent variable were a response to more than one independent variable, a multiple regression analysis model would result. For example, Eq. 5.5 below is a multiple regression model with two linear independent variables, X_1 and X_2, where B_0, B_1 and B_2 are parameter values and ε is the error term. The systematic part of Y in Eq. 5.5 is related to the independent variables by $B_0 + B_1X_1 + B_2X_2$ and the random part of the relationship is accounted for by ε.

$$Y_i = B_0 + B_1X_{1i} + B_2X_{2i} + \varepsilon \qquad \text{Eq. 5.5}$$

The most common method for estimating the parameters in Eq. 5.5 is known as the least squares method. The **least squares method** minimizes the sum of the squared errors, based on n sets of observations among the dependent and independent variables $[(Y_1, X_{11}, X_{21}), (Y_2, X_{12}, X_{22}), \ldots, (Y_n, X_{1n}, X_{2n})]$. The predicted or expected value of the dependent variable for Eq. 5.5 can be expressed as:

$$\hat{Y}_i = b_0 + b_1X_{1i} + b_2X_{2i} \qquad \text{Eq. 5.6}$$

where,

$\hat{Y}_i$	=	i^{th} predicted value of dependent variable,
b_0, b_1, b_2	=	parameter estimates,
X_{1i}	=	i^{th} value of independent variable X_1,
X_{2i}	=	i^{th} value of independent variable X_2, and
i	=	$1 \ldots n$.

16. The discussion contained in this Appendix is intended to only highlight the basic ideas underlying regression analysis. For a further treatment of this topic, the reader can refer to *Regression Analysis* by Draper and Smith (1981).

17. The computational aspects of regression analysis are easily and inexpensively handled via various statistical and spreadsheet software packages that run on personal computers. In addition, many pocket calculators can handle noncomplicated regression analysis problems.

In estimating the regression model shown in Eq. 5.5., based on the least squares method, the following three assumptions are made concerning the error term, ε: (1) the error is a random variable with an expected value of zero and a constant variance, σ^2, (2) the error is uncorrelated from one set of observations to any other set of observations, and (3) the error is a normally distributed random variable. If these assumptions are valid (which can easily be checked), it can be shown that the least squares estimators are unbiased, consistent, efficient, and sufficient.

Once a regression model has been hypothesized and the parameters estimated based on the sample data, it is important to ask the following question: How useful is the estimated regression equation in explaining the relationship between the dependent variable and the independent variable(s)? A common way of answering this question is by looking at the statistic known as R^2 (coefficient of determination), which can range from zero to one. As R^2 (adjusted for degrees of freedom) approaches unity, the greater the portion of the variability explained by the regression model. It is also important to check whether individual parameter estimates (and in turn, the associated variables) are statistically significant. This can be done by a "t" test and partial "F" test for individual parameter values.

PROBLEMS

Problem 5.1

It is often argued that cost allocation issues permeate nearly all managerial decisions. Explain this argument.

Problem 5.2

When a professor prepares a research proposal for external funding, it is normal for the budget to include an amount associated with recovering the university's overhead (i.e., indirect costs). Many universities use a flat overhead rate for such grants, in the vicinity of 35%.

Required:

A.   Does a 35% overhead rate for such grants seem reasonable? Explain.

B.   If a goal of a university were to maximize the dollar amount of external research grants received by its faculty and staff, is there some better rule for allocating costs than the one noted above? Explain.

C.   Is the goal of maximizing the dollar amount of the external research grants a good one for universities to pursue? Explain.

Problem 5.3

Discuss the rationale underlying the use of regression analysis for allocating indirect costs.

Problem 5.4 *(Adapted from CMA examination)*

Computer Information Services is a computer software consulting company. Its three major functional areas are computer programming, information systems consulting, and software training. Carol Birch, a pricing analyst in the Accounting Department, has been asked to develop total costs for the functional areas. These costs will be used as a guide in pricing a new contract. In computing these costs, Birch is considering three different methods of allocating overhead costs—the direct method, the step method, and the reciprocal method. Birch assembled the following data on overhead from its two service departments, the Information Systems Department and the Facilities Department.

	Service Department		Production Department			
	Infor-mation Systems	Facilities	Computer Programming	Consulting	Training	Total
Budgeted overhead	$50,000	$25,000	$75,000	$110,000	$85,000	$345,000
Information systems* (hours)		300	1,200	600	900	3,000
Facilities** (thousand square feet)	200		400	600	800	2,000
*Allocated on the basis of hours of computer usage.						
**Allocated on the basis of floor space.						

Required:

A.   Using computer usage time as the application base for the Information Systems Department and square feet of floor space for the Facilities Department, apply overhead from these service departments to the production departments, using the following two methods.

1.   Direct method.

2.   Step method.

B.

1.   Define the reciprocal method of allocating the costs of service departments.

2.   Would the reciprocal method be appropriate for Computer Information Systems?

C.   Rather than allocating costs, how might Computer Information Services better assign the Information Systems Department's costs?

Problem 5.5 *(Adapted from CMA examination)*

Sonimad Sawmill Inc. (SSI) purchases logs from independent timber contractors and processes the logs into the following three types of lumber products.

1. Studs for residential building (e.g., walls, ceilings).

2. Decorative pieces (e.g., fireplace mantels, beams for cathedral ceilings).

3. Posts used as support braces (e.g., mine support braces, braces for exterior fences around ranch properties).

These products are the result of a joint sawmill process that involves removal of bark from the logs, cutting the logs into a workable size (ranging from 8 to 16 feet in length), and then cutting the individual products from the logs, depending upon the type of wood (pine, oak, walnut, or maple) and the size (diameter) of the log.

The joint process results in the following costs and output of products for a typical month.

Joint production costs

Materials (rough timber logs)	$ 500,000
Debarking (labor and overhead)	50,000
Sizing (labor and overhead)	200,000
Product cutting (labor and overhead)	250,000
Total joint costs	$1,000,000

Product yield and average sales value on a per unit basis from the joint process are as follows.

Product	Monthly Output	Fully Processed Sales Price
Studs	75,000	$ 8
Decorative pieces	5,000	100
Posts	20,000	20

The studs are sold as rough-cut lumber after emerging from the sawmill operation without further processing by SSI. Also, the posts require no further processing. The decorative pieces must be planed and further sized after emerging from the SSI sawmill. This additional processing costs SSI $100,000 per month and normally results in a loss of 10 percent of the units entering the process. Without this planing and sizing process, there is still an active intermediate market for the unfinished decorative pieces where the sales price averages $60 per unit.

Required:

A. Based on the information given for Sonimad Sawmill Inc., allocate the joint processing costs of $1,000,000 to each of the three product lines using the

1. relative sales value method at split-off.

2. physical output (volume) method at split-off.

3. estimated net realizable value method.

B. Prepare an analysis for Sonimad Sawmill Inc. to compare processing the decorative pieces further as they presently do, with selling the rough-cut product immediately at split-off. Be sure to provide all calculations.

Problem 5.6 *(Adapted from CMA examination)*

Quick Telephone Response (QTR) was started several years ago to provide an outsource telephone service for the growing number of small, specialty catalog mail-order companies that commenced operations in recent years. Since most of the calls are received between 10 a.m. and 2 p.m., QTR began offering a telephone answering service to attempt to fill the remainder of the day for its operators. However, as outsource competition has recently increased, QTR analyzed its operations and concluded that it should focus on its core business of providing service to its mail-order clients only. To bring operating costs into line, QTR concluded that it should shed some of its full-time operators and replace them with part-timer operators in order to cover the peak mid-day calling period.

Weldon Miller, director of the Telephone Response Operations Department, engaged a consultant to assist in analyzing the situation and determining the number of full-time and part-time employees that will be required to meet QTR's variable operating schedule. Based on a study of one month's activity they concluded that the number of daily orders received for their specialty clients averaged 3,450 with the mid-day period averaging 2,250 orders. They calculated that there would be a need to retain twenty five (25) full-time employees. They further developed two regression analyses. Regression 1 relates to the average of 3,450 orders per day and Regression 2 relates to the average of

2,250 peak mid-day orders. The data resulting from these analyses are presented below.

Regression Equation: $E = a + bN$
where: E = Employees
N = Number of orders

	Regression 1	Regression 2
a	26.0265	31.6785
b	.0051	.0045
Standard error of coefficient	.0005	.0009
Standard error of the E estimate	4.623	4.228
Coefficient of determination (r²)	.563	.682
95% confidence for the E estimate	8.697	7.552

Required:
A. Refer to the regression data in the previous column for Quick Telephone Response (QTR).

   1. Calculate the number of part-time employees that will be needed each day using the regression results relating to the average number of daily orders handled. Round your response to the nearest whole number.

   2. Applying the regression results that relate to the average number of orders handled during the mid-day peak period, calculate the number of part-time employees that will be needed daily. Round your response to the nearest whole number.

   3. Of the two regression analyses used, select the regression analysis which appears to be the better one and explain the reason for your conclusion.

B. Describe at least two ways that Weldon Miller could improve the regression predictions.

6

ACTIVITY BASED
COSTING/MANAGEMENT

CHAPTER OUTLINE

- Activity Based Costing

- Global ABC Movement

- ABC Illustration

- Pros and Cons of ABC

- Activity Based Management

INTRODUCTION

This chapter addresses the approach to cost allocations known as **activity based costing (ABC)**. Although the concepts underlying activity based costing are not new, the enthusiasm by which managers, firms, and academicians have recently embraced ABC is nothing short of a cost management revolution.

As activity based costing has expanded in popularity, its focus has also shifted. The cost allocation aspects of ABC are often viewed as part of the activity based management process. The **activity based management (ABM)** process will also be discussed in this chapter.

ACTIVITY BASED COSTING

For many firms, indirect manufacturing costs are quite large in both absolute and relative terms. For example, it is not uncommon for these costs to represent more than 40% of the total manufacturing costs. In some highly automated operations, the indirect manufacturing costs could represent more than 75% of the total manufacturing costs. Hence, the proper allocation of indirect costs is an issue of critical importance to effective planning and control for a large number of firms.

As modern manufacturing firms became more automated and less labor intensive, the inappropriateness of using direct labor hours as the basis for allocating indirect manufacturing costs surfaced as a critical concern. Further, as noted in Chapter 5, to the extent that indirect costs are driven by several factors, a single cost driver of any sort is also inappropriate. The combination of these two concerns has led many firms to seek out more appropriate methods of allocating indirect manufacturing costs.

One method for allocating indirect manufacturing costs, which has received much attention since the mid 1980s, is **activity based costing (ABC)**.[1] In a 1997 survey of the members of the Cost Management Group of the Institute for Management Accountants, 39% of the responding firms have either implemented, or at least approved implementation, of ABC (Krumwiede and Jordan, 1998).

---

1. Although the discussion and example in this section focus on manufacturing firms, it should be noted that many nonmanufacturing firms have initiated an activity based costing system. For an interesting discussion on how ABC was implemented at Pennsylvania Blue Shield, see the paper by Norkiewcz (1994).

Activity based costing is generally thought of as being a two-stage procedure for allocating indirect costs. In the first stage, the activities which cause an organization to incur indirect costs are identified and the related costs of each activity are pooled together. In this context, an **activity** can be thought of as an act or effort directed at accomplishing a specific goal. In the second stage, the costs for each activity are allocated to the cost objective (e.g., product) based on the cost driver associated with the activity.[2] Figure 6.1 illustrates the general flow of indirect manufacturing costs under an ABC system.

GLOBAL ABC MOVEMENT

The U.S. has clearly been the incubator for the ABC movement. However, there is growing empirical evidence that ABC is no longer a predominately U.S. based phenomenon. Companies around the world have started to experiment with the use of ABC systems. For example, a survey of U.K. based firms, by Innes and Mitchell (1995), showed that almost 20% of the respondents were using ABC and an additional 27% were considering its adoption. A survey of Canadian firms, by Armitage and Nicholson (1993), showed that 14% of the respondents were using ABC and another 15% were considering its adoption. A survey of Irish firms, by Clarke (1992) showed that 14% were using ABC and another 34% were planning to adopt it. A survey of Swedish firms, by Ask and Ax (1992), showed that close to 23% were considering ABC.

ABC ILLUSTRATION

To illustrate the differences between allocating indirect manufacturing costs based on an ABC system versus a traditional single base costing system, consider the following example regarding the Neural Corporation. The Neural Corporation produces two types of bicycles: a deluxe model and a regular model. The materials cost for the bicycles is $40 for the deluxe model and $25 for the regular model. Both bicycles usually take one hour of labor to complete, at a cost of $15 per hour. The total indirect costs (assume all are variable) for the year are estimated to be $200,000

---

2. This discussion assumes that there is only one cost driver for each activity. If more than one cost driver describes an activity, a separate cost function for each activity could be developed. In such a case, the generic approach of using multiple regression analysis (discussed in the previous chapter) would be the most appropriate approach to allocating indirect costs. Further, even where ABC is used, an interesting evaluative technique would be for a firm to develop a regression model for allocating its costs and then to compare the results derived from such a model to the allocations derived under ABC.

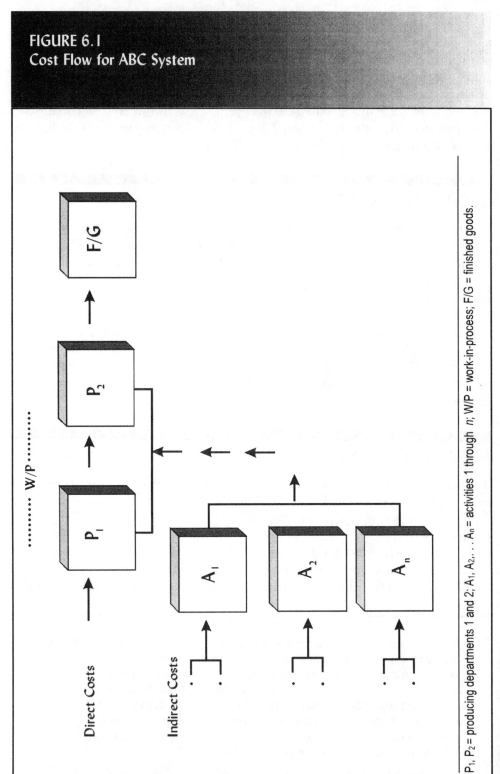

FIGURE 6.1
Cost Flow for ABC System

P_1, P_2 = producing departments 1 and 2; A_1, A_2, . . A_n = activities 1 through n; W/P = work-in-process; F/G = finished goods.

and, up until now, have been allocated based on direct labor hours. Neural Company estimates that its annual level of production for the deluxe bicycles will be 2,000 and 18,000 for the regular bicycles. Since each bicycle is expected to require one hour of direct labor to produce, the standard indirect cost per bicycle is estimated to be $10 (i.e., $200,000 / 20,000 hours). Given the above information, the standard cost of producing each bicycle would be $65 and $50 for the deluxe and regular models, respectively. Exhibit 6.1 provides a summary of this calculation.

Neural Company is considering adopting an ABC system for allocating its indirect costs. After careful analysis, it is decided that there are three major activities which drive the firm's indirect costs. These activities are purchasing, machine work, and machine setups. The cost drivers associated with these activities, in respective order, are purchase orders, machine hours, and number of machine setups. The amount of indirect costs driven by these activities, as well as the number of driver events for each product, are shown in part A of Exhibit 6.2. The materials and labor costs for Neural Company under the ABC system are the same whether an ABC or non-ABC system is in use. Given this information, the cost of producing the bicycles under an ABC system would be $97.50 for the deluxe model and $46.39 for the regular model. Part B of Exhibit 6.2 provides a summary of this calculation.

In the above example, all of the indirect costs were allocated to one activity or another. In many situations, a portion of these costs will not fit neatly into one activity or another and thus will have to be allocated by some other means.[3] Another point worth noting concerning the above example is the fact that the ABC allocation shifts costs from the high volume product (i.e., the regular bicycle) to the low volume product (i.e., deluxe bicycle). While this does not have to be the case, the fact that high volume products often subsidize low volume products under non-ABC allocation schemes is one of the main arguments advanced in favor of using ABC for allocating indirect costs. This latter fact results because ABC treats all costs as being variable in terms of the firm's activities (i.e., the traditional notion of fixed costs, in terms of units produced, is usually not considered in an ABC system). Finally, it should be noted that the above example assumes no interaction among activities. In reality, there may be various interactions among activities (including reciprocal interactions) that would need to be considered.[4]

---

3. This is similar to the point made in our discussion of service departments' costs. It was noted at that time that some indirect costs may not fall into homogeneous service department cost pools and will have to be allocated separately. A comparison of Figures 5.1 and 6.1 highlights the similarities between ABC and the allocation of service departments' costs.

4. Here again, the similarities between service departments' costs and activity based costs become apparent.

EXHIBIT 6.1
Neural Company
Product Costs Under a Non-ABC System

	Deluxe	Regular
Direct Materials	$40	$25
Direct Labor	$15	$15
Indirect Costs (overhead)	$10	$10
Total Costs	$65	$50

EXHIBIT 6.2
Neural Company
Product Costs Under an ABC System

A. Data

Driver Events	Deluxe	Regular	Total Events	Indirect Costs	Indirect Costs Per Event
Purchase Orders	15	5	20	$ 4,000	$200
Machine Hours	2,000	18,000	20,000	$100,000	$ 5
Machine Setups	120	40	160	$96,000	$600

B. Calculation of Cost Per Bicycle

	Deluxe	Regular
Direct Materials	$40.00	$25.00
Direct Labor	$15.00	$15.00
Indirect Costs (overhead)	$42.50[a]	$ 6.39[b]
Total Cost Per Bicycle	$97.50	$46.39

[a] Indirect costs per deluxe bicycle are derived as follows:
[(15 • $200) + (2,000 • $5) + (120 • $600)]/2,000 bicycles = $42.50

[b] Indirect costs per regular bicycles are derived as follows:
[(5 • $200) + (18,000 • $5) + (40 • $600)]/18,000 bicycles = $6.39

PROS AND CONS OF ABC

The fact that different methods for allocating indirect costs will most likely result in different final cost allocations is well known and has been illustrated earlier in this chapter. Accordingly, one should not be surprised to see a shift in product costs and profitability among different products as a result of a firm initiating an ABC system. However, it does not necessarily follow that the ABC system provides a preferred allocation scheme. The real issue, therefore, is whether or not ABC is an improvement over the firm's existing indirect cost allocation scheme. In this regard, many argue that ABC usually creates net value (i.e., the benefits exceed the costs) to a firm, whereas others argue it does not. More to the point, advocates of ABC argue that the following benefits will likely accrue from ABC: (1) a more accurate allocation of indirect costs; (2) a clearer understanding of the factors that drive indirect costs (including volume and nonvolume related cost drivers); (3) better pricing decisions; (4) identification of nonvalue added activities; and, (5) a more effective means of motivating and controlling performance and process improvements. Opponents of ABC often note that: (1) it is unnecessary in firms that already have a clear picture of the factors driving indirect costs via the use of a carefully developed multiple base approach to allocating indirect costs; (2) focusing on the allocation of indirect costs is not the key issue related to technological competitiveness; (3) if it is so good, why aren't more firms using it?; and (4) it tends to treat all indirect costs as if they are variable costs.

On balance, it would appear that the initiation of an ABC system may be beneficial for some firms but not for others. Thus, the fundamental question for a manager to address before agreeing to install an ABC system is: What can an activity based costing system offer my firm that cannot be derived from the existing costing system? For many firms, the answer to this question will be very little, at most. For other firms, the answer will be a great deal.

The empirical work to date seems to confirm the view that some firms will benefit from ABC whereas others will not. One problem in interpreting the empirical evidence is the self-selection bias. This problem is particularly prevalent in terms of the case studies conducted, in that the firms allowing researchers access to an "inside" examination of the effect of ABC tend to want their success stories told. In a study by Gordon and Silvester (1993) which examined the stock market performance effect of installing an ABC system across several manufacturing firms, the results were not supportive of the notion that ABC as a technique has generic net benefits. Shields (1995) and Gosselin (1997) also found that the benefits from ABC vary across firms. However, as pointed out by Gordon and Silvester, this does not preclude the fact that some specific firms may derive significant benefits from ABC. At Hewlett Packard, for example, an ABC system allowed engineers and production managers to more clearly see the relationship between design changes and product costs (Merz and Hardy, 1993).

ACTIVITY BASED MANAGEMENT

The process by which a firm manages its activities is often referred to as **activity based management (ABM)**. By focusing on activities as the unit of analysis, an ABM system facilitates improved management of the firm's activities. The key objective of ABM is to have an organization's activity performed in a "reasonably efficient" manner.[5] Hence, the initial step in carrying out ABM is to identify those activities which are running in an efficient manner. An activity which is being performed in an efficient manner can serve as a **benchmark** (i.e., unit of comparison) for improving other activities.

The efficiency of an activity ultimately needs to be viewed in terms of cost/benefit analysis. The key question to ask in this regard is as follows: Are the costs of the activity worth the benefits? The above question can only be answered through a careful analysis of the relevant costs and benefits. For some activities, it will be apparent that the benefits exceed the costs. In these cases, the management goal is to make sure the activity is performing in as efficient a manner as possible. For other activities, even the most efficient state may result in more costs to the organization than benefits. These latter activities can be thought of as non-value added activities and the management goal is to eliminate them.

A good example of the benefits that a firm can derive from an ABM system is provided by Sanyo Electric in Japan. According to Sakurai (1995), the introduction of ABM at Sanyo allowed the company to identify many non-value added activities and to shift employees from those activities to value added activities.

As noted above, the ultimate judgment of the worth of activities needs to be done on a cost/benefit basis and an ABC system can play an important role in this assessment. Indeed, an ABC system helps a firm shift its orientation toward activities and the related costs of carrying out those activities. The lack of a formal ABC system does not, however, preclude a firm from managing its activities, providing that cost information on the firm's activities is being gathered via some other mechanism. At the same time, the use of an ABC system does not guarantee a successful ABM approach.

Assessing the benefits of activities is often far more problematic than assessing the related costs. For many, if not most, activities, the level of analysis is such that benefits cannot be assessed in terms of specific revenues (or revenue equivalents). Hence, it is often necessary to assess the benefits of an activity in

---

5. The reader should recall from Chapter 2 that the term "efficient" refers to deriving the maximum output from a given level of input or, alternatively, using the minimal level of input for a given level of output. Rarely can the absolute efficiency of a task be assessed. Hence, the term "reasonably efficient" is used to reflect a realistic goal.

terms of nonfinancial measures. Measures that are commonly used in this latter regard are quality, output/input ratios, and activity completion (cycle) time. Unfortunately, there is no easy formula for comparing the nonfinancial benefits of an activity to the financial costs of such an activity. (More will be said about nonfinancial measures in Chapter 9.)

A key obstacle to successfully utilizing the concept of ABM is understanding the essence of an organizational activity and how various activities relate to one another. The more complicated an activity, and the greater its interaction with other activities, the harder it is to manage. Hence, organizations wanting to utilize ABM need to analyze individual activities and the relationships among various activities. In this regard, the work by MacKenzie (1976) provides a meaningful approach for such analysis.

According to MacKenzie (1976), the essence of an organization's activities (as well as the interrelationships among activities) is most appropriately viewed in terms of the interaction patterns among the individuals within the organization. In fact, MacKenzie argues that the right way to think of the structure of an organization is via the activity oriented interaction patterns among individuals. Managing activities, according to this view, is actually the process of managing the structure of an organization or, in terms of the lowest common denominator, managing the interaction patterns among individuals.

Of course, to the extent a firm is utilizing ABM in conjunction with other new management techniques, such as TQM (total quality management), JIT (just-in-time production system), and/or FMS (flexible manufacturing systems), it is difficult to isolate the costs and benefits of any one technique over another. In essence, the key is to use these various techniques in a way that enhances a firm's strategies for overall competitiveness, irrespective of the labels.

CONCLUDING COMMENTS

Despite the growing tendency for firms to initiate (to one degree or another) ABC systems, it must not be forgotten that ABC is essentially a multiple base method for allocating indirect costs. The key objectives underlying its use are to get a clear understanding of the activities that cause indirect costs and to develop a meaningful way to allocate, via cost drivers, the costs related to each activity. Other approaches, such as the use of multiple regression analysis models discussed in the previous chapter, offer viable, and in many cases preferred, alternatives for meeting the same objectives. Indeed, the empirical evidence clearly shows that the benefits of ABC are not uniform across firms. One factor, among several, that Shields (1995) found to be associated with ABC success is competitive strategy. A study by Frey and Gordon (1998) also found competitive strategy to be an important factor associated with the benefits derived from ABC. In the final analysis, the long-term legacy of ABC to the field of cost management may well rest in the fact that it helped focus attention on the need for firms to use multiple base cost allocation methods, rather than in terms of the longevity of the ABC technique itself.

Once firms focus on understanding the costs of their activities, the logical next step is to compare these costs to the related benefits. By doing a cost/benefit analysis of individual activities, an organization is able to manage such activities based on a relative measure of efficiency. The process of managing activities is often referred to as activity based management (ABM).

PROBLEMS

Problem 6.1

The issue of "Allocating Indirect Costs" has been of importance to most firms for decades. However, since the early 1980s this issue has taken "center stage" in many, if not most, cost management discussions.

Required:

A.   Explain the reasons why the issue of allocating indirect costs has become so important in the past decade.

B.   Assume your boss is considering the introduction of an ABC system in order to get a better handle on indirect costs and the various activities creating these costs. The new system is estimated to cost your firm $800,000. Before going ahead with the new ABC system, your boss asks you to present the argument against the idea (i.e., your task is to play "devil's advocate").

Problem 6.2

The interest in ABM is largely an outgrowth of the developments regarding ABC over the past decade. Nevertheless, the ABM concept could be utilized even in a firm that does not have an ABC system. Explain this latter line of thinking.

Problem 6.3 *(Adapted from CMA examination)*

Redwood Company sells craft kits and supplies to retail outlets and through its catalog. Some of the items are manufactured by Redwood while others are purchased for resale. For the products it manufactures, the company currently bases its selling prices on a standard costing system that accounts for direct material, direct labor, and the associated overhead costs. In addition to these standard product costs, Redwood incurs substantial selling costs, and Roger Jackson, controller, has suggested that these selling costs should be included in the product pricing structure.

        After studying the costs incurred over the past two years for one of its products, skeins of knitting yarn, Jackson has selected four categories of selling costs and developed cost drivers (allocation bases) for each of these costs. The selling costs actually incurred during the past year and the cost drivers are shown below.

Cost Category	Amount	Cost Driver
Sales commissions	$675,000	Boxes of yarn sold to retail stores
Catalogs	295,400	Catalogs distributed
Cost of catalog sales	105,000	Skeins sold through catalog
Credit and collection	60,000	Number of retail orders
Total selling costs	$1,135,400	

The knitting yarn is sold to retail outlets in boxes, each containing twelve skeins of yarn; the sale of partial boxes is not permitted. Commissions are paid on sales to retail outlets but not on catalog sales. The cost of catalog sales includes the wages of personnel who take the catalog orders and telephone costs. Jackson believes that the selling costs vary significantly with the size of the order; order sizes are divided into three categories as shown below.

Order Size	Catalog Sales	Retail Sales
Small	1-10 skeins	1-10 boxes
Medium	11-20 skeins	11-20 boxes
Large	Over 20 skeins	Over 20 boxes

An analysis of the previous year's records produced the statistics shown in the chart below.

	ORDER SIZE			
	Small	Medium	Large	TOTAL
Retail Sales in Boxes (12 skeins per box)	2,000	45,000	178,000	225,000
Catalog Sales in Skeins	79,000	52,000	44,000	175,000
Number of Retail Orders	485	2,415	3,100	6,000
Catalogs Distributed	254,300	211,300	125,200	590,800

Required:

A.   Define the concept of activity-based costing and provide two examples of cost drivers that are not related to selling costs.

B.   Prepare a detailed schedule showing Redwood Company's total selling cost for each order size and the per skein selling cost within each order size.

C.   Explain how the analysis of the selling costs for skeins of knitting yarn is likely to impact future pricing and product decisions at Redwood Company.

Problem 6.4 *(Adapted from CMA examination)*

Alyssa Manufacturing produces two items in its Trumbull Plant: Tuff Stuff and Ruff Stuff. Since inception, Alyssa has used only one manufacturing overhead pool to accumulate cots. Overhead has been allocated to products based on direct labor hours.

Until recently, Alyssa was the sole producer of Ruff Stuff and was able to dictate the selling price. However, last year Marvella Products began marketing a comparable product at a price below the standard costs developed by Alyssa. Market share has declined rapidly, and Alyssa must now decide whether to meet the competitive price or to discontinue the product line. Recognizing that discontinuing the product line would place additional burden on its remaining product, Tuff Stuff, Alyssa is using activity-based costing to determine if it would show a different cost structure for the two products.

The two major indirect costs for manufacturing the products are power usage and set-up costs. Most of the power usage is used in fabricating, while most of the set-up costs are required in assembly. The set-up costs are predominantly for the Tuff Stuff product line.

A decision was made to separate the Manufacturing Department costs into two activity centers.

Fabricating   - using machine hours as the cost driver (activity base).

Assembly   - using the number of set-ups as the cost driver (activity base).

Manufacturing Department
Annual Budget Before Separation of Overhead

	Total	Tuff Stuff	Ruff Stuff
		Product Line	
Number of Units		20,000	20,000
Direct labor*		2 hours per unit	3 hours per unit
Total direct labor	$800,000		
Direct material		$5.00 per unit	$3.00 per unit
Budgeted overhead:			
Indirect labor	$ 24,000		
Fringe benefits	5,000		
Indirect material	31,000		
Power	180,000		
Set-up	75,000		
Quality assurance	10,000		
Other utilities	10,000		
Depreciation	15,000		

*Direct labor hourly rate is the same in both departments.

Manufacturing Department
Cost Structure After Separation of Overhead into Activity Pools

	Fabrication	Assembly
Direct labor	75%	25%
Direct material (no change per product)	100%	0%
Indirect labor	75%	25%
Fringe benefits	80%	20%
Indirect material	$ 20,000	$11,000
Power	$160,000	$20,000
Set-up	$ 5,000	$70,000
Quality assurance	80%	20%
Other utilities	50%	50%
Depreciation	80%	20%

Activity base:	Product Line	
	Tuff Stuff	Ruff Stuff
Machine hours per unit	4.4	6.0
Number of set-ups	1,000	272

Required:

A. By allocating overhead based on direct labor hours, calculate the

1. total budgeted cost of the Manufacturing Department.

2. unit standard cost of Tuff Stuff.

3. unit standard cost of Ruff Stuff.

B. After separation of overhead into activity pools, compute the total budgeted cost of the

1. Fabricating Department.

2. Assembly Department.

C. Using activity-based costing, calculate the unit standard costs for

1. Tuff Stuff.

2. Ruff Stuff.

Problem 6.5 *(Adapted from CMA examination)*

Hawthorn Company manufactures three lawncare component parts: fuel systems, transmission assemblies, and electrical systems. For the past five years, manufacturing overhead has been applied to products on standard direct labor hours for the units actually produced. The standard cost information is shown below.

The current direct labor rate is $10 per hour. New machinery that highly automates the production process, was installed two years ago and greatly reduced the direct labor time to produce the three products. The selling price for each of the three products is 125 percent of the manufacturing cost.

Hawthorn's segment of the lawncare component industry has become very competitive, and the company's profits have been decreasing. Jim Briggs, controller, has been asked by the president of the company to analyze the overhead allocations and pricing structure. Briggs thinks that future allocations should be based on machine hours and direct labor hours rather than the current allocation method which is based on direct labor hours, only. Briggs has determined the additional product information shown below.

Standard Cost Information			
	Fuel Systems	Transmission Assemblies	Electrical Systems
Units produced and sold	10,000	20,000	30,000
Standard labor hours	2.0	1.5	1.0
Standard direct material cost per unit	$25.00	$36.00	$30.00
Budgeted and actual manufacturing overhead		$3,920,000	

Additional Product Information			
	Fuel Systems	Transmission Assemblies	Electrical Systems
Standard machine hours	2.0	4.0	6.0
Manufacturing overhead			
Direct labor hours		560,000	
Machine hours		3,360,000	

Required:

A.   By allocating all of the budgeted overhead based on direct labor hours, calculate the unit manufacturing cost and unit sales price for each of the three products manufactured at Hawthorn Company.

B.   Prepare an analysis for Hawthorn Company using the appropriate cost driver(s) determined by Jim Briggs for manufacturing overhead. Calculate the unit manufacturing cost and unit sales price for each of the three products.

C.   Based on your calculations in Requirements A and B, prepare a recommendation for the president at Hawthorn Company to increase the firm's profitability.

PRICING DECISIONS

CHAPTER OUTLINE

INTRODUCTION

Chapters 2 through 6 focused on cost issues and their relationship to profits. The focus of this chapter is on the way firms make pricing decisions and the effect of such decisions on the generation of revenues and, in turn, profits.

There are many different approaches that firms can, and do, take in making pricing decisions. The approaches discussed in this chapter are marginal analysis, full costs-plus target profits, variable costs-plus percentage markup, and target costing. The discussion of these approaches will be in terms of pricing decisions related to selling products to customers who are external to the firm. The subject of transfer pricing, which deals with pricing decisions related to the internal transfer of products among subunits of the same organization, will be discussed in Chapter 10.

MARGINAL ANALYSIS

In microeconomics, it is usually assumed that managers focus on maximizing company profits. As shown in Chapter 2, the sales level which maximizes profits is also the point where the marginal revenue from the last unit of a product sold is equal to that unit's marginal cost.[1] By substituting the optimal sales level into the product's demand function, the optimal sales price is readily determined. This approach to pricing is sometimes referred to as the **marginal analysis** approach and can be illustrated with the aid of Figure 7.1. In this figure, the firm is assumed to be the only supplier to the market (i.e., a monopoly) and the demand for the firm's product is assumed to be inversely related to price.[2] Marginal revenue equals marginal cost at an output level of $X^\star$ and a price of $P^\star$. In order for the firm to sell more units than $X^\star$, it would have to lower its price per unit below $P^\star$. However, the increase in revenues derived by selling additional units would be less than the increase in costs to produce and sell these extra units. That is, the marginal revenue would be less than the marginal cost for output to the right of $X^\star$ and thus the firm would earn more profits by charging a price of $P^\star$ and having output of $X^\star$. On the other hand, if the firm were to raise its price beyond $P^\star$, it would sell less units than $X^\star$. In this case, the firm would lose more revenue than it would save in cost. In other words, with output to the left of $X^\star$, the

---

1. As in Chapter 2, the discussion in this chapter assumes that all units produced (or purchased) are sold, thereby ignoring the issues surrounding inventory buildup.

2. This assumption means that high prices encourage a relatively low volume of units sold, while low prices encourage a relatively high sales volume. The relationship between changes in the unit price of a product and the changes in the number of units sold is referred to as price elasticity of demand. Appendix 7.1 provides a technical discussion of the price elasticity of demand concept.

FIGURE 7.1
Monopoly Pricing

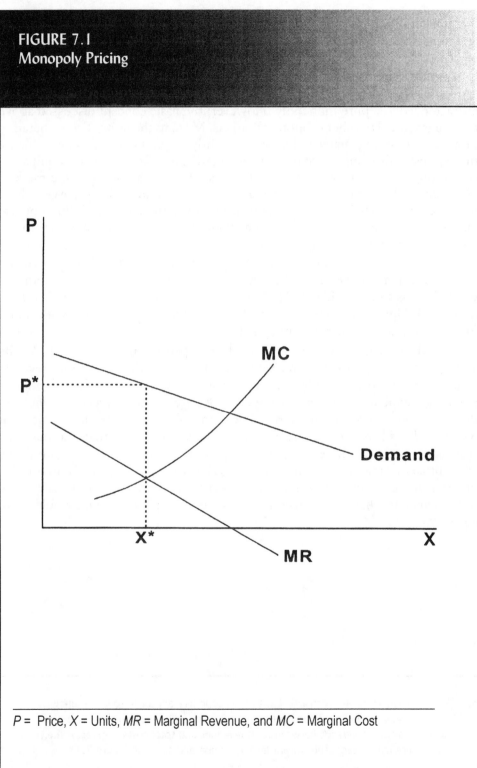

P = Price, X = Units, MR = Marginal Revenue, and MC = Marginal Cost

marginal revenue exceeds the marginal cost and the firm would be better off returning to the $P\star$ and $X\star$ position. Hence, profits are maximized where MR equals MC. At this point, $X\star$ is the level of output, $P\star$ is the product's price, and total revenues are equal to $P\star \bullet X\star$.[3]

Of course, very few firms operate in an economic environment characterized as a pure monopoly. However, the basic concept discussed above may be extended to other economic markets. More to the point, firms operating in a market having many sellers with slightly differentiated products (i.e., a monopolistically competitive market) or a market having a few major companies accounting for the majority of the industry's sales (i.e., an oligopolistic market) would normally face demand, marginal revenue, and marginal cost curves which have the same general characteristics as those shown in Figure 7.1. Thus, optimal price-output decisions in these markets would be derived in a similar fashion to that described above.

The demand and cost curves for firms operating in a perfectly competitive market (i.e., a market having many sellers with similar products) would look as shown in Figure 7.2. Notice in this figure that the demand curve is horizontal. Hence, the demand curve has only one price associated with it and that price is equal to the firm's marginal revenue.

Maximizing profits in a perfectly competitive market would also be accomplished by producing and selling at the point where marginal revenue equals marginal cost, $X\star$, only now the firm is a price taker at $P\star$. Hence, under a perfectly competitive market, pricing decisions are technically a *fait accompli* and the focus shifts to controlling costs. The firm is able to sell as many units as it wishes at $P\star$. However, the marginal revenue would be less than the marginal cost if the firm sells more units than $X\star$, and the marginal revenue would be greater than the marginal cost if the firm sells less units. Accordingly, equilibrium in terms of maximum profits is again reached at an output of $X\star$ and a sales price of $P\star$, which is where MR equals MC. Total revenue, at this point, would again equal $P\star \bullet X\star$.

---

3.   The above discussion is consistent with the economics approach to C-V-P analysis presented in Chapter 2. Referring to Figure 2.2, it will be recalled that output of X_2 is where the difference between total revenues and total costs is greatest (i.e., profits are maximized). This output level is comparable to X^* in Figure 7.1.

FIGURE 7.2
Pricing Under Perfect Competition

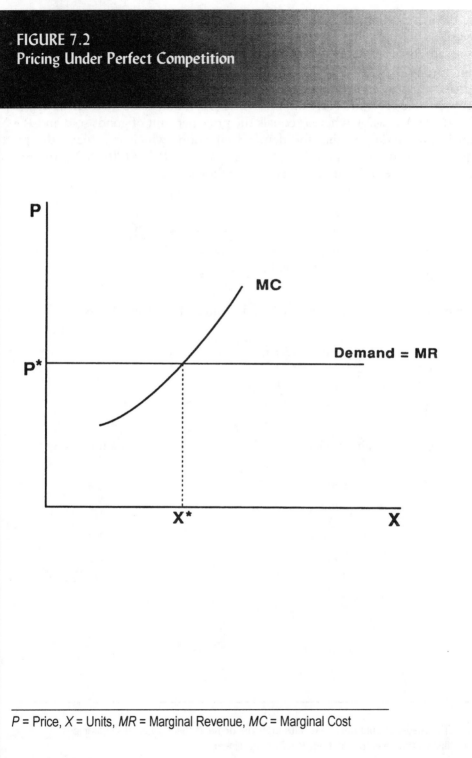

P = Price, X = Units, MR = Marginal Revenue, MC = Marginal Cost

An example will help illustrate the marginal analysis approach to pricing decisions. Assume that the fixed costs for High Style Co., a single product retail store, are equal to $5,000 and its variable costs per unit sold are $4. Total costs can therefore be depicted as: $5,000 +$4X, where X represents the number of units purchased and sold by High Style Co. Since profits (π) represent the difference between total revenues (TR) and total costs (TC), they can be written as $\pi = (P \bullet X) - (\$5,000 + \$4X)$, where P equals the price per unit of goods sold and $P \bullet X$ equals TR. Assuming that the demand equation (which is actually the price equation) facing the product of High Style Co. is: $P = \$100 - \$.2X$, the profit equation for the firm can be rewritten as follows:[4]

$$\pi = TR - TC$$
$$\pi = [(\$100 - \$.2X)X] - [(\$5,000 + \$4X)]$$
$$\pi = \$100X - \$.2X^2 - \$5,000 - \$4X$$
$$\pi = -\$.2X^2 + \$96X - \$5,000$$

The profit maximizing values for X and P can be found as follows:

$$\frac{d\pi}{dX} = -.4X + 96 = 0$$
$$.4X = 96$$
$$X = 240$$

Substituting this value back into the demand equation to obtain P, we get:

$$P = 100 - .2X$$
$$= 100 - (.2)(240)$$
$$= \$52$$

---

4.   The reader should note that, although the demand function in this example is linear, the revenue function, $P \bullet X$, is nonlinear.

Thus, in order to maximize profits, High Style should sell 240 units at a price of $52 per unit, yielding a *TR* of $12,480. The marginal revenue and marginal cost for the last unit sold at this level are equal to $4.[5] The firm's maximum profit in this example would be $6,520, as shown below:

$$
\begin{aligned}
\pi \quad &= \quad P \bullet X - (\$5,000 + \$4X) \\
&= \quad (\$52)\,(240) - [\$5,000 + (\$4)(240)] \\
&= \quad \$12,480 - \$5,960 \\
&= \quad \$6,520
\end{aligned}
$$

The above discussion demonstrates that the marginal analysis approach to pricing relies on information related to both revenues (i.e., market demand) and costs. The management accounting system can play an important role in gathering and processing this information. However, as noted in Chapter 2, it is usually extremely difficult, if not impossible, to obtain the information required to accurately derive a firm's economic cost and revenue curves. For example, even though many argue for a variable costing system on the basis of a marginal analysis approach to pricing, the reality is that economic based marginal costs usually cannot be derived from accounting based variable costs. As a result, firms often turn to more practical, accounting based pricing approaches, including the ones discussed below.

5.   The solution in this example is easily verified by noting that the marginal cost for the product sold is a constant $4, given the cost function is equal to:

$5,000 + $4X (i.e., $\dfrac{dTC}{dX}$ = $4). The marginal revenue, at the optimal output

level of 240 units, is also $4 (i.e., $\dfrac{dTR}{dX}$ = $100 - [$.4(240)] = $4).

FULL COSTS-PLUS TARGET PROFITS

There are many cost based approaches to pricing decisions. These approaches are often viewed as being more practical than the marginal analysis approach discussed above because the costs are usually derived from accrual accounting data and the goal is to satisfy, rather than maximize, with respect to profits. One commonly advocated approach considers both variable and fixed costs, as well as target profits. This approach is sometimes referred to as a **full costs-plus target profits**. Prices under this approach are derived as shown below.[6]

$$P = VC + \frac{FC + \pi}{X_N}$$ Eq. 7.1

where,

P	=	product price
VC	=	variable costs per unit
FC	=	total fixed costs,
X_N	=	normal level of output
π	=	target profits, which equal target return on investments (ROI) multiplied by related investments.

An example of the basic calculation involved in establishing prices based on full costs-plus target profits follows. Assume that the normal sales level, X_N, for a small, one product manufacturing firm, Nat, Inc., is estimated at an average of 1,000 units per month, or 12,000 per year. The combined manufacturing and nonmanufacturing variable costs are estimated to be $20 per unit. The combined manufacturing and nonmanufacturing fixed costs are estimated to be $80,000 per year. Thus, the average full costs for this product are estimated to be $26.67 (i.e., $20 + ($80,000 / 12,000)). The target profits (derived from a satisfactory return on

---

6. This approach to pricing is closely related to the C-V-P approach to target profits discussed in Chapter 2. Indeed, with minor reworking, Eq. 7.1 becomes:

$$X_N = \frac{FC + \text{Target Profits}}{P - VC}$$

The difference between this formulation and the formulation for determining the number of units required to earn a target profit, X_π in Eq. 2.2, is that here a given (normal) level of output is assumed and the object is to solve for the desired price. In Eq. 2.2, price is assumed and the desired sales level is unknown.

investments) are $100,000 for the year. The selling price, P, for Nat's product would be:

$$P = \$20 + \frac{\$80,000 + \$100,000}{12,000} = \$35,$$

and the total revenue would be $420,000 (i.e., $35 x 12,000).[7] Once a price is derived, the firm should assess whether or not the market demand for the product will support the price. If the market will not support the price, the firm can decide either against entering the market for the product or to try and reduce the price via a cost and/or profit reduction. In other words, even under cost based approaches to pricing, it is essential to consider market conditions.

Full costs-plus target profits pricing has many advocates. Support for this method is based on several factors, including the following three. First, the method relies on accounting data which, although subject to limitations, is usually available. Second, full costs-plus target profits pricing allows a firm to work toward a profit objective which is well understood by users of accounting data. This second point is especially true when the target profits are derived from a target ROI, which is a well established yardstick of firm performance.[8] The third reason many advocate the use of full costs-plus target profits pricing concerns its perception of fairness. That is, it seems fair for a firm to attempt to earn a satisfactory level of profits.[9] Therefore, from a regulatory point of view, the procedure has much support.

VARIABLE COSTS-PLUS PERCENTAGE MARKUP

Another form of cost based pricing starts with variable costs and adds a percentage markup (based on variable costs) to cover fixed costs plus profits. This approach is sometimes referred to as a **variable costs-plus percentage markup**. Prices under this approach are derived as shown below.

$P = VC + \% \ Markup \bullet VC$

Eq. 7.2

---

7. Some manufacturing firms choose to consider only manufacturing costs in the VC and FC parts of Eq. 7.1. Where this is done, the target profits need to incorporate a recovery of the nonmanufacturing costs as well as a return on the investments.
8. Of course, the notion of a target ROI is a satisfying, rather than maximizing, concept. However, given the difficulties associated with maximizing, satisfying is often the more realistic approach.
9. In contrast, many argue that it is not only fair, but appropriate, for firms to strive toward profit maximization rather than profit satisfaction (e.g., Friedman, 1970).

where,

P	=	product price
VC	=	variable costs per unit
% Markup	=	percentage markup on variable costs.

In Eq. 7.2, the percentage markup is intended to incorporate both the fixed costs per unit and the profit per unit desired by the firm. Thus, the difference between this approach and the full costs-plus target profits pricing approach discussed above is really one of form rather than substance. Returning to our previous example, if the markup were 75% of VC, the same sales price of $35 [i.e., $20 + (75% x $20)] would be obtained. Of course, as with any form of cost-plus pricing, before trying to sell a product at a particular price the firm needs to assess whether the market conditions will support such a price.

Nonmanufacturing firms also recognize the need to consider fixed as well as variable costs in setting prices. In this regard, it is interesting to consider the way consulting firms set their prices. It is common for consulting firms to determine the prices of their services in terms of particular consulting jobs. In pricing a particular job, a variant of variable costs-plus percentage markup pricing is often utilized. The approach frequently begins by estimating the total direct labor costs related to the job. This is done by estimating the number of direct hours needed for the job, according to the class of personnel required (e.g., partner, supervisor, staff consultant), and then multiplying the respective hours by an hourly rate of pay. Next, the price of the job is determined by multiplying the total direct labor costs of the job by a factor (sometimes called multiplier), which is intended to cover all indirect costs (including both variable and fixed items), plus provide for profits.

An example of how a consulting firm, GRN and Associates, might come up with a bid price for a job to install an ABC costing system is illustrated in Exhibit 7.1. For the job in question, it is estimated that to install the system it would require 50 hours by partners, 200 hours by supervisors and 1,000 hours by staff consultants, at respective hourly rates of $120, $60, and $30. Using a multiplier of 3 to cover all indirect costs and a desired profit, the bid price works out to be $144,000.

EXHIBIT 7.1
GRN and Associates, Bid Price for Consulting Job to Install an Activity-Based Costing System

Personnel	Estimated Hours	Hourly Labor Rate	Direct Labor Costs
Partners	50	$120	$6,000
Supervisors	200	60	12,000
Staff Consultants	1,000	30	30,000
	Total Direct Labor Costs =		$48,000

Bid Price of Job: $48,000 x 3[a] = $144,000

[a] Multiplier of 3 is intended to cover all indirect costs (of both a variable and fixed nature) as well as a desired profit.

CONTRIBUTION MARGIN PARADOX AND PRICING

It is interesting at this point to revisit the concept of the **contribution margin paradox** raised in Chapter 2. The idea underlying the contribution margin paradox is that a product can be priced to have a positive contribution margin, while at the same time lose money. This paradox is due to the fact that fixed costs can exceed the contribution margin. In other words, a pricing strategy which generates a positive contribution margin (i.e., prices exceed variable costs) does not guarantee that total revenues will cover total costs. Most managers understand the contribution margin paradox, as evidenced by their emphasis on covering fixed as well as variable costs in setting prices. For example, in a study based on 22 U.S. and 22 Canadian manufacturing firms, Gordon et al. (1981) found that 83% of the executives in charge of pricing considered fixed as well as variable costs in making pricing decisions. However, these executives also understood that for one-time special purchases, variable costs may be the only relevant costs to consider. Accordingly, they expressed an interest in having information on the variable costs, as well as the full costs of their products. Similar findings have been reported in other studies (e.g., Govindarajan and Anthony, 1983; Cornick et al., 1988; Shim and Sudit, 1995).

To see the above points more clearly, let us once again return to the example of Nat, Inc. Assume the firm is currently operating only at 90% of normal sales level. At this rate, the firm will only sell 10,800 (i.e., 12,000 x .9) units by the end of the year. One of Nat's regular domestic customers offers to buy an extra 1,000 units at a price of $24 per unit. If Nat, Inc. accepts the offer, its contribution margin and profits would ostensibly go up by $4,000 (i.e., 1,000 x $4). In other words, the $24 per unit covers the variable costs per unit of $20, plus has a contribution margin of $4 per unit. However, by selling some units to one of its regular customers at a price of $24, Nat realizes that it will open itself up to renegotiations for all of the units purchased by this customer, as well as other domestic customers. Since $24 is not a sustainable price (i.e., it is below the full costs of $26.67 per unit), Nat rejects the offer.

Now suppose Nat, Inc. is contacted by a company in a foreign country, which has never bought any units of this product from Nat in the past. In fact, the company in question, FR, Inc., usually purchases a poorer quality substitute product from a foreign source. The poorer quality substitute is all that is needed by FR, Inc. However, due to a labor strike at FR's regular supplier, Nat is offered $24 per unit plus shipping costs, for 1,000 units. This is a one-time offer, which is unlikely to be repeated. After much consideration, it is determined that by selling these 1,000 units to FR, Inc., Nat's domestic customers will not be affected. Under this scenario, Nat decides to take the order because its contribution margin and profits go up by $4,000 (i.e., 1,000 x $4), and regular orders at a price of $35 are deemed unaltered.

TARGET COSTING

As noted earlier in this chapter, for some products there is a well established market price. For other products, a target price (possibly set at a level which will enable the firm to obtain a target share of the market) can be set. Assuming profit maximization is not the driving force, some firms reverse the cost-plus pricing approaches discussed above. This is done by shifting the focus to managing costs, such that a desirable profit level is achieved given the established or targeted price. For example, assume MAR, Inc. is considering the introduction of a new household appliance product. Given the close substitutes offered by competitors, the firm decides that the new product should be introduced at a targeted sales price of $80 per unit. The gross profit (i.e., revenues less cost of goods sold) per unit required to cover nonmanufacturing (i.e., selling and administrative) costs, plus a desired net profit per unit, is determined to be $25. Hence, the target cost of developing and manufacturing this product would be $55 (i.e., $80 - $25) per unit.

The above approach to managing costs is often referred to as **target costing**. Although technically a costing concept, target costing is inextricably intertwined with pricing considerations. Many firms use target costing as a way to focus on managing costs, rather than recovering costs through some form of cost-plus pricing mechanism. Of course, the logical follow-up step to target costing as a method of managing costs would be to attempt to reduce the target cost in successive periods. To the extent that the product could be manufactured in subsequent periods for less than the target cost, the firm could either earn a larger profit or lower the price, depending on which seemed more appropriate given the demand for the product.

Japanese firms are often credited with popularizing the target costing concept over the past few decades. However, the idea of focusing on costs to achieve a target profit, given an established price, is as old as discussions concerning competitive economic markets. Nevertheless, Japanese firms have certainly given new life to the notion of reducing costs via target costing. In discussing this emphasis on reducing costs by Japanese firms, many authors often make a distinction between the cost reduction process related to the development phase of a new product and the cost reduction process related to the production phase of products (e.g., Monden and Hamada, 1991; Cooper and Slagmoulder, 1998). These authors refer to the former cost reduction process as target costing and the latter as **kaizen costing.** J. Fisher (1995), in his discussion of target costing at Matsushita Electric Industrial Corporation and Toyota Motor Corporation,[10] also emphasizes that the focus of target costing is on reducing costs at the planning and product design stages, rather than the production stage

---

10. Toyota Motor Corporation is generally credited with having popularized, if not developing, the modern view of target costing.

of a product. The approach taken in this book is to view the target costing concept as being concerned with managing all manufacturing costs (i.e., planning, product design, and production costs). Of course, the target costing concept could be extended to include nonmanufacturing costs, although most discussions of the concept do not make this extension.

An interesting example of target costing is provided by Morgan (1993) in his case study from Tantalus Company. That study illustrates how the desired profit utilized in target costing is often derived from a target return on sales (i.e., profits divided by sales). In addition, the study also shows how Tantalus Company was able to achieve an acceptable target cost via successive rounds of cost management.

COSTS VS. MARKET CONSIDERATIONS

As indicated in the above discussion, pricing decisions for some products are initially set into motion by first considering costs. In contrast, pricing decisions for other products are initially driven by market concerns. In the final analysis, however, both costs and market concerns need to be considered in deriving prices. Stated differently, both supply considerations (which are determined by costs) and demand considerations (which are determined by market conditions) are critical aspects of pricing decisions.

The cost side of pricing is derived largely from a firm's management accounting system. Accordingly, management accountants have given, and continue to give, a significant amount of attention to the subject of pricing decisions. Questions like the following are at the heart of this attention. Should fixed, as well as variable, costs be included in cost-plus pricing models? How do cost allocation issues affect pricing decisions? What is the relationship between an ABC system and pricing decisions? How will cost accumulation procedures (e.g., job order costing vs. process costing) affect pricing decisions? The answers to these questions seem to vary, depending (i.e., contingent) on the circumstances surrounding the firm and the product being sold.

SENSITIVITY ANALYSIS

A valuable aspect of a well-designed management accounting system is its ability to incorporate sensitivity analysis (i.e., ask "what if" type questions). The area of pricing decisions is particularly well suited for such an analysis. More specifically, it is both natural and necessary to ask questions like the following: What will happen to profits if costs increase (decrease) by 5 or 10 percent? What will happen to revenues, costs, and profits if prices increase (decrease) by 5 or 10 percent? What will happen to the sales volume of our product(s) if competitors raise (lower) their prices by 5 or 10 percent?

Let us return to the High Style Co. example discussed earlier in this chapter. This time, however, we will assume that while $4 is the most likely variable cost per unit, it is also possible for the actual cost to vary between $3 and $6 per unit, considered in increments of $1.00. Based on this additional information, it is reasonable to question the initially derived optimal sales price of $52. In fact, by going back to the original calculations and replacing the variable costs of $4 per unit with $3, $5, and $6, it can be seen how sensitive the initially derived price of $52 is to the original point estimate of $4 in variable costs. We can also look at the sensitivity of final profits to the revised estimates of variable costs. The results of this exercise are provided in Exhibit 7.2 (the reader should verify the numbers shown under the optimal sales level, price, and profits).

CONCLUDING COMMENTS

Pricing decisions are of fundamental importance to the survival of a firm. The conceptual approaches toward pricing decisions are largely grounded in microeconomic concepts, with marginal analysis at the center. This approach assumes that firms are profit maximizers and that their revenue and cost functions are nonlinear. In contrast, pricing based on cost schemes usually assumes that firms are profit satisfiers and that cost and revenue curves are linear within the normal range of operations. These latter assumptions are usually associated with accounting concepts and are similar to the ones discussed under cost-volume-profit analysis in Chapter 2.

Although the microeconomic underpinnings of pricing decisions are apparently well understood by managers, the principles underlying marginal analysis and profit maximizing are not easily implemented in most firms. Thus, most pricing managers seem to follow a profit satisfying approach, which combines cost based pricing tempered by market considerations.[11] Further, the empirical evidence points out that the information utilized cuts across the tripartite classification scheme discussed in the first chapter of this book. As Gordon et al. (1981, pp. 45-46) noted in discussing the results of their empirical study of 22 U.S. manufacturing firms and 22 Canadian manufacturing firms, most managers in charge of pricing decisions want nonfinancial, externally oriented, and ex ante information, as well as the financial, internally oriented, and ex post information.

---

11.   Loeb and Surysekar (1995) show that under special conditions cost-based pricing is not optimal.

EXHIBIT 7.2
High Style Company Sensitivity Analysis[a]

Variable Costs (Per Unit)	Fixed Costs	Optimal Sales Level (In Units)[b]	Optimal Price (Per Unit)	Optimal Profits
$3.00	$5,000	242 1/2	$51.50	$6,761.25
$4.00	$5,000	240	$52.00	$6,520.00
$5.00	$5,000	237 1/2	$52.50	$6,281.25
$6.00	$5,000	235	$53.00	$6,045.00

[a] Demand function is assumed to be: P = $100 - $.2X

[b] Although the optimization problem permits a solution with half units, from a practical point of view only whole units can be sold.

The need for information that traditionally is not included in most formal management accounting systems places managers in charge of pricing in the position of having to follow one of two strategies. First, they can turn to informal information sources for the required information. The informal sources may be internally or externally generated. Either way, they are likely to be incomplete, unreliable, and/or untimely in terms of meeting the manager's needs. An alternative strategy is to take an expanded view of the data base supporting the management accounting system. That is, nonfinancial, ex ante, and external information, as well as the more traditional financial, ex post, and internal information, can be built into the formal MAS. Numerous information services exist which provide macroeconomic forecasts, replacement cost data, and competitor analyses on a timely and inexpensive basis. The developments with microcomputers and the Internet have done much to advance this latter strategy.

The discussion in this chapter has implicitly assumed that firms either sell one product or that the information on the various products can be disentangled. Of course, nearly all firms sell more than one product and disentangling information related to one product from that concerning other products is often difficult, if not impossible, to do. Where the information related to various products cannot be disentangled, simple solutions to pricing decisions do not exist. Nevertheless, the underlying concepts discussed in this chapter provide a good framework for exploring more complex solutions.

Pricing decisions related to products transferred among subunits within the same firm raise a host of additional concerns. These concerns are discussed in Chapter 10. However, before addressing these concerns, it is helpful to first consider the way firms measure performance. The next chapter covers this topic.

APPENDIX 7.1:
Price Elasticity of Demand

The relationship between the price of a product (goods or services) and the number of units sold (i.e., demanded) plays a central role in microeconomics. This relationship is expressed in terms of the ratios of the percentage change in the number of units sold to the percentage change in the price of the product, i.e.,

$$\left(\frac{\Delta X}{X}\right) / \left(\frac{\Delta P}{P}\right)$$

which is referred to as the **price elasticity of demand**, or e_p. In the limiting case, e_p can be derived through calculus by:

$$e_p = \frac{dX}{dP} \bullet \frac{P}{X} \qquad\qquad \text{Eq. 7.3}$$

For normal products, e_p is negative in that an inverse relationship exists between the number of units sold and the price of a product. However, an important issue is the strength of this inverse relationship. For certain points along a product's demand curve, the absolute value of e_p is greater than 1 (i.e., $|e_p| > 1$) and said to be price elastic. For other points along the same demand curve, the absolute value of e_p is less than 1 (i.e., $|e_p| < 1$) and said to be price inelastic. Unit elasticity exists where $|e_p| = 1$. These concepts are illustrated in Figure 7.3. Total revenues derived from a product can be increased by reducing the product's price when $|e_p| > 1$ and increasing the product's price when $|e_p| < 1$.

FIGURE 7.3
Price Elasticity Concepts

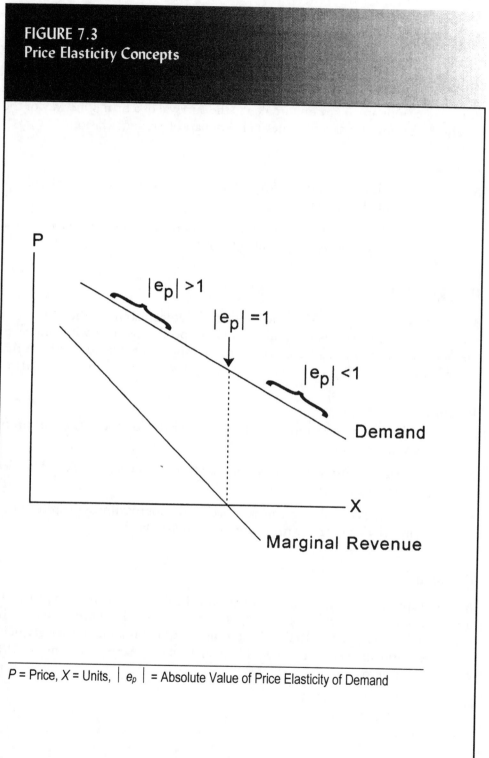

P = Price, X = Units, $\left| e_p \right|$ = Absolute Value of Price Elasticity of Demand

PROBLEMS

Problem 7.1

Pricing decisions are of key importance to the survival of a firm. One way or the other, cost accounting data becomes a critical part of pricing decisions.

Required:

A.   Discuss how cost accounting data is used when pricing decisions are largely market driven.

B.   Define "target costing" and explain what, if anything, is novel about the use of target costing by Japanese firms.

Problem 7.2

Many firms use cost-plus pricing techniques for at least some of their products. One common approach is to combine a target profit objective with full costs. Despite the common use of such an approach, opponents like to point out that cost-plus pricing (of any sort) does not result in maximizing the profits of a firm.

Required:

A.   Explain why cost-plus pricing approaches do not result in profit maximization.

B.   Do mangers using cost-plus pricing approaches ignore the marketplace for the product? Explain.

C.   Given that cost-plus pricing approaches do not maximize the profits of a firm, why do so many firms use these approaches?

Problem 7.3

In this chapter, an example was given on how the marginal analysis approach to pricing would solve for the price output combination where profits would be maximized. The Appendix to the chapter discussed the notion of price elasticity of demand and showed $| e_p |$ would equal 1 where marginal revenues (*MR*) were equal to zero.

Required:

A. Using the example provided in this chapter (i.e., where $P = \$100 - \$.2X$, and $TC = \$5,000 + \$4X$), prove that the $|\, e_p \,|$ is equal to 1 where MR is equal to zero.

B. Derive the $|\, e_p \,|$ for this example where profits are maximized.

Problem 7.4

The ZIP Corporation owns a chain of hotels operating in various countries. At a recent pricing meeting, Ms. Jennifer Agarwal, who recently joined the company after completing her MBA degree, suggested a new strategy for the firm. Since many of the firm's hotels are located close to major airports around the world, her suggestion is to set a partial-day rate for renting out rooms between the hours of 9 a.m. and 5 p.m. Her thinking, in this regard, is that many of the hotels' regular guests arrive at the room late in the evening and leave early in the morning to catch airline flights. At the same time, there are many business people who would like to rent a hotel room for part of the day for work-related activities.

Although other hotel chains have used a partial-day pricing strategy, ZIP corporation has avoided such a policy. The corporation's Vice-President in charge of pricing likes Ms. Agarwal's suggestion, but first wants to know the pros and cons of the proposal.

Required:

Prepare a memo for ZIP Corporation's Vice-President discussing the pros and cons of Ms. Agarwal's suggestion.

Problem 7.5 (Adapted from CMA examination)

Award Plus Co. manufactures medals for winners of athletic events and other contests. Its manufacturing plant has the capacity to produce 10,000 medals each month; current monthly production is 7,500 medals. The company normally charges $175 per medal. Variable costs and fixed costs for the current activity level of 75 percent are shown below.

Current Product Costs	
Variable costs	
Manufacturing	
Labor	$ 375,000
Material	262,500
Marketing	187,500
Total variable costs	825,000
Fixed costs	
Manufacturing	275,000
Marketing	175,000
Total fixed costs	450,000
Total costs	$1,275,000

Award Plus has just received a special one-time order for 2,500 medals at $100 per medal. For this particular order, no variable marketing costs will be incurred. Cathy Senna, a management accountant with Award Plus, has been assigned the task of analyzing this order and recommending whether or not the company should accept or reject it. After examining the costs, Senna suggested to her supervisor, Gerard LePenn who is the controller, that they request competitive bids from vendors for the raw materials as the current quote seems high. LePenn insisted that the prices are in line with other vendors and told her that she was not to discuss her observations with anyone else. Senna later discovered that LePenn is a brother-in-law of the owner of the current raw materials supply vendor.

Required:

A.   Identify and explain the costs that will be relevant to Cathy Senna's analysis of the special order being considered by Award Plus Co.

B.   Determine if Award Plus Co. should accept the special order. In explaining your answer, compute both the new average unit cost for Award Plus and the incremental unit cost for the special order.

Problem 7.6 *(Adapted from CMA examination)*

The Midwest Division of the Paibec Corporation manufactures sub-assemblies that are used in the corporation's final products. Lynn Hardt of Midwest's Profit Planning Department has been assigned the task of determining whether a component, MTR-2000, should continue to be manufactured by Midwest or purchased from Marley Company, an outside supplier. MTR-2000 is part of a sub-assembly manufactured by Midwest.

Marley has submitted a bid to manufacture and supply the 32,000 units of MTR-2000 that Paibec will need for 1998 at a unit price of $17.30. Marley has assured Paibec that the units will be delivered according to Paibec's production specifications and needs. While the contract price of $17.30 is only applicable in 1998, Marley is interested in entering into a long-term arrangement beyond 1998.

Hardt has gathered the following information regarding Midwest's cost to manufacture MTR-2000 in 1997. These annual costs will be incurred to manufacture 30,000 units.

Direct material	$195,000
Direct labor	120,000
Factory space rental	84,000
Equipment leasing costs	36,000
Other manufacturing overhead	225,000
Total manufacturing costs	$660,000

Hardt has collected the following additional information related to manufacturing MTR-2000.

- Direct materials used in the production of MTR-2000 are expected to increase eight percent in 1998.

- Midwest's direct labor contract calls for a five percent increase in 1998.

- The facilities used to manufacture MTR-2000 are rented under a month-to-month rental agreement. Thus, Midwest can withdraw from the rental agreement without any penalty. Midwest would have no need for this space if MTR-2000 is not manufactured.

- Equipment leasing costs represent special equipment that is used in the manufacture of MTR-2000. This lease can be terminated by paying the equivalent of one month's lease payment for each year left on the lease agreement. Midwest has two years left on the lease agreement, through the end of 1999.

- Forty percent of the other manufacturing overhead is considered variable. Variable overhead changes with the number of units produced, and this rate per unit is not expected to change in 1998. The fixed manufacturing overhead costs are not expected to change whether or not MTR-2000 is manufactured. Equipment other than the leased equipment can be used in Midwest's other manufacturing operations.

John Porter, divisional manager of Midwest, stopped by Hardt's office to voice his concern regarding the outsourcing of MTR-2000. Porter commented, "I am really concerned about outsourcing MTR-2000. I have a son-in-law and a nephew, not to also mention a member of our bowling team, who work on MTR-2000. They could lose their jobs if we buy that component from Marley. I really would appreciate anything you can do to make sure the cost analysis comes out right to show we should continue making MTR-2000. Corporate is not aware of the material increases and maybe you can leave out some of those fixed costs. I just think we should continue making MTR-2000!"

Required:

A.   Prepare an analysis of relevant costs that shows whether or not the Midwest Division of Paibec Corporation should make MTR-2000 or purchase it from Marley Company for 1998.

B.   Based solely on the financial results, recommend whether the 32,000 units of MTR-2000 for 1998 should be made by Midwest or purchased from Marley. Show supporting calculations.

Problem 7.7 *(Adapted from CMA examination)*

When Mayfair Corporation moved to the suburbs 15 years ago, a decision was made to provide cafeteria services for its 200 employees as there were no restaurants or delicatessens within the immediate vicinity. In order to provide food prices at an attractive level to the employees, the company currently subsidizes the cafeteria services. Mayfair is in the process of reviewing the cafeteria services as cost cutting measures are needed throughout the organization to keep the price of its products competitive. Two alternatives are being evaluated: downsize the cafeteria staff and offer a reduced menu or contract with an outside vendor.

The current cafeteria operation has four employees with a combined annual salary of $110,000 plus additional employee benefits at 25 percent of salary. The cafeteria operates 250 days each year, and the costs for utilities and equipment maintenance average $30,000 annually. The daily sales include 100 entrees at $4.00 each, 80 sandwiches or salads at an average price of $3.00 each, plus an additional $200 for beverages and desserts. The cost of all cafeteria supplies is 60 percent of revenue.

The plan for downsizing the current operation envisions retaining two of the current employees whose base annual salaries total $65,000. An entree would no longer be offered, and prices of the remaining items would be increased slightly. Under this arrangement, it is expected that only 150 employees would use the cafeteria; however, the average price of a sandwich or salad would increase to $3.60. The additional revenue for beverages and desserts is expected to increase to $230 each day. Because of the elimination of the entree, the cost of all cafeteria supplies is expected to drop to 50 percent of revenue. All other conditions of operation would remain the same. Mayfair is willing to continue to subsidize this reduced operation but will not spend more than 20 percent of the current subsidy.

A proposal has been received from Wilco Foods, an outside vendor who is willing to supply cafeteria services. Wilco has proposed to pay Mayfair $1,000 per month for use of the cafeteria and utilities; Mayfair would be expected to cover equipment repair costs. In addition, Wilco would pay Mayfair four percent of all revenues received above the breakeven point; this payment would be made at the end of the year. All other costs incurred by Wilco to supply the cafeteria services are variable and equal 75 percent of revenue. Wilco plans to charge $5.00 for an entree, and the average price for a sandwich or salad would be $4.00. All other daily sales are expected to average $300. Wilco expects that 160 employees will purchase entrees, salads, or sandwiches in the cafeteria daily and has evaluated the probability of daily purchases of entrees as follows.

Entrees	
Number	**Percent**
50	.40
70	.40
90	.20

Required:

A.   Determine if the plan for downsizing the current cafeteria operation would be acceptable to Mayfair Corporation. Support your conclusion with appropriate calculations.

B.   Is the Wilco Foods proposal more advantageous to Mayfair Corporation than the downsizing plan? Support your conclusion with appropriate calculations.

FINANCIAL PERFORMANCE MEASURES

CHAPTER OUTLINE

■ Subunit Level Financial Performance Measures

■ Firm Level Financial Performance Measures

■ Managerial Compensation and Performance

INTRODUCTION

There are many factors which need to be considered when evaluating the performance of an organization and/or its subunits. These factors relate to both financial (e.g., profits) and nonfinancial (e.g., customer satisfaction) aspects of performance. The focus of this chapter is on financial performance measures. Such measures are considered at both the subunit and firm levels. There are five reasons why financial performance measures are very important. First, managers concerned with efficiently allocating scarce organizational resources are keenly interested in the financial performance of their organizations. Second, stockholders and creditors place great emphasis on financial performance in deciding whether or not to invest in a firm. Third, financial performance is directly correlated to a firm's ability to pay its employees and managers. Fourth, managerial incentive compensation schemes are commonly based on financial performance measures. Fifth, understanding the strengths and weaknesses of financial performance measures provides an important foundation for evaluating the strengths and weaknesses of nonfinancial performance measures.

The fact that the focus of this chapter is on financial performance measures is in no way intended to suggest that nonfinancial performance measures are unimportant. Indeed, there is a growing recognition that globally competitive firms need to give serious attention to nonfinancial performance measures. Accordingly, nonfinancial performance measures will be discussed in the next chapter.

Whether discussing the subunit or firm level, it is important to keep in mind that performance measures facilitate the control side of managerial accounting. As such, an overriding concern is that performance measures should be chosen in a manner that helps align the actions of managers with the objectives of the organization.

SUBUNIT LEVEL FINANCIAL PERFORMANCE MEASURES

A key feature of modern organizations is the notion of decentralization. **Decentralization** refers to an organizational structure based on subunits, whereby subunit managers have decision making autonomy. One reason for decentralization is that it allows decisions to be made at the subunit level, where a comparative advantage exists in gathering and processing relevant information. Another reason for decentralization is that it allows managers in large organizations to have a workable level of span of control. A further reason for decentralization is that decision making autonomy and concomitant responsibility provide a strong motivational force for subunit managers to achieve success.

Once a firm has decided to decentralize, the next step is to choose the form of its subunits. The forms available can be thought of in terms of the set of activities for which managerial responsibility can be established. The notion of holding individuals responsible for a specific set of activities, and devising an accounting system based on those activities, is often referred to as **responsibility accounting**. In this regard, it is generally agreed that managers should only be held responsible for activities over which they have control.[1]

The management accounting system is intertwined with the way many firms choose the form of their subunits. In fact, the activities and organizational form of subunits are often structured around accounting based measures of subunit performance. The use of cost centers, profit centers, and investment centers are key examples of this point and will provide the basis of our discussion of subunit performance measures. Although the literature usually discusses these three forms of organizational structure as being independent of each other, in reality these concepts are not mutually exclusive. It is possible, and even likely, for firms to have cost centers within profit centers, and both cost and profit centers within investment centers.

Cost Centers

A **cost center** is an organizational arrangement whereby the performance of a subunit and its managers is evaluated in terms of costs. Evaluating the performance of subunits and managers in terms of costs is ubiquitous in most organizations. In some cost centers, a neatly specified relationship between the costs of inputs and the level of physical outputs exists. In such a case, performance can be measured by comparing actual costs to prespecified input-output cost relationships. An example of a cost center for which a direct relationship can be established between the cost of inputs and the level of physical outputs is a production department within a manufacturing firm. The discussion in Chapter 4, concerning cost variances under a standard costing system, is an illustration of how a cost center can be evaluated in terms of input-output relationships.

In other cost center situations, neatly specified input-output relationships do not exist. For example, the activities of a marketing department usually do not lend themselves to the development of neatly specified input-output relationships. In cases like this one, actual costs are often compared to expected costs without reference to specific output levels.

---

1. This argument notwithstanding, there are circumstances under which it is optimal to evaluate a manager's performance based on signals derived from outcomes which are beyond her (his) control (Antle and Demski, 1988).

A major objection to treating organizational subunits as cost centers is that comparability across subunits is difficult, at best. The fact that one subunit has lower total costs than another does not necessarily reflect superior performance. If it did, the best thing a manager could do would be to close down the subunit and reduce costs to zero. Of course, such an approach would not be a reflection of a high performing subunit. It is also difficult to compare the performance of subunit managers on any sort of cost-per-output basis unless outputs are similar, in which case the outputs normally would be grouped under the same subunit. Finally, the fact that one subunit does a better job at meeting its budgeted costs than another subunit, without regard to the value of what those costs accomplished, does not necessarily mean that the subunit is performing better than the other subunit. The same concerns would exist regarding the comparison of costs for a given subunit across different time periods.

The above concerns regarding cost centers have led many organizations to evaluate subunits in terms of the value of outputs relative to the cost of inputs. A common method for conducting such an evaluation is through the use of profit centers as a means of subunit decentralization.

Profit Centers

A **profit center** is an organizational arrangement whereby the performance of a subunit and its managers is evaluated in terms of profits. Hence, the focus of a profit center is on earning a profit for the subunit. The cost of inputs are therefore judged in relation to the revenues generated by the subunit's outputs.

To illustrate the use of profit centers, assume that the Jess Co. sells two products, A and B. The company has divided itself into two profit centers, SU_1 and SU_2, with SU_1 being responsible for product A and SU_2 being responsible for product B. Mr. Harris is in charge of SU_1 and Ms. Sellers in charge of SU_2. The revenues and costs data for last year's performance is provided in Exhibit 8.1.

As the new company controller, you are provided with Exhibit 8.1 and asked to advise the president as to which subunit manager, Mr. Harris or Ms. Sellers, is doing a better job. In carrying out this assignment, you are initially struck by the fact that SU_1 has higher net operating profits than SU_2. However, SU_2 has higher controllable profits than SU_1. Hence, an issue that must be addressed is whether the controllable or net operating profits shown in Exhibit 8.1 is a better measure of performance. When measuring the performance of the subunit's manager, controllable profits are usually preferred due to the principle that one should only be held responsible over those things under her/his control. In terms of assessing the ultimate contribution of the various subunits to the firm, net operating profits will often be the dominant concern, especially if there were a strong rationale underlying the procedure for allocating corporate controlled costs.

EXHIBIT 8.1
Jess Co.
Comparison of Profit Centers

	SU_1	SU_2
Revenues	$2,000,000	$4,000,000
Variable Costs	1,200,000	3,000,000
Contribution Margin	800,000	1,000,000
Controllable Fixed Costs	100,000	50,000
Controllable Profits	$ 700,000	$ 950,000
Allocated Corporate Costs (not controllable at subunit level)	200,000	500,000
Net Operating Profits	$ 500,000	$ 450,000

Measuring subunit performance based on profits is widely accepted in practice, especially in terms of comparing actual with budgeted profits. For example, in a study by Scapens and Sale (1985), it was found that 45.4% of 205 U.S. firms and 50.5% of 211 U.K. firms used target profits in evaluating the performance of divisional managers. This empirical evidence notwithstanding, it should be apparent that profits alone do not represent the entire performance picture. What is needed is an evaluation of profits relative to the amount of capital investment required to generate such profits. This concern is relevant when comparing the profits of different subunits for a given time period or comparing the profits of a given subunit over several time periods. It is this need for a measure of profitability which has led many firms to evaluate subunits in terms of investment centers.

Investment Centers

An **investment center** is an organizational arrangement whereby the performance of a subunit and its managers is evaluated based on a rate of profit (i.e., a measure of profitability) per unit of investment. The accounting measure of a rate of profit per unit of investment is usually referred to as **return on investment (ROI)** or **accounting rate of return (ARR)** and is computed by dividing a subunit's profits by its investment level. This performance measure can be expressed algebraically as follows:

$$ROI = \frac{AP}{I} \qquad\qquad \text{Eq. 8.1}$$

where,

AP	=	accounting profits (income), and
I	=	accounting value of investments (assets).

In choosing the figures for profits and investments to use in calculating Eq. 8.1, various options exist. Most firms, however, divide controllable profits by controllable investments to arrive at a subunit's controllable ROI. This approach is usually justified based on the principle of holding managers responsible only for those items over which they have control. Returning to the Jess Co. presented in Exhibit 8.1, assume that the total controllable investment level for SU_1 is $3,500,000 and for SU_2 it is $5,000,000. Thus, based on controllable profits and controllable investments, the ROI for SU_1 is 20% (i.e., $700,000/$3,500,000) and the ROI for SU_2 is 19.0% (i.e., $950,000/$5,000,000).

As with profits, measuring subunit performance based on *ROI* is widely accepted in practice. In the Scapens and Sale (1985) study noted above, it was also found that 51.7% of the U.S. firms and 44.7% of the U.K. firms used such a measure in evaluating the performance of divisional managers. Nevertheless, as a measure of performance, *ROI* has several problems. First, and foremost, an accounting rate of return is not equal to a true rate of return (often called the economic or internal rate of return).

A true rate of return is usually described in terms of an investment in a single project. In the single project case, the **internal rate of return** (sometimes called economic rate of return) is equal to that discount rate which sets the future expected net cash flows from the project (i.e., investment) equal to the cost of the investment. (In the case of an organizational subunit, the internal rate of return would be computed in the same way, only now the investment must be viewed in terms of the cost of the entire subunit rather than a single project.) Although the internal rate of return is a valid measure of efficiency and thus performance, the problems associated with measuring future cash flows limit its usefulness. The calculation of an internal rate of return can be illustrated algebraically as follows:

$$CF_0 = \sum_{t=1}^{n} \frac{CF_t}{(1+IRR)^t} \qquad \text{Eq. 8.2}$$

where,

CF_0	=	initial cost of investment,
CF_t	=	net cash flow in period t,
n	=	economic life of capital project, and
IRR	=	internal rate of return.

A comparison of Eq. 8.1 with Eq. 8.2 highlights some of the major differences between the accounting notion of rate of return and its economic counterpart. Whereas the accounting notion of *ROI* is historical (i.e., ex post) in nature, the economic notion is future (i.e., ex ante) oriented. Further, the accounting concept of *ROI* considers only one period's rate of return, whereas the economic concept considers the return over the entire life (i.e., n) of a project (or organizational unit). Finally, the accounting concept of *ROI* is based on accrual concepts of income (including depreciation), whereas the economic concept is based on discounted cash flows.[2,3]

A second problem with using the *ROI* as a measure of subunit performance concerns the issue of goal congruency between subunits and the organization as a whole. If a given subunit has an average *ROI* which exceeds the *ROI* of an incremental project, then the subunit's *ROI* would decrease by accepting the new project. However, it may be that the *ROI* for the incremental project is above the average *ROI* for the firm as a whole because other subunits have a lower average *ROI* than the one in question. Hence, even if *ROI* were a valid measure of efficiency, maximizing a subunit's *ROI* would not be synonymous with maximizing the *ROI* of a firm.[4]

Both of the above problems related to *ROI* are relevant whether comparing the *ROI* of different subunits for a given time period or comparing the *ROI* of a given subunit over different time periods. Hence, some firms have turned to residual income (*RI*) as a measure of subunit performance.

Residual Income

Residual income (RI) is computed by deducting a capital charge from profits, where the capital charge is usually thought of in terms of the firm's cost of capital multiplied by the investments utilized to generate profits. Algebraically, this can be expressed as follows:

$$RI = AP - (I \bullet k) \hspace{5cm} \text{Eq. 8.3}$$

---

2. For a more rigorous discussion of the similarities and differences between accounting and economic rates of return, the reader is referred to the papers by Harcourt (1965), Livingstone and Salamon (1970), Stauffer (1971), Gordon (1974a), Fisher and McGowan (1983), Gordon and Stark (1989), and Kelly (1996).

3. More will be said about the economic rate of return in Chapter 12, where capital budgeting is discussed.

4. This problem also exists if a firm were to attempt to maximize the *IRR* of its divisions.

where,

AP	=	accounting profits,
I	=	accounting value of investments,
k	=	cost of capital.

As a performance measure, *RI* lies somewhere between profits and return on investment in that it provides a partial mechanism for considering the level of investment utilized in generating subunit profits. Thus, measuring a subunit's performance based on *RI* is equivalent to establishing the subunit somewhere between a profit and investment center.

To illustrate the use of residual income as a subunit performance measure, let us return to Exhibit 8.1. Recall from the discussion of investment centers that the controllable investment levels were assumed to be $3,500,000 for SU$_1$ and $5,000,000 for SU$_2$. Further, assume the firm charges each division 15% (its estimated cost of capital[5]) of its controllable investments. Given this information, the controllable *RI* would be $175,000 for SU$_1$ [i.e., $700,000 - (.15 x $3,500,000)] and $200,000 for SU$_2$ [i.e., $950,000 - (.15 x $5,000,000)]. Exhibit 8.2 summarizes the information for the Jess Co. regarding controllable profits, *ROI* and *RI*. As is evident from Exhibit 8.2, the choice of performance measure can affect the relative performance of the subunits' managers.[6]

There are many arguments for and against residual income. For example, proponents often argue that *RI* is a valid measure of economic performance because maximizing a subunit's residual income is congruent with maximizing the value of the firm. It is also often argued that the *RI* concept provides a mechanism for making divisional risk adjustments by applying different cost of capital charges to different divisions. In contrast, opponents of residual income often point out that it is largely derived from accrual accounting concepts and thus is not a true measure of economic performance. In fact, larger subunits will often have a higher *RI* than smaller subunits (providing they are able to earn a rate of profit in excess of the percentage charge on capital). As for the idea of using differing cost of capital charges for different divisions, opponents of *RI* are quick to note that the concept of a subunit cost of capital is illusive, at best.[7,8]

---

5. The cost of capital concept will be discussed in detail in Chapter 12.

6. In reality, there is a large overlap between profit and investment centers because profit centers usually have control over some investments and most investment centers do not have control over all of their investments.

7. It is sometimes suggested that *RI* be computed as a percentage of investments. However, this solution brings us back to the ratio problem associated with *ROI*.

8. For a more rigorous discussion of the strengths and weaknesses of residual income, the reader is referred to the papers by Amey (1975), Tomkins (1975a, 1975b), and Scapens (1978, 1979).

EXHIBIT 8.2
Jess Co. Comparison of Controllable Profits, ROI and RI

	SU$_1$	SU$_2$
Controllable Profits	$700,000	$950,000
Controllable ROI[a]	20%	19%
Controllable RI[b]	$175,000	$200,000

[a] Based on controllable investment levels of $3,500,000 and $5,000,000 in SU$_1$ and SU$_2$, respectively.

[b] Based on controllable investment levels noted above and a capital charge equal to 15% of the subunit's investment level.

Several empirical studies have examined whether residual income is used as a subunit performance measure in large corporations. In general, these studies have shown that residual income has received mixed acceptance as a subunit performance measure. For example, Reece and Cool (1978) found that 28% of 1,000 large U.S. industrial firms used *RI* along with *ROI*, while only 2% used *RI* alone. Another 65% of the firms used *ROI* by itself. Scapens and Sale (1985) found that 28.8% of U.S. firms and 37.4% of U.K. firms used residual income.

FIRM LEVEL FINANCIAL PERFORMANCE MEASURES

Managerial planning and control take place at all levels of an organization. Hence, management accounting systems need to be concerned with measuring performance at the firm level, as well as at the subunit level. Senior managers, board of directors, stockholders, and creditors are especially concerned with firm level performance. Accordingly, we now turn our attention to several commonly used firm level performance measures.

Profits

One measure of firm level performance commonly used in practice is net profits and the derivative concept of earnings per share.[9] Evidence attesting to the importance attached to profits and earnings per share by practitioners can be found in business publications and corporate annual reports. *Business Week*, for example, annually lists both profits and earnings per share for the 1,000 most valuable U.S. companies (Byrd, 1994). In the opening paragraph of his letter to stockholders, the highly successful Chairman and President of Marriott International Corporation highlights growth in net income in discussing the firm's banner 1995 year (Marriott, 1996). Articles about the increase or decrease of firm level profits (both actual and anticipated) also appear in the daily business press (e.g. *The Wall Street Journal*). At the firm level, profits are often evaluated in terms of a given firm over several time periods. Hence, it is common to see (e.g., in annual corporate reports) a comparison of firm profits over several years (e.g., 3-5 years).

---

9. The terms **profits, income** and **earnings** are used interchangeably in this text, as is common in the literature and in practice.

Not surprisingly, profits as a measure of performance has the same major deficiency at the firm level as it does at the subunit level. That is, it is difficult to gauge performance based on profits unless the level of capital investment required to generate such profits is considered. To rectify this deficiency, return on investment is a commonly used measure of firm level performance.

Return on Investment

As is the case at the subunit level, firm level return on investment (ROI) can be expressed in generic terms as shown in Eq. 8.1 (i.e., $ROI = AP/I$). Although many variations exist, ROI at the firm level is often computed by either dividing the firm's net profits by stockholders' equity or by dividing the firm's operating profits by total assets (capital).[10] In the *Business Week* article by Byrd (1994) referred to above, both of these measures are provided for the 1,000 most valuable U.S. companies. For both of these measures, the intent is to capture the firm's rate of return per dollar of investment. However, in the former case (i.e., net income divided by stockholders' equity) the emphasis is on the return on the assets financed by stockholders,[11] whereas in the latter case (i.e, operating profits divided by total assets) the emphasis is on the return related to all of the assets of the firm, regardless of how the assets were financed.

The fact that ROI is a popular measure of firm level performance does not negate the argument made earlier in this chapter that ROI is not equal to a true rate of return. Accordingly, whether looking at ROI at the firm level or the subunit level, it does not reflect a valid measure of how efficiently a firm is allocating its resources.[12]

---

10. For a discussion of the strengths and weaknesses of various ROI computations at the firm level, the reader is referred to the paper by Gordon (1976).

11. A related measure of return on stockholders' equity is the notion of **earnings per share (EPS)**. This measure does not, however, take into consideration the amount of investment required to generate such earnings and usually considers only the return to common stockholders.

12. Brief and Lawson (1992) argue that, while not a valid measure of profitability, the accounting rate of return does have a useful role to play in terms of the valuation process.

At the firm level, the computation shown in Eq. 8.1 is often divided into the two major components of profit margin [i.e., accounting profits (*AP*) divided by total revenues (*TR*)] and capital turnover [i.e., total revenues divided by investments (*I*)]. This reformulation of *ROI* is expressed algebraically as follows (see Appendix 8.1 for a further discussion of financial statement ratios):

$$ROI = \frac{AP}{TR} \bullet \frac{TR}{I} \qquad\qquad\qquad \text{Eq. 8.1a}$$

By reformulating the *ROI* into the two components shown in Eq. 8.1a, the relationship between short-run and long-run profit planning comes into focus. Whereas short-run profit planning is primarily concerned with issues related to the profit margin (often called operating profitability), long-run profit planning shifts its concern toward capital turnover and the related issue of capital budgeting (a topic discussed in Chapter 12). Of course, the short- and long-run aspects of profit planning are, in many ways, inexplicably intertwined. Nevertheless, from a practical point of view, most firms find it helpful to highlight the importance of operating profitability separate from capital investment decisions. For example, in his letter to stockholders for the year ending 1996, the dynamic CEO of Black & Decker Corporation noted that improving operating profitability was one of the firm's primary objectives (Archibald, 1997).

The computation of return on investment up to this point has purposely avoided the issue of financial leverage (i.e., the ability of a firm to use debt, as opposed to equity, in its capital structure). However, we can easily consider this factor by slightly modifying Eq. 8.1a to consider the return on stockholders' equity (*ROE*), as shown in Eq. 8.1b below (where *SE* equals the stockholders' equity portion of the firm's capital structure):

$$ROE = \left[\frac{AP}{TR} \bullet \frac{TR}{I}\right]\frac{I}{SE} \qquad\qquad \text{Eq. 8.1b}$$

An important point should be noted in comparing Eq. 8.1b to Eq. 8.1a. Accounting profits (*AP*) now need to be thought of as net income, since this is the portion of income left over for stockholders.

Residual Income

Although initially utilized to measure subunit performance, an interesting development has occurred in many large (especially U.S.) corporations. That development is the use of residual income (*RI*), as defined in Eq. 8.3 [i.e., $RI = AP - (I \bullet k)$], at the firm level. In the study by Healy (1985), for example, it was pointed out that many firms have incentive schemes for senior executives based on the concept of residual income. These schemes vary in detail, but essentially deduct a capital charge from a firm's profits to arrive at a base for deriving executive bonuses.

There seems to be a growing belief that residual income at the firm level is a meaningful economic measure of value added. An article in *Fortune*, by Tully (September, 1993), makes this point and cites several firms (e.g., Coca-Cola, AT&T, and Quaker Oats) which are using a stylized version of residual income (under the new name of <u>economic value added</u>) as a measure of firm performance. Since the first article in *Fortune*, a plethora of other articles have taken up the argument in favor of economic value added as a measure of firm performance (e.g., Tully, 1994; Fisher, A.B., 1995). At the same time, a rapidly growing number of firms are using economic value added as a key measure of performance [e.g., see DiCamillo (1997) for an interesting discussion of why Polaroid Corporation has focused on using this measure).

RI at the firm level is similar to *RI* at the subunit level in that it lies somewhere between the notions of profits and return on investment. The measure still relies on accrual accounting numbers and, despite claims to the contrary, is not a true measure of economic performance. Nevertheless, many U.S. firms are embracing the *RI* concept as very useful, if not perfect, performance measure. Thus, it is helpful to examine the relationship between *RI* and *ROI*. Through simple algebraic manipulation, it is possible to derive the following equation. (Problem 8.1 asks for such a derivation.)

$$RI = (ROI - k) \bullet I \qquad\qquad\qquad \text{Eq. 8.4}$$

or

$$ROI - k = RI/I \qquad\qquad\qquad \text{Eq. 8.4a}$$

Eq. 8.4a can be thought of as a value added return (*VAR*) or risk-adjusted *ROI*. Although not a perfect measure, *VAR* seems to have at least two advantages over *RI*. First, it takes into account the size of the firm being evaluated. Second, a risk-adjusted *ROI* allows managers, investors, and creditors to easily compare the performance of one firm against other firms. As such, it explicitly recognizes the fact that larger firms are expected to earn more residual income than smaller firms.

Cash Recovery Rate

In an effort to come up with a measure of firm performance that can be derived from accounting based data, and at the same time capture the economic notion of return, accounting researchers have devoted much time and effort to examining various alternative measures of return. One such measure, initially discussed by Ijiri (1979,1980), is the **cash recovery rate (CRR)**. The cash recovery rate (*CRR*) is derived by dividing the operating cash flows for a year by the gross fixed investment, as shown in Eq. 8.5.

$$CRR = \frac{CF_A}{GI}$$
Eq. 8.5

where,
CF_A =   annual cash flows from operations, and
GI =   gross fixed investments.

Ijiri demonstrated that the *CRR* can be used to estimate a firm's internal rate of return, by setting the reciprocal of the *CRR* equal to the present value of an annuity formula. The assumptions required to make such a conversion appropriate include: (1) the firm must be mature and invest in a similar composite asset mix from year to year and (2) the firm must reinvest all of its cash flows. However, as Salamon (1982) pointed out, if firms reinvest 100% of their cash flows, then the firm's growth rate will converge toward the true *IRR* and in turn the firm's *ROI* will converge toward the true *IRR*.[13] Hence, under the circumstances described by Ijiri, the *ROI* will serve as a valid proxy for the *IRR* and hence there is no need to utilize a *CRR* for such purposes.

---

13. For a more technical discussion of this point, the reader is referred to the papers by Livingstone and Salamon (1970), Stauffer (1971), Gordon (1974b), and Gordon and Stark (1989).

Salamon (1982) went on to show that the *CRR* was a useful concept, even if the 100% reinvestment assumption were dropped. More specifically, Salamon empirically showed that if it could be assumed, on *a priori* basis, that a group of firms had a similar cash flow pattern, then: (1) a conditional *IRR* (*CIRR*) could be estimated for the group of firms and (2) the relative rankings of these firms would remain the same (statistically speaking) under variously assumed *a priori* cash flow patterns. This was an important finding (which was extended by Gordon and Hamer, 1988) in that it allows for the relative rankings of firms by their *CIRRs*, without making any claim to actually deriving the true *IRR*. Unfortunately, the assumption that a group of firms with similar cash flow patterns could be identified on *a priori* grounds is itself quite tenuous. Further, cash recovery rates have many of the same measurement errors that are inherent in other accounting based measures.[14]

Stock Market Returns

The above discussion has focused on accounting based measures of performance. However, many argue that all of these measures suffer from at least the following three fundamental problems. First, accounting measures are ex post in nature. Hence, the future implications of past actions are not addressed. Second, accounting measures of performance do not consider the risk associated with particular actions. Third, it is often argued that accounting measures lend themselves to managerial manipulation.

In light of the above problems with accounting measures, many believe that firm performance is best gauged in terms of market based measures. In this regard, it is often argued that stock returns provide the best gauge of firm performance. In efficient capital markets, expected stockholders' returns are in direct relation to the level of risk associated with the return. Hence, if the stockholders of a firm wish to earn above normal returns, they must assume above normal risk. Accordingly, performance is gauged in terms of the risk-return trade-off. The risk adjusted return for stockholders in firm *i*, period *t*, based on the capital asset pricing model (*CAPM*), can be expressed as follows:

$$R_{i,t} = R_{f,t} + \beta_i \left(R_{m,t} - R_{f,t} \right) + \varepsilon_{i,t} \qquad \text{Eq. 8.6}$$

---

14.   For a further discussion on the CRR, the reader is referred to the papers by Griner and Stark (1988, 1991), Salamon (1985), and Stark (1993).

where,

$R_{i,t}$ = stock return for firm i in period t, which is equal to the change in the period's stock price plus dividends during the period, divided by the stock price at the beginning of the period [i.e., $(P_{t-1} - P_t + D_t)/P_{t-1}$]

β_i = beta (i.e., measure of risk) for firm i,

$R_{m,t}$ = market return in period t,

$R_{f,t}$ = risk-free return in period t,

$\varepsilon_{i,t}$ = error term for firm i in period t.

On an ex ante basis, stockholders can expect to earn only a normal return for the level of risk assumed. In other words, the ex ante expected return for Eq. 8.6 is equal to the risk-free rate, plus a risk premium based on the firm's beta multiplied by the difference between the overall market rate of return and the risk-free rate of return [i.e., $R_{f,t} + \beta_i (R_{m,t} - R_{f,t})$]. Of course, on an ex post basis, some stockholders will *beat* the market whereas others will be *beaten* by the market. In terms of determining whether or not the stockholders of a specific firm have beaten or been beaten by the market, a measure of *excess return* can be derived from Eq. 8.6 by computing the difference between the actual and expected return (i.e., the error term in Eq. 8.6).[15]

Measuring firm performance based on stock market returns is not problem free. For any given time period, the price of a firm's stock may fluctuate (up or down) for macroeconomic reasons beyond the control of corporate managers. In addition, stock prices may fluctuate for psychological reasons that have little, or nothing, to do with the economic performance of a firm. For example, the psychological aspects of stock price movements are evident when a company's earnings fall short of analysts' expectations even though the company is doing quite well in economic terms (Lev 1992).

---

15. For a more rigorous discussion of the excess return notion, the reader is referred to the paper by Kolodny et al. (1989).

Finally, the argument that stock market return is a good measure of firm performance is based on the assumption that stock markets are efficient (i.e., that stock prices reflect all publicly available information). Although a large body of research suggests that the assumption is reasonably accurate (at least in the U.S.), the efficiency of stock markets (especially on a global basis) is far from uncontested. For all these reasons, stock prices tend to provide a very noisy (i.e., imprecise) measure of firm performance. These concerns notwithstanding, stock market returns are commonly computed and utilized as a measure of firm performance by corporate executives, stockholders, and creditors alike.

Tobin's q

In recent years, various performance measures which attempt to combine market based data with accounting based data have surfaced. One such attempt is known as Tobin's q (named after Nobel Laureate James T. Tobin, who is credited with initiating the measure). This measure is calculated as follows:

$$q = MV/RC$$
Eq. 8.7

where,

q	=	Tobin's q,
MV	=	total market value of firm (including stock and debt),
RC	=	replacement cost of firm's tangible assets.

Technically speaking, Tobin's q is more a measure of monopoly power and over (under) investment than it is a measure of either firm profitability or efficiency. This fact, coupled with the difficulties involved in measuring the ratio's denominator,[16] have thus far restricted the use of Tobin's q primarily to research studies (i.e., the measure has not been widely used in practice). Nevertheless, the measure has caught the attention of a rapidly growing number of researchers and one day may become popular among practitioners.

Market Value Added

Although Tobin's q has attracted little attention among practitioners, a closely related measure has attracted much attention among corporate executives. This closely related measure is called **market value added** and is defined as the difference between the market value and accounting book value of a firm (see Eq. 8.8). A comparison of Eq. 8.7 and Eq. 8.8 shows the close similarity between Tobin's q and market value added.

---

16. For a discussion of these difficulties, see Myers, Gordon, and Hamer (1991).

$$MVA = MV - BK \qquad\qquad\qquad\qquad \text{Eq. 8.8}$$

where,

MV = total market value of a firm (including stock and debt),

BK = accounting book value of a firm.

The theoretical basis for using market value added can be most easily seen from its relationship to a firm's assets and link to residual income. As pointed out by Peasall (1982), the present value of a firm's future cash flows can be separated into two major components. The first is the book value of a firm's assets. The second is the present value of the firm's future stream of residual income. An interesting aspect of this relationship is that it holds true, regardless of accounting conventions, provided the firm's cost of capital is properly computed and the residual income stream is treated as an infinite stream (or, if treated as a finite stream, the salvage value of the firm is equal to the firm's remaining book value). Hence, if we deduct the book value of a firm's assets from its present value, the net present value is equal to the present value of the firm's future residual income. To the extent that the present value of a firm is accurately estimated via its market value, the market value added serves as a surrogate measure of the firm's net present value. It is this net present value which market value added is trying to approximate.

Before leaving this measure, a few words of caution seem in order. First, the justification for using this measure is highly dependent on the market place being able to accurately estimate the firm's true economic value. Second, on a period to period basis (e.g., a year), it is not possible to claim that the change in market value added is directly related to the period's residual income.[17]

---

17. For a further discussion of this latter point, the reader is referred to the article by Egginton (1995) on the issue of periodic consistency (or lack thereof) related to residual income.

MANAGERIAL COMPENSATION AND PERFORMANCE

The owners of many firms have expressed a growing concern regarding the relationship between compensation and performance of top executives. This concern is directly related to the agency issues raised in Chapter 1 and is sometimes referred to as pay-for-performance. Nowhere is the concern regarding pay-for-performance more prevalent than in U.S. corporations. Several business publications (e.g., *Business Week, The Wall Street Journal*) publish the total annual compensation for senior executives at various U.S. corporations. The sums involved are often staggering. In a segment entitled "Easy Money in Hard Times," on the popular U.S. television show called *60 Minutes* (11/10/91), it was noted that some U.S. senior executives are paid huge bonuses (e.g., millions of dollars) even in years when their companies apparently have poor performance.

The *60 Minutes* segment highlighted the important issue concerning whether or not U.S. senior executives are overpaid. Many argue they *are* overpaid. In contrast, there are many who believe that the high pay given to U.S. senior managers is usually justified and even desirable. Murphy (1986), for example, makes a cogent argument that executives are worth the huge sums they receive. This latter argument is supported by several empirical studies. For example, in an article by Boschen and Smith (1995), they found a strong correlation between the pay and performance of senior executives. Their findings are particularly noteworthy because they rigorously demonstrated that the pay senior executives receive in a current year is not only a function of the current performance, but also the performance of the previous four years. Further, in the study by Lambert and Larcker (1985b), it was shown that even the adoption of large "golden parachutes"[18] has a positive effect on the shareholder wealth (i.e., the stock market return) of firms. Finally, there is a growing trend for many companies to actually eliminate the CEO's bonus during a poor performance year.

---

18. Golden parachutes provide payments to senior executives when their employment agreements are terminated due to a change in corporate control (e.g., an acquisition of the company). In essence, golden parachutes represent a form of bonus payment to executives who are being removed from their positions.

In light of our earlier discussion in this chapter, it should be obvious that the pay-for-performance concern is itself conditional on how performance is measured. In other words, different performance measures can provide different performance signals regarding a similar situation. Thus, any link (or lack thereof) between managerial compensation and performance is itself affected by the way performance is measured. Among those firms trying to get a closer link between managerial compensation and performance, various types of incentive compensation schemes are being utilized. Some of these schemes are based on accounting measures of performance. One such accounting based measure of performance attracting growing attention, in regards to managerial incentive compensation plans, is the stylized version of residual income called economic value added.[19] Other schemes are based on stock market measures of firm performance. Given the strengths and weaknesses of both accounting and market based measures of performance, it is not surprising that most major firms are using a combination of both measures in establishing executive compensation packages. Further, several firms are developing compensation packages by "benchmarking" against rival firms. However, the issue still remains as to which measures of performance should be included in the benchmark.

CONCLUDING COMMENTS

The ability to measure subunit and firm level performance is a fundamental concern to firms interested in efficiently allocating scarce resources. Unfortunately, there is no simple procedure for deriving a valid and reliable single or composite measure. This is especially true in multinational corporations, where country differences come into play. Hence, firms tend to use a combination of numerous short-run and long-run measures. These measures range from a financial to a nonfinancial nature, from an ex post to an ex ante nature, and from an internal to an external focus. Regardless of which measures are used, the ultimate objective is to provide an indication of the firm's (and subunit's) long-run economic viability.

---

19. In Chapter 11, compensation schemes based on short-term budgeted profits will be discussed. In Chapter 12, the relationship between long-term incentive schemes and capital investments will be discussed.

As environments change, an organization's needs change with respect to performance measures. For example, the type of performance measures required seem dependent upon whether a firm is confronting a growing, declining, or stable economy. Under periods of rapid growth, emphasis on market-based measures of performance may be most appropriate. However, under periods of economic stability, the most appropriate focus may well be on accounting-based measures of performance. The increased emphasis on profits and cost measures by many Japanese firms provides evidence for this contingency view of performance measures (Sakurai, 1995).

Globally competitive firms have become keenly aware of the importance of nonfinancial, as well as financial, measures of performance. The next chapter will consider some of the key nonfinancial measures used by major corporations around the world.

APPENDIX 8.1:
Additional Financial Statement Ratios

The emphasis in this chapter has been on analyzing the performance of subunits and firms from a managerial perspective. Of course, many parties which are external to the firm are also concerned with firm level performance. For example, stockholders and creditors are keenly interested in a firm's performance and follow such measures as return on investment, return on equity, and stock market returns. Further, as noted in the chapter, the use of a variant of firm level residual income (often under the name of economic value added) has become a widely utilized performance measure by external users of financial information.

In addition to the ones discussed in this chapter, there are many other financial performance measures that both managers and external parties to the firm consider. Many of these measures are essentially ratios based on a firm's publicly available financial statements. Some of the more commonly utilized ratios, not discussed in the chapter, are briefly noted below.

1. Current Ratio = Current Assets / Current Liabilities

A firm's current ratio is a direct derivative from its **working capital**, which is defined as current assets minus current liabilities. The current ratio indicates the firm's ability to pay its short-term debt on a timely basis. As such, it is often thought of as a measure of the firm's liquidity. Since some of the firm's current assets may not be very liquid (i.e., not easily converted to cash), it is common for firms to reduce current assets by such items as inventory before computing the current ratio.

2. Times Interest Earned Ratio = Operating Income / Interest Expense

The times interest earned ratio measures a firm's ability to cover (sometimes called service) its annual interest payments. This ratio is closely associated with the ratio of financial leverage discussed in this chapter.

3. Inventory Turnover Ratio =
Cost of Goods Sold / Average Inventory

Manufacturing firms incur substantial costs by having funds tied up in inventory. Accordingly, it is commonly believed that firms should turn over their inventory as quickly (i.e., as many times) as possible, as measured by the above ratio. Of course, this concern is directly related to the push for just-in-time inventory systems discussed in Chapter 3.

4. Accounts Receivable Collection Period =

$$\frac{\text{Credit Sales}}{\text{Average Accounts Receivable}} \quad x \quad \frac{1}{\text{365 Days}}$$

The accounts receivable collection period provides a firm with a measure of the average time (in days) it takes to collect credit sales (total sales are usually used because cash and credit sales are rarely separated on financial statements). From a cash management perspective, it is important for firms to keep the accounts receivable collection period as low as possible, which is another way of saying that firms should try to collect credit accounts as quickly as possible.

5. Dividend Payout Ratio = Dividends Paid / Net Income

A firm's dividend payout ratio depends on many factors. For example, high growth firms usually plow back most of their earnings into investment opportunities and will have a low dividend payout ratio. In contrast, some firms try to maintain a high payout ratio as a means of attracting capital from those stockholders who count on dividends as part of their fixed annual income.

PROBLEMS

Problem 8.1

Show how the relationship between residual income and return on investment, illustrated in Eq. 8.4, was derived.

Problem 8.2

Exhibit 8.2 in the chapter shows that SU_1 has controllable ROI of 20% and RI of $175,000. SU_2 has controllable ROI of 19% and RI of $200,000.

Required (Show all work):

A.   At what k would the two divisions have an equal amount of RI?

B.   Provide a graph that shows the relationship between RI and ROI for the example underlying Exhibit 8.2.

C.   Which of the two subunits, SU_1 or SU_2, is doing a better job of performance?

Problem 8.3

In recent years, there has been a major push toward the use of firm level nonfinancial performance measures. Some believe that these measures should replace financial performance measures, while others believe that both financial and nonfinancial performance measures are needed.

Required:

A.   Discuss the argument for and against the use of nonfinancial performance measures.

B.   What are the problems associated with combining financial and nonfinancial measures for evaluating the performance of firms?

Problem 8.4

A.   Briefly define and explain the theoretical justification for residual income (recently referred to as economic value added) and market value added as measures of firm level performance.

B.   Discuss the weaknesses of economic value added and market value added.

C.   Several of the class projects addressed issues related to performance measures. One project discussed the balanced scorecard approach. Another project addressed the relationship between a company's life cycle and performance measures. Another project addressed the relationship between pay and performance in the baseball industry. Briefly discuss the findings of any one of those projects (but not your own project) and provide a short critique of that project.

Problem 8.5

Many believe that CEOs (Chief Executive Officers) in U.S. firms are overpaid. Others believe that CEOs are worth every penny they receive. This controversy seems to center around the incentive compensation packages that CEOs receive, rather than their fixed salaries.

Required:

A.   Why have U.S. firms moved to a situation where incentive compensation packages are such a large portion of CEO pay?

B.   Do you believe that U.S. CEOs are overpaid? Explain.

Problem 8.6 *(Adapted from CMA examination)*

Domi Products, a multi-divisional manufacturing company, measures performance and awards bonuses to division managers based upon divisional operating income. Under the current bonus plan, common company-wide operating expenses are allocated evenly to all five of its divisions. For example, if rent were $50,000, each division would be charged $10,000. In planning next year's budget, corporate management has requested that the division managers recommend how common expenses should be distributed to the divisions. The division managers met and jointly developed an incentive plan that would more equitably distribute common expenses on the basis of resources used and measure each division manager's performance based on return on assets (*ROA*), with divisional bonuses based on a target *ROA*. They jointly presented their recommendation to corporate management.

Required:

A.   Describe at least three problems that Domi Products could encounter when using return on assets (ROA) as the basis of performance measurement.

B.   1.   Define the residual income approach to segment performance measurement.

        2.   Determine if Domi Products should implement this approach instead of the ROA approach.

C.   Discuss the behavioral implications of:

        1.   the division manager's involvement in the corporate budgeting process, and

        2.   the decision to more equitably allocate common costs.

9

NONFINANCIAL
PERFORMANCE MEASURES

INTRODUCTION

Financial performance measures were discussed in the previous chapter. Many of these measures were based on accounting data, whereas other measures were based on market data. However, the need for firms to be globally, as well as locally, competitive has been accompanied by a keen awareness of the importance of nonfinancial performance. Thus, a rapidly growing body of literature argues that nonfinancial, as well as financial, measures of firm performance need to be considered. Several of these measures, as well as some of the issues surrounding the use of such measures, will be discussed in this chapter. It should be noted at the onset, however, that nonfinancial measures of firm performance are viewed as a complement to, rather than as a substitute for, financial measures of firm performance.

ARGUMENTS FOR NONFINANCIAL MEASURES

The argument that nonfinancial measures of firm performance need to be considered is not new to the accounting literature. For example, over 25 years ago the American Accounting Association appointed a blue-ribbon committee of accounting scholars to examine the issues surrounding the use of nonfinancial measures of performance (Jensen et al., 1971). There have been many other articles written in the accounting journals during the 1970s which called for the addition of nonfinancial information into formal accounting systems (e.g., Gordon and Miller, 1976). Nevertheless, it is only in recent years that the advocates for incorporating nonfinancial performance measures into management accounting systems have shared centerstage for the debate over how to measure firm performance.

The contemporary concern for nonfinancial measures of firm performance has two arguments at its core. First, it is often argued that nonfinancial measures are the *leading* indicators of firm performance, whereas financial performance measures are the *lagging* indicators. This leading vs. lagging argument usually has associated with it a long-run vs. short-run perspective. In other words, it is often claimed that nonfinancial measures are good predictors of a firm's long-run future performance and that financial measures are associated with a firm's past, or at best, contemporary performance. Of course, the validity of this claim is an empirical question. Unfortunately, to date there is little empirical evidence to either refute or support the claim, although the evidence which does exist seems to favor the argument.

The second argument usually associated with the contemporary concern for nonfinancial measures of performance is that organizations need to combine (or balance) the financial and nonfinancial measures of performance. This argument is often discussed in terms of the *balanced scorecard,* a term made popular in an excellent series of articles by Kaplan and Norton (1992, 1993, 1996). As discussed by Kaplan and Norton, the nonfinancial measures are intended to capture the following three dimensions of firm performance: a firm's relationship with its customers, a firm's business operations, and a firm's growth. Advocates of the balanced scorecard approach usually claim that nonfinancial measures, in combination with financial measures, are required to facilitate the pursuit of a firm's strategy. The empirical evidence clearly demonstrates that firms have begun to recognize the importance of considering nonfinancial, as well as financial, performance measures.

KEY NONFINANCIAL MEASURES

As illustrated in Figure 9.1, the nonfinancial performance measures considered in this chapter are product quality, customer satisfaction, productivity, and market share. Although this list is by no means all inclusive, these measures are among the ones most often discussed. In addition, these four measures capture the attributes which underly the contemporary arguments in favor of utilizing nonfinancial performance measures. That is, these measures are usually thought of as leading indicators of a firm's performance. In addition, they capture the basic dimensions underlying the nonfinancial aspects of firm performance usually associated with the balanced scorecard approach.

One nonfinancial performance measure commonly discussed is **product quality**. There are, of course, numerous dimensions to product quality.[1] One such dimension, which has received much attention among manufacturing firms, has to do with the percentage of defective products. The lower the percentage of defects, the higher the quality. There are two separate, albeit related, aspects to this defect measure. First, the percentage of defects internal to the firm, which require either reworking or scrapping. Second, the percentage of defects sent to customers (i.e., defects which are external to the firm). These latter defects could be gauged by customer returns and/or service requirements during the product's warranty period. This type of defect is far more costly to correct than the reworking or scrapping kind, especially when the long-term cost of ill feelings by customers is factored into the equation.

---

1.   The term *quality* is often used in a generic sense to cover a host of nonfinancial aspects of a firm's performance. The Malcolm Baldridge National Quality Award, established by Public Law 100-107, has provided much impetus for this view in the U.S. The approach in this chapter is to concentrate on the measurement aspects of nonfinancial performance, hence, a micro view is taken toward quality.

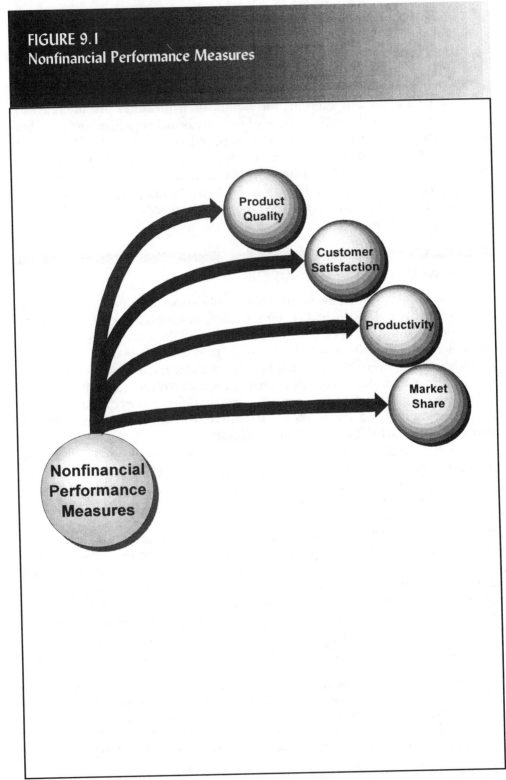

FIGURE 9.1
Nonfinancial Performance Measures

In the automobile industry, product quality has become almost synonymous with the notion of firm success. To see this point, all one has to do is to go back in time and look at what happened with U.S. automobile companies. For many years, U.S. auto firms seemed to be operating with an approach that considered a certain percentage of defects as being justified. In essence, this approach assumes that the costs are less by letting defects flow through the system and correcting the defective units in response to customer complaints. Unfortunately, this approach had the long-term effect of encouraging customers to look elsewhere for more reliable automobiles. Indeed, by emphasizing quality, auto manufacturers from other countries (especially Japan) managed to capture a large share of the U.S. automobile market. In an effort to regain the lost market share (or at least stem the loss), U.S. auto manufacturers now place great emphasis on product quality.

Measuring product quality has become a key concern of all well-managed corporations. At Whirlpool, for example, the CEO singles out this item for mention, in his letter to shareholders for the year ending 1995, with specific reference to the firm's reduced service incidence rates in North America and Europe (Whitwam, 1996). The highly regarded CEO of General Electric, along with the other senior officers of the corporation, place great emphasis on quality. In their letter to Share Owners and Employees for the year ending 1997, it is specifically noted that General Electric uses the term **Six Sigma** to highlight its focus on near perfect quality for all of its products and services (Welch et al., 1998).

Another nonfinancial performance measure commonly discussed is **customer satisfaction**. Although no simple measure exists for this notion, there are several indicators which can be considered. For example, percentage of returns and warranty work represent two aspects of customer satisfaction. The lower the percentage, the higher the level of customer satisfaction. In addition, some firms conduct surveys to gauge customer satisfaction with their products. Finally, the percentage of repeat business represents an important long-run measure of customer satisfaction. The higher the percentage, the higher the level of customer satisfaction.

Of course, customer satisfaction and product quality are often highly correlated. In the above discussion concerning the auto industry, for example, it was the lack of quality which led to customer *dissatisfaction* and, in turn, problems for the U.S. auto firms. At the same time, customer satisfaction and product quality are not synonymous concepts. For many products, customers are willing to trade-off quality for price. In other words, where the price of one product is substantially lower than that of a competitive product, quality differentials are accepted and even expected. The key, however, is for organizations to understand where such price-quality differentials will be accepted and to make sure that competitors' products of a similar price are not at a higher quality.

One more measure of nonfinancial performance often considered is **productivity**. Generally speaking, productivity can be thought of as a ratio of outputs to inputs (i.e., a measure of efficiency). For example, physical units of output per employee hour worked, or sales dollar per dollar of labor cost, could be used to represent productivity. Other measures of productivity include through-put times (i.e., the time it takes to produce a product from start to finish) and product delivery times.

A field study of seven Canadian firms by Armitage and Atkinson (1990), left little doubt of the importance attached to productivity measures by organizations. This was true regardless of the industry represented by the firm studied. Of course, the measure of productivity most emphasized did vary with the nature of the firm.

The percentage of the industry **market share** controlled by a firm is often used as a nonfinancial measure (although some would argue that it is a financial measure) of performance. Indeed, market share (usually derived by dividing a firm's sales by the industry's sales) is viewed as a key performance indicator by many of the world's leading firms. For example, in his letter to Shareholders, Customers, and Friends for the year ending 1995, the chairman of the globally oriented Ford Motor Company highlights the firm's market share success in the U.S., Europe, Taiwan, Australia, and Japan (Trotman, 1996). Market share presumably serves as a proxy for long-term acceptability and, in truth, growth of a product. That is, the larger a firm's market share, the more likely its sales will continue to grow well into the future.

Of course, market share and profitability are not synonymous concepts. In fact, as we know from basic microeconomics, a firm's point of sales maximization and its point of profit maximization are rarely the same. This point is especially true as we move from an expanding market to a declining one. Hence, an issue of concern is the trade-off between profitability and market share. This trade-off has become a key concern for many firms in the 1990s. This concern has hit even Japanese companies, which are notorious for concentrating on market share rather than profits (Chandler, 1992).

The argument for nonfinancial performance measures is more complex than is often recognized. Few would disagree that a firm which ultimately goes bankrupt needs to be judged as an economic failure. This is true no matter how high the rating a firm receives on quality and/or customer satisfaction. In the same vein, a firm which maintains financial vitality over the long-run, needs to be judged as an economic success. In other words, in the long-run, a firm's economic success or failure is ultimately judged in financial terms. When contemporary financial and nonfinancial performance measures provide similar signals regarding the long-run economic health of a firm, it is a moot issue as to which measures are more valuable. Hence, the only interesting case is where the contemporary financial and nonfinancial measures provide conflicting signals regarding the long-run. In such a case, the question which needs to be answered is: What combination of measures provide the most accurate signal as to the firm's long-run economic viability? In thinking about the nonfinancial performance measures discussed above, this question should be kept in mind. In this regard, it seems wise to remember that even the icons of nonfinancial performance measures recognize the importance of bottom line numbers during periods of economic decline. For example, as noted in the previous chapter, within the past few years the Japanese automobile manufacturers seem to be shifting some of their attention toward cost control and profit concerns.

NONFINANCIAL PERFORMANCE MEASURES AND STRATEGY

As discussed in Chapter 3, the term cost management is used to refer to the generic concept of managing a firm's costs. The key in this regard is to get the maximum output for a given level of costs or, alternatively, to have the minimum costs for a given level of output. In other words, the firm should manage its costs to be as efficient as possible.

As indicated above, cost management is not intended to curtail operations. Indeed, effective cost management will consider costs in light of the firm's strategic positioning relative to its competitors, as well as in terms of the firm's level of operations. The way a firm positions itself in the long-run relative to its competitors can be thought of as the firm's **strategy**. Thus, in managing its costs, the firm should simultaneously consider its strategy. The notion of managing costs within the context of a firm's strategy has become known as **strategic cost management**. Strategic cost management can be thought of as a subset of strategic management accounting in a fashion comparable to the way cost management is a subset of management accounting.

Ceteris paribus, the more a firm uses its management accounting system to facilitate its strategic decisions, the greater is the need for *nonfinancial*, external and ex ante information (e.g., see Gordon et al., 1978; Larcher, 1980, and Gordon and Pinches, 1982). Thus, it should be no surprise that firms which more heavily utilize their management accounting systems for strategic, as well as *non-strategic*, decisions will place greater emphasis on nonfinancial information in measuring performance. Accordingly, the increased use of management accounting systems by many firms to facilitate strategy over the last decade has further added to the increased emphasis placed on nonfinancial performance measures over the same time period. For example, if a firm decides that it wants to position its products, vis-à-vis its competitors' products, in terms of the highest quality, then the MAS should incorporate measures of product quality (e.g., percentage of internal defects). Of course, using a firm's MAS for strategic decision purposes in no way mitigates its use for *non-strategic* purposes.

A recent survey conducted by the Cost Management Group (1997), of the Institute of Management Accountants, indicated that a large percentage (i.e., 76%) of the responding members see the concept of strategic cost management as being of importance to the future success of their firms. In fact, 41% of the responding members indicated that their firms had already implemented a strategic cost management program.

CONCLUDING COMMENTS

There is no "silver bullet" in terms of measuring firm performance. This fact is true whether using financial or nonfinancial measures. In fact, there is a growing belief that the right way to measure firm performance (as well as subunit performance) is via a combination of nonfinancial and financial measures. The empirical evidence is clearly showing that firms are pointing in this direction. The task at hand, however, is to figure out ways to combine such measures in a meaningful way. In recent years, this task has become an issue of concern to many researchers and corporations around the globe. Further, the push for greater use of nonfinancial measures of firm performance has also led many corporations to include such measures as part of their managerial incentive compensation packages.

PROBLEMS

Problem 9.1

Discuss the general arguments in favor of using nonfinancial, as well as financial, measures of performance.

Problem 9.2

Define the four non-financial performance measures listed below, and provide specific indicators of each of these concepts.

A.   Product Quality

B.   Customer Satisfaction

C.   Productivity

D.   Market Share

Problem 9.3

A fundamental task confronting researchers and corporations is determining an appropriate mechanism for combining financial and nonfinancial measures of performance. This task is particularly daunting in the situation where contemporary financial and nonfinancial measures are providing conflicting signals.

Required:

In outline form, provide a blueprint for combining financial and nonfinancial measures of firm performance.

Problem 9.4

Many corporations are claiming that nonfinancial performance measures are of key importance to them. Indeed, as noted in this chapter, letters to stockholders by CEOs often mention this very fact. However, many would argue that for a firm to "walk the talk" in this area, it is necessary for the incentive compensation packages for CEOs to include a component which based on such nonfinancial measures of performance.

Required:

By searching the proxy statements of firms, find at least one where the CEO's incentive compensation is at least partially determined based on nonfinancial performance measures. (Proxy statements are now available via several sources on the Internet.)

Problem 9.5 *(Adapted from CMA examination)*

Bergen Inc. produces telephone equipment at its Georgia plant. In recent years, the company's market share has been eroded by stiff competition from Asian and European competitors. Price and product quality are the two key areas in which companies compete in this market.

Jerry Holman, Bergen's president, decided to devote more resources to the improvement of product quality after learning that his company's products had been ranked fourth in product quality in a 1991 survey of telephone equipment users. He believed that Bergen could no longer afford to ignore the importance of product quality. Holman set up a task force that he headed to implement a formal quality improvement program. Included on the task force were representatives from engineering, sales, customer service, production, and accounting as Holman believed this was a company-wide program, and all employees should share the responsibility for the success of the program.

After the first meeting of the task force, Sheila Haynes, manager of sales, asked Tony Reese, production manager, what he thought of the proposed program. Reese replied, "I have reservations. Quality is too abstract to be attaching costs to it and then to be holding you and me responsible for cost improvements. I like to work with goals that I can see and count! I don't like my annual bonus to be based on a decrease in quality costs; there are too many variables that we have no control over!"

Bergen's quality improvement program has now been in operation for eighteen months, and the cost report, shown below, has recently been issued.

As they were reviewing the report, Haynes asked Reese what he thought of the quality program now. "The work is really moving through the Production Department," replied Reese. "We used to spend time helping the Customer Service Department solve their problems but they are leaving us alone these days. I have no complaints so far. I'll be anxious to see how much the program increases our bonuses."

Cost of Quality Report by Quarter (in thousands)						
	6/30/92	9/30/92	12/31/92	3/31/93	6/30/93	9/30/93
Prevention costs:						
Machine maintenance	$215	$ 215	$ 202	$ 190	$ 170	$ 160
Training suppliers	5	45	25	20	20	15
Design reviews	20	102	111	100	104	95
	240	362	338	310	294	270
Appraisal costs:						
Incoming inspection	45	53	57	36	34	22
Final testing	160	160	154	140	115	94
	205	213	211	176	149	116
Internal failure costs:						
Rework	120	106	114	88	78	62
Scrap	68	64	53	42	40	40
	188	170	167	130	118	102
External failure costs:						
Warranty repairs	69	31	24	25	23	23
Customer returns	262	251	122	116	87	80
	331	282	146	141	110	103
Total quality cost	$ 964	$1,027	$ 862	$ 757	$ 671	$ 591
Total production	$4,120	$4,540	$4,380	$4,650	$4,580	$4,510

Required:

A.   Identify at least three factors that should be present for an organization to successfully implement a quality improvement program.

B.   By analyzing the Cost of Quality Report presented, determine if Bergin Inc.'s quality improvement program has been successful.

C.   Discuss why Tony Reese's current reaction to the quality improvement program is more favorable than his initial reaction.

D.   Jerry Holman believed that the quality improvement program was essential and that Bergin Inc. could no longer afford to ignore the importance of product quality. Discuss how Bergen could measure the opportunity cost of not implementing the quality improvement program.

TRANSFER PRICING

CHAPTER OUTLINE

- Negotiated Transfer Price

- Market Based Transfer Price

- Cost Based Transfer Price

- Transfer Pricing and Taxation in Multinational Corporations

INTRODUCTION

Chapter 7 focused on pricing decisions made by a firm selling its products to customers external to the firm (i.e., in the external market place). This chapter will concentrate on transfer pricing decisions. **Transfer pricing** is concerned with establishing the price one subunit charges another subunit within the same organization for the internal transfer of intermediate products.[1] Hence, transfer pricing is a critical issue whenever the output of one organizational subunit serves as input to another subunit and the performance of each subunit is to be judged as an independent operation.

The total profits of a firm may be affected by the transfer prices among subunits, even though the revenues of the selling subunits are exactly offset by the expenses of the buying subunits. The reason for this peculiarity is due to the fact that transfer prices may affect the quantity of intermediate goods produced and purchased internally. In turn, the total revenues and costs of each subunit, as well as the firm as a whole, are affected. In addition, transfer prices will affect the overall profits of a firm via their tax implications.

There are two central, although often conflicting, objectives associated with transfer pricing decisions. First, a transfer price should *motivate subunits to operate in an autonomous fashion*. For example, if the performance of subunits is measured in terms of profits, a transfer price should motivate each subunit to strive to increase profits. Second, a transfer price should *encourage subunits to pursue goals which are congruent with the goals of the entire organization*. Thus, if the goal of the firm is to maximize (or more realistically, continually improve) profits, a transfer price should discourage subunits from increasing their own profits whenever such increases result in decreasing profits to the firm as a whole.

Transfer pricing concerns are ubiquitous in large organizations. In fact, it is almost impossible to think of a large decentralized organization where the goods and services of some subunits do not serve as the inputs for other subunits. For example, transferring unfinished goods from one stage of production to another stage of production, is essentially a transfer pricing concern. An information system department, which provides computer services to other organizational departments, is another example of a transfer pricing concern.[2]

---

1. As noted elsewhere in this book, the term **products** refers to services as well as physical goods.
2. Although the focus is different, the notions of transfer pricing and cost allocations are inextricably intertwined (Cohen and Loeb, 1988).

The primary focus in this chapter will be on discussing the following three generic methods of transfer pricing: (1) negotiated, (2) market-based, and (3) cost based. The effect of different national tax laws on transfer pricing decisions in multinational corporations will also be of particular concern in this chapter.

NEGOTIATED TRANSFER PRICE

The fact that subunits are part of the same organization implies that there are some economies to interdependencies. In other words, there are economies to transacting operations among subunits of a given firm rather than across separated firms in the open market place. These economies can be thought of as the economics of internal organization, as discussed by such individuals as Coase (1937) and Williamson (1981, 1988). In essence, the **economics of internal organization** perspective argues that firms organize in ways to create internal markets that serve as substitutes for external markets to run their economic activities. The objective, in this regard, is to find the point whereby the costs of organizing an incremental transaction are the same whether carried out within the firm or through an exchange in the open market (Coase, 1937). To the extent that the subunits are expected to operate in an autonomous fashion, freely negotiated transfer prices among subunits are desirable.

A **negotiated transfer price** is one that is determined through negotiations between the buying (i.e., acquiring) and selling (i.e., transferring) subunits, without interference from corporate headquarters. These negotiated prices within the internal organization (i.e., internal market place) are presumably derived via a process which is similar to the way negotiated prices are derived in the external market place. In fact, both buying and selling subunits will consider external markets as a baseline for internal transfers. Hence, assuming an external market exists for the intermediate product, a starting place for a negotiated transfer price will often be the amount the selling department could receive for the intermediate product via sales to an external market purchaser and the amount the buying subunit would have to pay for similar units from an external market seller. These amounts would then be adjusted for differential transaction costs associated with doing business within, rather than outside, the firm as a whole.

On the surface, it would appear that a negotiated price is a simple procedure for handling transfer pricing decisions. However, this is often not the case, especially where profit sharing is involved. There are numerous scenarios which can arise whereby one subunit is in a stronger internal bargaining position than another and, as a result, only willing to settle upon a transfer price which is unacceptable to the other subunit. Consequently, an internal transfer of goods may not result and the firm as a whole could be worse off than if such a transfer did occur. For example, assume Engine United, Inc. is a firm which has a selling and buying subunit, hereafter referred to as S and B, respectively. S produces specialized rubber gaskets and B uses these gaskets in the final production of small engines intended for garden equipment. These engines are ultimately sold by B to garden equipment manufacturers for $65 per engine. Until this year, B always bought S's entire production of 10,000 gaskets at a price of $5 per gasket. Each engine sold by B uses 1 gasket and B sells an average of 10,000 engines per year.

Both S and B are evaluated as profit centers (i.e., responsible for both revenues and costs) within Engine United, Inc. The most recent calculations by S show variable costs equal to $3.10 per gasket and total fixed costs of $10,000. The fixed costs incurred by S are from depreciation on specialized equipment which has neither an alternative use nor resale value. Besides the cost of the gaskets, B incurs additional variable costs of $35 per engine and total fixed costs of $100,000. As shown in the first column of Exhibit 10.1, S earns $9,000 when all 10,000 gaskets are sold to B for $5 per unit. As shown in the second column of Exhibit 9.1, B earns $150,000 when the internal transfer takes place at the transfer price of $5 per gasket.

A couple of years ago another company started to sell similar (in terms of quality and supplier dependability) gaskets at a price of $4 per gasket. At the recent transfer price negotiations, B has informed S that the maximum amount it will pay for the rubber gaskets is $4 per unit (i.e., the open market price). If S will not sell the gaskets for that price, B plans to go to the external market place supplier. B takes this stand because it would earn an additional $10,000 profit on the engines at the $4 per gasket price being requested by the external supplier. As shown in the third column of Exhibit 10.1, B earns a total profit of $160,000 when the gaskets are purchased from the external supplier as compared to the $150,000 when they are purchased from S.

The major problem resulting from the above scenario is as follows. If B pays anything above $4 per gasket, its potential profits will decrease. At the same time, S only earns a profit after receiving $4.10 (i.e., $3.10 + $10,000/10,000 units) per gasket. However, in terms of goal congruency, the firm as a whole would lose money (at least in the short-run) if B went to the external supplier and paid more than the $3.10 variable cost per gasket incurred by S. In other words, from the firm's point of view, the fixed costs incurred by S are sunk costs (i.e., costs that have been incurred, but are not relevant to the decision under consideration). Hence, the subunits and firm as a whole seem to be on horns of the following dilemma. If the subunits are allowed to negotiate in a truly

EXHIBIT 10.1
Engine United, Inc.
Negotiated Transfer Price Illustration

	(1) Selling Subunit	(2) Buying Subunit (Internal Purchase)	(3) Buying Subunit (External Purchase)
Sales	$50,000	$650,000	$650,000
Variable Costs	31,000	400,000[a]	390,000[b]
Contribution Margin	19,000	250,000	260,000
Fixed Costs	10,000	100,000	100,000
Profits	$9,000	$150,000	$160,000

[a] Consisting of $50,000 (10,000 x $5) transferred-in costs, plus $350,000 (10,000 x $35) additional variable costs incurred in the subunit.

[b] Consisting of $40,000 (10,000 x $4) costs for gasket purchases from outside supplier, plus $350,000 additional variable costs incurred in the subunit.

autonomous fashion, an internal transfer of gaskets will likely not occur. Yet, if goal congruency is to be maintained, a transfer of goods (at least in the short-run) should occur. One way out of this dilemma, at least for the short-run, would be for corporate headquarters to step in and treat S as a cost center. This solution would eliminate the profit sharing element of the transfer price by letting S concentrate on cost control rather than profits. Under this solution, the market price of $4 per gasket could be the transfer price and B could continue to operate as a profit center. Of course, this solution changes the transfer pricing mechanism from a negotiated price to a market price and the notion of being completely autonomous subunits is lost. At the same time, it eliminates the profit incentive from S. Further, an important issue for the firm to address is whether or not S will be able to produce the intermediate product at, or below, the external market price in the long-run. If not, a good case could be made for not replacing the fixed assets of S and, in effect, gradually phasing out the selling subunit's operation.

MARKET BASED TRANSFER PRICE

A **market based transfer price** is derived from the price charged by an external market supplier. When the external market for the intermediate product is perfectly competitive (in the sense discussed in Chapter 7), the market based transfer price method usually dominates all other methods. The reason is that, in purely competitive markets, the selling subunit could sell to the external market all of the units it could produce at the market price and the buying subunit could buy from the external market as many units as needed at the same price. Hence, even with free negotiations, it is reasonable to expect both subunits to settle on a transfer price which is equal to (or slightly modified due to transaction cost savings) the external market price. However, few products are bought and sold in a perfectly competitive market.

When an imperfectly competitive external market exists for the intermediate product, there is no simple market price solution to the transfer price issue. In fact, the price at which the buying subunit can buy the product from external market suppliers will itself vary depending on the number of units bought from such suppliers. At the same time, the price charged and the number of units sold to external customers by the selling subunit will be affected by the specific imperfections existing in the external market place. These imperfections usually lead the internal selling subunit to argue for a transfer price which is higher than the average external market price, based on difficult-to-quantify factors such as higher quality and shorter lead-times for delivery. In contrast, the buying subunit will usually argue for a transfer price which is lower than the average external market price, claiming that the selling subunit will not incur the uncertainties and selling costs associated with the external market place. Either way, the simple notion of using a market based transfer price breaks down when there are imperfectly competitive markets for intermediate products. Instead, the solution tends to move back toward some form of negotiated price. However, since one subunit is often in a stronger position than the other, corporate headquarters may once again need to resolve transfer pricing disputes to ensure goal congruency.

COST BASED TRANSFER PRICE

A **cost based transfer price** is derived from the costs of the intermediate product. If the selling (i.e., transferring) subunit is being treated as either a profit or investment center, some form of cost-plus is used to set a cost based transfer price. The plus factor may be based either on the selling subunit's total costs or variable costs. Either way, the intention is for the *plus* to allow the selling division to earn an acceptable level of profits (or return on investment) after considering all costs. If the selling subunit is being treated as a cost center, then a cost based transfer price is usually set equal to the full costs of the transferring department. This was the implicit assumption in the way goods were transferred from one producing department to another in Chapters 3 and 4, with the exception of the discussion on variable costing.

There are several problems with cost based transfer pricing schemes. One such problem is that the selling subunit may have little or no incentive to be cost efficient. This tendency is especially prevalent where the selling subunit is treated as either a profit or investment center *and* the transfer price is derived based on a cost-plus system. Hence, to the extent that cost efficiency is an organizational objective, goal congruency may be lost. Even where the selling subunit is treated as a cost center, goal congruency is difficult to achieve under a cost based transfer pricing scheme. To see this latter point, consider the example provided below whereby Dehy Company has a selling subunit which transfers an intermediate product, Product X, to a buying subunit based on full costs (i.e., variable and fixed costs).[3] In this example, the selling subunit is treated as a cost center and the buying subunit is treated as a profit center.

Suppose that the selling subunit of Dehy Co. has indirect costs of $1,000,000 (all of which are fixed) per year. The selling subunit's normal annual volume of activity is 100,000 direct labor hours, although currently it is operating far below this level. Indirect costs are applied based on normal volume of direct labor hours in this company. Hence, each unit of Product X (as well as the many other products produced by this subunit) will be allocated $10 of indirect costs per direct labor hour. Product X requires .1 direct labor hour per unit, so it is allocated $1 of indirect cost per unit. Also assume that the selling subunit incurs $2 of direct variable costs per unit of Product X. Using a full cost transfer pricing scheme, the buying subunit must pay the selling subunit $3 ($1 fixed + $2

---

3. This example was provided by Professor Martin P. Loeb.

variable costs) for each unit of X. Next, suppose the buying subunit transforms one unit of the intermediate product to one unit of a final product, Product Y, at a variable cost of $4 per unit. For simplicity, it is assumed that the buying subunit incurs no fixed costs. Hence, for each unit of Y the buying subunit incurs variable costs of $7 ($3 transfer costs + $4 additional variable costs).

Now suppose the buying subunit is deciding on a final selling price for Product Y of either $8 or $7.40 per unit. It estimates that at a price of $8 it can sell 1,000 units of Y and at $7.40 it can sell 2,000 units. The contribution margins for each of Dehy's subunits and the firm as a whole, derived under both prices for the final product, Y, are shown in Exhibit 10.2.

As part A of Exhibit 10.2 shows, if the buying subunit charges $8.00 for the final product, the sales from Y will contribute $1,000 to its profits. The contribution margin to the firm as a whole will be $2,000 under this scenario. As part B of Exhibit 10.2 shows, if the buying subunit charges $7.40 for the final product, sales from Y will contribute $800 to the subunit's profits. The contribution margin to the firm as a whole will be $2,800 under this scenario. Hence, the buying subunit, acting to maximize its own profits, will sell Product Y for $8 and demand 1,000 units of the intermediate product X. However, the firm as a whole would be better off if 2,000 units were transferred because an additional $1,000 (1,000 units x $1 per unit fixed cost) of the selling subunit's fixed costs would be covered. This extra recovery of $1,000 fixed costs, when offset against the $200 reduction in the buying subunit's profits, means that the firm as a whole is $800 better off. The explanation for the above goal incongruency is that the $1 of fixed production costs represented variable costs to the buying subunit, while for the firm as a whole the fixed production costs are unavoidable and, hence, not relevant to the short-run pricing decision of the final product.

As suggested by the above illustration, cost based transfer prices may encourage profit driven buying subunits to behave in a fashion which does not maximize the overall profits of the firm. At the same time, where producing (i.e., transferring) subunits are treated as cost centers, cost based transfer prices often do not provide an incentive for these subunits to be cost efficient. One noted exception to this situation is when the external market for the intermediate product is perfectly competitive. Under this scenario, a transfer price equal to the producing subunit's marginal cost (in an economics sense) would encourage both the buying and producing subunits to behave in a fashion which is optimal from the overall firm's perspective. To see this point, recall that in a perfectly competitive market each seller is a price taker. Hence, the incentive is to produce and sell the number of units whereby the marginal cost (from the last unit) is equal to the price (which is also the marginal revenue). Given perfectly competitive intermediate markets, the marginal cost rule is equivalent to a market price rule, and subunits, as well as the entire firm, are able to optimize. Unfortunately, once the unlikely assumption of a perfectly competitive intermediate product market is relaxed, the marginal cost rule breaks down. That is, when the competitive market assumption is dropped, the marginal cost

EXHIBIT 10.2
Dehy Company
Cost Based Transfer Price Illustration

A. Price of Product Y = $8; 1,000 units

	Selling Subunit	Buying Subunit	Firm-Wide
Revenues	$3,000	$8,000	$8,000
Variable Costs	$2,000	$7,000	$6,000[a]
Contribution Margin	$1,000	$1,000	$2,000

[a] Firm-wide variable costs are derived from the sum of $2 in the selling subunit and $4 in the buying subunit, multiplied by 1,000 units.

B. Price of Product Y = $7.40; 2,000 units

	Selling Subunit	Buying Subunit	Firm-Wide
Revenues	$6,000	$14,800	$14,800
Variable Costs	$4,000	$14,000	$12,000[b]
Contribution Margin	$2,000	$ 800	$ 2,800

[b] Firm-wide variable costs are derived from the sum of $2 per unit in the selling subunit and $4 per unit in the buying subunit, multiplied by 2,000 units.

transfer price rule requires *a priori* knowledge of the optimal quantity to be sold, since, at different quantities, different marginal costs will exist. For example, in an imperfectly competitive external intermediate market, the producing subunit's optimal quantity of production and, in turn, transfer price, are dependent on the buying subunit's demand. Yet, the buying subunit's demand is dependent on the producing subunit's transfer price. Hence, a simultaneous solution for the producing subunit's transfer price and the buying subunit's demand needs to be derived, which itself negates meeting the transfer pricing objective of having autonomous subunits.[4]

Although cost based transfer prices have serious deficiencies, they are commonly used in practice. A classic study by Vancil (1978) showed that 46.8% of the 249 participating firms used some version of cost based transfer prices. Negotiated prices were used by 22.2% of the firms included in the study and market prices by 31.0%. Although the Vancil study was conducted many years ago, more recent studies confirm the fact that various forms of cost based transfer prices are widely used by firms. These studies also show that negotiated and market based transfer prices are commonly used. Further, it is common for different transfer pricing methods to be used in various places within the same firm.[5] This latter point is especially true for large multinational corporations, as pointed out by Al-Eryani, Alam, and Akhter (1990). Indeed, as pointed out by Eccles (1983) based on interviews of nearly 150 executives from 13 companies, the type of transfer pricing used in practice is highly contingent upon the organization's situation and goals.

TRANSFER PRICING AND TAXATION IN MULTINATIONAL CORPORATIONS

Once the assumption that the organizational subunits involved in the transfer of goods are all operating within one country (e.g., the U.S.) is relaxed, the transfer pricing problem takes on many new, and more complex, dimensions. One such dimension, which has a significant impact on transfer pricing, is the differing national corporate tax rates which exist across countries.

---

4.   For a further discussion of the marginal cost transfer pricing rule, the reader is referred to Hirshleifer's (1956) classic paper on the subject.

5.   Various hybrid systems also are used by many firms. In this latter regard, a dual pricing system, whereby the producing subunit gets credit for one transfer price and the buying subunit is charged another (usually lower) price, is frequently used. Of course, the use of a dual pricing system would necessitate an adjustment at corporate headquarters to eliminate any overstated (double counted) profits.

As a general rule of thumb, global corporate taxes are reduced and net profits increased when subunit profits are shifted from high taxing countries to low taxing countries. One way of accomplishing such a shift is via transfer prices. More to the point, high transfer prices shift profits toward the transferring (i.e., selling) subunit, while low transfer prices shift profits toward the acquiring (i.e., buying) subunit. Hence, when the transferring subunit is in the low (high) taxing country, the best strategy is to set the transfer price as high (low) as possible.

Minimizing the taxes on profits via transfer pricing decisions is a key objective for multinational corporations. In direct response to this situation, most industrialized countries have tax laws which are designed to prevent multinational corporations from shifting profits, and in turn tax revenues, in an unfair manner via transfer pricing maneuvers. In the U.S., for example, Section 482 of the Internal Revenue Service (IRS) Code is aimed at preventing tax evasion via such practices. The general thrust of the IRS Code is to have transfer prices reflect an *arm's length* transaction (i.e., a transaction where the buying and selling of subunits act as if they were independent of one another). Nevertheless, it is difficult to enforce the tax code in this area. In fact, in a U.S. General Accounting Office (GAO, 1993) report by Dr. Natwar Gandhi on transfer pricing,[6] it was noted (p. 3) that "For each year from 1987 through 1990, about 72 percent of foreign-controlled corporations paid no U.S. income tax, compared to about 59 percent of U.S.-controlled corporations." Although pointing out that transfer pricing abuse is not proved by these statistics, the GAO report does allude to the potential of transfer pricing abuse as a contributing factor. Unfortunately, as also pointed out in the GAO report, the courts have had very limited success in correcting this situation.

The concern for shifting profits via transfer pricing mechanisms is not limited to highly developed countries. Indeed, countries with rapidly emerging economies, that are experiencing significant direct foreign investments, are also keenly interested in this issue. A recent study by Chan and Chow (1997) examined this concern with respect to China, where many believe that profits are being shifted out of the country via transfer pricing techniques. Although their study did not confirm the shifting of profits argument, this is clearly an important issue for newly emerging economies.

---

6. This report was presented in testimony before the U.S. Senate Committee on Governmental Affairs.

It is difficult to argue against the importance of minimizing corporate taxes (within the constraints of the law) via transfer pricing schemes. However, transfer pricing schemes also have important implications in terms of their effect on performance evaluation. For example, by transferring an intermediate product based on costs alone, all of the potential profits from the product accrue to the buying subunit. Hence, it is important for firms to recognize the potential dysfunctional evaluation consequences of shifting profits from one subunit to another based on tax concerns alone. The transfer pricing approach which minimizes taxes may well result in a poor allocation of profits for performance evaluation purposes. One way to correct this situation is to use one transfer pricing method for tax purposes and another for performance evaluation purposes. However, besides being expensive, a dual transfer pricing system like the one suggested above gives the *prima facie* appearance of unlawfully evading taxes. Consequently, it is common for firms to use the same transfer price system for both tax and subunit performance evaluation purposes.

CONCLUDING COMMENTS

Transfer pricing decisions are a major concern to large decentralized organizations. In fact, the benefits associated with being a decentralized subunit of a large organization are, in part, dependent on an effective transfer pricing scheme. Unfortunately, under most circumstances the conflicting objectives of transfer pricing make it impossible to derive an optimal transfer pricing approach. In some circumstances, negotiated transfer prices may work best while in other circumstances either a market based or cost based approach may be the best strategy. In the final analysis, the transfer pricing system should be linked to the firm's organizational structure and performance evaluation system.

A legitimate goal for corporations is to minimize their overall taxes paid. This goal has important implications for transfer pricing decisions, especially among multinational corporations. In fact, despite the potential dysfunctional performance evaluation consequences, the empirical evidence suggests that tax concerns are a dominant factor in determining transfer prices for multinational corporations.

PROBLEMS

Problem 10.1

Transfer pricing is an issue that confronts nearly all major organizations. The three most commonly used transfer pricing methods appear to be: (1) negotiated transfer prices, (2) market-based transfer prices, and (3) cost-based transfer prices.

Required:

A.   Briefly define each of the above three methods for deriving transfer prices.

B.   Are there any conditions under which one transfer pricing method clearly dominates the other methods in terms of being an ideal solution? Explain your answer to this question.

C.   Tax considerations are often viewed as being a key issue in selecting one transfer pricing method. Explain *why* and *how* tax concerns can cause a firm to choose one transfer pricing method over another.

Problem 10.2

In charging users for its services, a University's Computer Center needs to establish a transfer price. Should this price be based on variable costs only, full costs (i.e., variable plus fixed costs), or some other method? Explain your position.

Problem 10.3 *(Adapted from CMA examination)*

Ajax Consolidated has several divisions. One of its divisions, the Mining Division, refines toldline which is then transferred to the Metals Division. The toldline is processed into an alloy by the Metals Division and is sold to customers at a price of $150 per unit. The Mining Division is currently required by Ajax to transfer its total yearly output of 400,000 units of toldline to the Metals Division at a total manufacturing cost plus 10 percent. Unlimited quantities of toldline can be purchased and sold on the open market at $90 per unit. While the Mining Division could sell all the toldline it produces at $90 per unit on the open market, it would have to incur a variable selling cost of $5 per unit.

Brian Jones, manager of the Mining Division, is unhappy with having to transfer the entire output of toldline to the Metals Division at 110 percent of cost. In a meeting with the management of Ajax, he said, "Why should my division be required to sell toldline to the Metals Division at less than market price? For the year just ended in May, Metals' contribution margin was over $19 million on sales of 400,000 units while Mining's contribution was just over $5 million on the transfer of the same number of units. My division is subsidizing the profitability of the Metals Division. We should be allowed to charge the market price for toldline when transferring to the Metals Division."

Presented below is the detailed unit cost structure for both the Mining and Metals Divisions for the fiscal year ended May 31, 1993.

Cost Structure Per Unit		
	Mining Division	Metals Division
Transfer price from Mining Division	---	$66
Direct material	$12	6
Direct labor	16	20
Manufacturing overhead	32[1]	25[2]
Total cost per unit	$60	$117

[1] Manufacturing overhead cost in the Mining Division is 25 percent fixed and 75 percent variable.

[2] Manufacturing overhead cost in the Metals Division is 60 percent fixed and 40 percent variable.

Required:

A.   Explain why transfer prices based on cost are not appropriate as a divisional performance measure.

B.   Using the market price as the transfer price, determine the contribution margin for both the Mining Division and the Metals Division for the year ended May 31,1993.

C.   If Ajax Consolidated were to institute the use of negotiated transfer prices and allow divisions to buy and sell on the open market, determine the price range for toldline that would be acceptable to both the Mining Division and the Metals Division. Explain your answer.

D.   Which one of the three types of transfer prices—cost-based, market-based, or negotiated—is most likely to elicit desirable management behavior at Ajax Consolidated and thus benefit overall operations? Explain your answer.

Problem 10.4

A United Kingdom based electronics firm is considering the possibility of opening a manufacturing plant in either Africa or Asia. The initial impetus for considering this strategy is the high labor costs in the U.K., relative to both Africa and Asia. During a meeting of key executives of the U.K. firm, the Corporate Controller mentions the fact that, due to transfer pricing concerns, tax considerations are critical in deciding where to locate the plant. The Controller also notes that foreign currency issues need to be considered before finalizing the location decision. The Corporate Attorney jumps into the discussion and raises the fact that political risk and repatriation issues also need to be considered. The Vice President of Finance notes that the firm needs to consider whether it wants to raise the capital for the plant in the host country or home country (i.e., U.K.). Finally, the Director of Human Resources argues that, although the labor costs should be cheaper by opening the new plant in either Africa or Asia, there are many other important labor related issues that need to be addressed. By this time, the firm's President is becoming overwhelmed.

Required:

Prepare a brief report for the President that:

A.   summarizes the issues involved in the above noted decision, and

B.   provides a strategy for combining the various concerns involved in the decision.

BUDGETING FOR CURRENT OPERATIONS AND CASH FLOWS

CHAPTER OUTLINE

■ Operating Budgets

■ Cash Flow Budgets

■ The Cash is Sovereign Myth

INTRODUCTION

A **budget** is a formal plan for future activities, usually expressed in financial terms. The term **budgeting** refers to the process by which budgets (plans) are prepared. A comparison of actual with budgeted results provides control. Hence, budgets are an integral part of the planning and control of organizations.

Besides facilitating planning and control, budgets also serve to motivate, coordinate, communicate, and authorize organizational activities. Budgets motivate individuals within organizations by establishing targets (i.e., goals) which they can work toward achieving. Budgets help to coordinate the various activities of an organization by combining several activities into a formal plan. The mere act of getting involved in the budgeting process opens up the communication channels among the budgeting participants. Finally, budgets serve as an authorizing device in that authority to spend funds is often provided (especially in governmental organizations) by the budget.

Most firms prepare a separate budget for current operating activities, long-term capital investments, and cash flows. The budget for current operating activities is usually referred to as the **operating budget** and the budget for capital investments is usually referred to as the **capital budget**.[1] The budget related to cash flows is usually referred to as the **cash flow budget**. This chapter will discuss budgets for current operating activities, with a focus on the planning, control, and motivational aspects of such budgets. Cash flow budgets will also be discussed in this chapter. Capital budgets will be the focus of Chapter 12.

---

1.   In the central government of most industrialized countries, the operating and capital budgets are combined into a unified budget, as discussed by Gordon (1983).

OPERATING BUDGETS

Planning

The operating activities of a firm can be thought of as a recurring process whereby inputs are transformed into outputs. The outputs represent the firm's products (either physical goods or services) and the inputs can be thought of as the factors of production (i.e., resources) required to produce those products. The planning part of operating budgets focuses on the forecasting of the next period's (e.g., next year's) normal operations in terms of the costs of the inputs and the revenues generated by the outputs.[2] In essence, the firm-wide goal of budgeting for operations can be thought of as culminating in a forecasted (sometimes called *pro forma*) statement of earnings,[3] based on the rules of accrual accounting.

The mechanics of deriving operating budgets can vary greatly across firms. For example, in a small manufacturing firm it may be possible to begin with a forecast of sales for the operating period under consideration (i.e., a sales budget). This forecast would likely be based on a combination of past experiences and future expectations. Once the sales budget is derived, the expected sales (in units), adjusted for a projected decrease (or increase) in existing inventories, would permit the sequential calculation of the production budget, the budget for manufacturing costs, and the budget for cost of goods sold. In turn, the requisite administrative and sales expense budget could be estimated. After these numbers have been derived, the next period's budgeted income can be determined. An illustration of this approach is provided below.

Assume Tri Company is a small manufacturing firm which produces one basic model of office chairs. It is estimated that each chair will be sold for $30 to various retail stores and will cost (on average, at a normal volume of production) $8 in materials, $7 in labor, and $6 in indirect costs (i.e., a total of $21 per chair) to manufacture. Based on a combination of past sales and economic forecasts, the company expects to sell approximately 40,000 chairs during the next year. In line with the company's efforts to eliminate the costs associated with carrying inventories, there are currently neither materials nor work-in-process inventories and only 1,200 chairs in finished goods inventory. Administrative and selling expenses for the next year are estimated to be $40,000 and $20,000, respectively. Given these facts, Tri Company's budgeted earnings (ignoring taxes) and related components are shown in the first column of Exhibit 11.1.

---

2. In governmental organizations, a large part of the revenues are generated via taxes rather than from fees for direct services.
3. The terms **earnings**, **income**, and **profits** are used interchangeably in this chapter, as elsewhere in this book.

EXHIBIT 11.1
Tri Company: Comparison of Budgeted and
Actual Earnings Statement for Year Ending 199X

	(1) Budgeted	(2) Actual	(2) - (1) Variance
Revenues	$1,200,000[a]	$1,131,000[c]	$(69,000)[e]
Cost of Goods Sold	840,000[b]	819,000[d]	21,000
Gross Profits	360,000	312,000	(48,000)
Administrative Expenses	40,000	45,000	(5,000)
Selling Expenses	20,000	25,000	(5,000)
Earnings	$300,000	$242,000	$(58,000)

[a] Budgeted revenues are derived as follows: 40,000 chairs x $30 = $1,200,000.

[b] Budgeted cost of goods sold are derived as follows: 40,000 chairs x $21 = $840,000. Assuming the company strives to have zero inventories, the budgeted production would be: 40,000 - 1,200 (finished goods inventory) = 38,800 chairs.

[c] Actual revenues are based on: 39,000 chairs x $29 = $1,131,000.

[d] Actual cost of goods sold is based on: 39,000 chairs x $21 = $819,000.

[e] Brackets indicate an unfavorable variance on earnings.

Of course, in a large multidivisional organization, budgeting for operations becomes much more complicated than illustrated above. Each subunit must budget its own revenues and costs, in the context of the overall plan for the entire organization. At the corporate level, the complexities of coordinating subunits' operating budgets are positively related to the size and number of units involved. Hence, whereas a bottom-up (in terms of managerial levels) approach to budgeting may be the starting position for most large organizations, the efficient allocation of resources in these organizations often requires a top-down rebudgeting process.

The degree to which operating budgets mirror past activities varies among firms and subunits. Nevertheless, in most organizations it is common to begin the planning phase of operating budgets by assuming existing operating activities are to continue into the future at one level or another.[4] This approach is usually referred to as **incremental budgeting** because it assumes the budget consists of a base portion plus (or minus) some incremental (or decremental) portion. The **base** is that portion of the budget which is assumed to remain constant from one budget to the next. The **incremental** portion of the budget is that part which is driven by changes in the budget related activities.

A common criticism of the incremental budgeting approach is that many activities included in the base portion of the budget are perpetuated well beyond their useful economic life. Hence, many argue for an alternative approach toward budgeting. One such alternative is **zero base budgeting (ZBB)**. Under zero base budgeting, there is no base (i.e., the base is zero) and the entire budget is open for scrutiny and evaluation. Each organizational activity, often called decision unit, requires justification on a cost/benefit basis and is ranked relative to other activities. The advocates of ZBB argue that this approach toward budgeting enhances an organization's efficiency and flexibility to make changes. That is, under a ZBB system, the continuation of existing organizational activities would have to be economically justified in the same way that new activities would need to be justified.[5] Existing activities which cannot be justified on a cost/benefit basis are more likely to be discontinued under ZBB than an incremental budgeting system. At the same time, new activities would have a greater likelihood of being selected for implementation. Nevertheless, the application of ZBB to all organizational activities on a period to period basis would be extremely time consuming and, as such, likely cost more than its worth. As a result, even the

---

4. Of course, in start-up firms, this assumption would not be possible. For an interesting example of how R&D (research and development) drove the operating budget of Phanton Technology International, Inc., see the article by Pouliot (1991).

5. The ZBB approach has been utilized in private and public organizations. For a further discussion of ZBB, see the General Accounting Office (1979) report and the papers by Gordon, Haka and Schick (1984), and Gordon and Seilers (1984).

staunchest supporters of ZBB usually argue that a combination of the ZBB and incremental approaches toward budgeting provides the most efficient practice.

The part of the budgeting process leading up to the various operating budgets is essentially an exercise in planning. Alternative operating activities are identified and developed, and the course of action chosen. The budget itself represents a formal statement of the plan of action selected. Once plans are set in motion, the next step is to evaluate the plan by comparing the actual results with the expected results. In many organizations, this comparison takes place at frequent intervals (e.g., quarterly or monthly) and budgets are revised accordingly, with moving one year budgets being continually prepared at each interval.

Control

The comparison of actual results to expected results represents the control part of the budgeting process. The fact that operating budgets represent a formal plan of future activities means that the opportunity to exercise control is a natural outgrowth of budgeting. For example, let us return to the Tri Company, which developed a budgeted income statement for the forthcoming year. The actual amounts for revenues, cost of goods sold, and administrative and selling expenses were: $1,131,000, $819,000, $45,000 and $25,000, respectively. These amounts are shown in the second column of Exhibit 11.1. The differences between budgeted and actual amounts, which are often referred to as variances, are shown in the third column. The budget variances shown in Exhibit 11.1 could be used as the basis for appropriate actions regarding operating improvements at Tri Company. Budget variances are also used as a performance evaluation device.

It is common for firms to calculate operating budget variances, especially for the cost components of the budget. It is far less common for firms to conduct a formal analysis of these variances. However, there is nothing preventing firms from analyzing budget variances in a fashion similar to that done for standard cost variances discussed in Chapter 4. For example, let us return to the Tri Company illustration and analyze the revenues and cost of goods sold variances. These variances can be divided into a price and volume variance. An analysis of the data in Exhibit 11.1 reveals that actual sales were 39,000 chairs at a price of $29 per chair. Hence, there was a $39,000 [39,000 x ($30 - $29)] unfavorable budget sales price variance and a $30,000 [(40,000 - 39,000) x $30] unfavorable sales volume variance. The combination of these two variances makes up the $69,000 revenue variance shown in Exhibit 11.1. Actual cost of goods sold in this example turned out to be $21 as expected. Hence, the cost of goods sold variance of $21,000 is due solely to the sales volume being 1,000 units lower than expected (i.e., 1,000 x $21). If one thinks of standard costs as a form of budgeted costs, the analogy between analyzing budget variances and standard cost variances is both direct and obvious.

Once managers know that budget variances will be computed and used as an evaluation device, it is common for them to behave in a fashion which is consistent with maximizing their performance in terms of such variances. The behavior which is consistent with such a goal is not, however, as straightforward as some may initially think. For example, should a manager try to minimize unfavorable cost variances, maximize favorable revenue variances or try to achieve or exceed a budgeted profit target? The answer to these questions will, in part, be determined by the type of incentive compensation scheme the firm has for its managers.

Many individuals argue that firms need to develop budget-based (e.g., budgeted profit) incentive schemes, taking into consideration the way the firm is organized and the principal-agent relationships involved. These schemes can include a fixed portion (so as to limit a manager's downside risk) and a variable portion. Figure 11.1 illustrates such a compensation scheme, where the variable portion of compensation kicks in at budgeted profits of π_1 and is capped when profits equal π_2. The fixed portion of compensation in Figure 11.1 is equal to C_1 and the variable portion can go as high as the difference between C_2 and C_1 (i.e., the maximum total compensation is C_2). Empirical studies in the area indicate that a large number of firms have developed such incentive schemes and that managers attempt to maximize their total compensation accordingly (e.g., see Healy, 1985).

Motivation

The fact that operating budgets will motivate (influence) the behavior of individuals is well documented, dating back at least as far as Argyris' (1952) classic work in the area. However, an issue of much contention concerns the best way to use operating budgets to motivate people (Hopwood, 1972; Otley, 1978). The budget-based incentive scheme illustrated in Figure 11.1 is premised on the argument that individuals are motivated by financial concerns. While this seems to be the case for most people, the degree to which individuals are motivated by financial incentives varies greatly. For most people, nonfinancial concerns are also very important in motivating their behavior.

FIGURE 11.1
Budget-Based Compensation Scheme

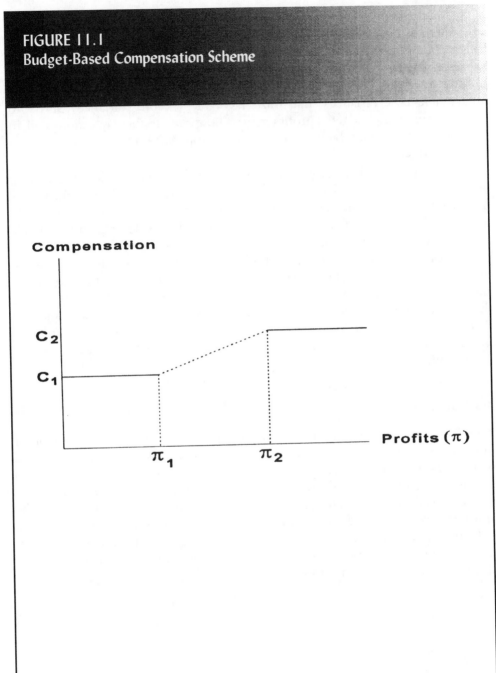

One nonfinancial aspect of budgeting which often motivates individuals is the sense of commitment to a jointly derived goal. In fact, it is widely believed that the strongest commitment to achieving (or exceeding in the positive sense) budget targets will result when budgeting is a participative process. This belief has been the outgrowth of much research on the subject during the past few decades. However, the research in the area has shown that there are many intervening variables which moderate the motivational effect of participative budgeting on performance (Brownell, 1982), where performance itself is viewed as being a function of motivation and ability.[6] Hence, whereas the consensus still seems to be that those individuals affected by budgets should participate in the budgeting process, the exact relationship between participative budgeting and motivation (and in turn performance) appears to be contingent on numerous environmental, organizational, and personal factors.

Another nonfinancial aspect of budgeting which motivates the performance levels of individuals has to do with an individual's need for achieving goals. It is generally agreed that an individual's motivation to perform is positively affected by the establishment of specific goals (e.g., see Locke et al., 1981). The issue, however, which has arisen in the budgeting literature, is whether budget goals (targets) should be set at easy, moderate, or difficult (even impossible) to achieve levels. The consensus which seems to be forming in this regard is that budgets are most effective in motivating behavior (and in turn performance) when set at achievable, though challenging, levels. The empirical evidence provided by Merchant and Manzoni (1989) has greatly solidified this consensus.

Given the potential number of financial and nonfinancial factors which may affect the relationship between budgets and motivation, it is not surprising that the literature in the area is confusing to most readers. By utilizing **expectancy theory**, Ronen and Livingstone (1975) were able to provide important insight into unraveling this confusion. Specifically, they showed that budgets affect the motivation of individuals in terms of intrinsic (i.e., internally derived) and extrinsic (i.e., externally derived) rewards, as well as in terms of the probabilities individuals assign to achieving budgets and in turn receiving rewards for such achievements. Hence, to the extent that these various factors work in different directions, it is natural to expect budgets to have differing motivational effects on individuals. The problem facing most organizations is developing an integrated approach toward the factors affecting the motivational aspects of operating budgets.

---

6. In the psychology based literature, an individual's performance, P, is often viewed as being determined by the interaction of her (his) motivation, M, and ability, A, i.e., $P = f(M \bullet A)$.

CASH FLOW BUDGETS

A fundamental concern to firms is the prevention of interruptions in activities due to cash shortages.[7] At the same time, firms do not want to have too much cash on hand because cash will usually generate less than an optimal return.[8] Hence, it is important for firms to anticipate their future cash position via the preparation of a cash flow budget.

The underpinnings of preparing a cash flow budget can be thought of in terms of two basic steps. First, the cash excess (shortage) at the beginning of a period is determined. This amount is derived based on the difference between the cash on hand at the beginning of the period and the desired cash level. Second, the cash inflows and outflows during the subsequent time interval (e.g., month, quarter, or year) are estimated.

One way to organize the budgeted cash inflows and outflows is in terms of operating, investing, and financing activities.[9] An advantage of this approach is that the cash flow budget can be linked to the firm's budget for operating activities (discussed in the previous section of this chapter) and its capital budget (discussed in the next chapter). Another advantage of this approach is that the cash flow budget at the firm level will be consistent with the statement of cash flows contained in the firm's financial reports. (Appendix 11.1 provides the 1997 statement of Cash Flows for IBM.)

An illustration of a quarterly cash flow budget is provided in Exhibit 11.2. This illustration is for DAS Corporation and assumes that the cash on hand at the beginning of the quarter is $600,000. The desired cash level is assumed to be $1,000,000. The first step in preparing the cash flow budget for DAS Corporation is the determination of the cash shortage of $400,000 at the beginning of the period. In order for the firm's ending cash balance to equal the desired level of $1,000,000, this shortage needs to be considered.

---

7. The term cash, as used in this section, refers to cash and cash equivalent items (i.e., items that can be easily and quickly converted into cash, such as U.S. Treasury Bills).

8. If holding cash were viewed as an attractive investment option, the argument would be to close down operations and invest all of a firm's assets in risk-free cash type accounts.

9. Since a large part of financing activities are handled at the firm level, cash flow budgets for subunits will show only limited financing activities.

EXHIBIT 11.2
DAS Corporation Cash Flow Budget
For January 1—March 31, 199X

Step I.

Cash on hand at beginning of period	$600,000
Minimum desired cash balance	1,000,000
Cash excess (shortage) at beginning of period—Actual	$(400,000)

Step II.

Cash Provided by Operations—Budgeted	
Net Income	900,000
Add:　Depreciation	50,000
Increase in accounts payable	10,000
Deduct:　Increase in accounts receivable	(15,000)
Total	$945,000
Cash Provided by Capital Investments—Budgeted	
Sale of capital investments	100,000
Capital expenditures	(1,200,000)
Total	$(1,100,000)
Cash Provided by Financing—Budgeted	
Issuance of long-term debt	260,000
Sale of capital stock	300,000
Dividends paid	(5,000)
Total	$　555,000
Cash at End of Period—Budgeted	$1,000,000

The second step is to budget the period's cash inflows and outflows. The total amounts in this regard are a net cash inflow of $945,000 from operations, a net cash outflow of $1,100,000 from investments, and a $555,000 net cash inflow from financing. These amounts, plus the subcomponent parts, are shown in Exhibit 11.2, under the section headed up as Step II.

At the end of the period, the budgeted cash flows can be compared to actual cash flows and the variance between these two amounts can be analyzed. This comparison and analysis represents the control side of cash flow budgeting. Where the firm level cash flow budget is prepared on an annual basis, the actual amounts for the cash provided by operations, investments, and financing will be the same as those shown in the DAS Corporation's annual statement of cash flows (assuming DAS uses the indirect method for computing cash flows from operations).

THE CASH IS SOVEREIGN MYTH

The theoretical value of a firm is well known to be equal to the present value of its future stream of cash flows. This basic axiom is reiterated in nearly every university-level accounting, economics, and finance course, as well as in countless discussions among corporate executives. Of course, firms do not know the exact nature of all their future cash flows. Nevertheless, many believe that by looking at realized periodic (e.g., on a year-to-year basis) cash flows, a firm is in a better position to predict future cash flows and thus firm value, than by looking at realized periodic accrual accounting numbers (e.g., earnings). Hence, we often hear the phrase, "Cash is King (or Queen)."

The above line of argument is dead wrong! Indeed, empirical evidence shows that realized accounting earnings often do a better job of predicting future cash flows and, in turn, firm value than do realized cash flows. This is true even when the cash flows in question are limited to those from operations. If this seems surprising, consider the following. The whole idea underlying accrual based accounting earnings is to record revenues as earned and expenses as incurred. This accrual process reduces the "lumpiness" resulting from the timing of actual cash collections and payments. In addition, the accounting accrual process focuses attention on matching revenues with related expenses, which also reduces the "lumpiness" associated with realized cash flows.

In essence, the accrual accounting system has been designed to mitigate the noisy performance signal provided by cash flows. Why unravel this entire system to get back to cash flows? One reason to unravel the accrual accounting system might be the commonly held belief that accounting numbers lend themselves to being easily "managed." However, the same criticism holds true for cash flows! Remember, cash flows and the accrual accounting process are inextricably intertwined. Indeed, cash flows from operations is generally computed by adding back depreciation (and/or amortization) to accounting operating income. Further, cash flows from financing and/or investment activities are intentionally, and rightly, "managed."

Is there any time when the adage "Cash is Sovereign" holds true? Yes! When a firm becomes "cash poor" (i.e., it needs to be extremely worried about having cash available to pay off its debts as they mature), it becomes a "slave to cash." Under that scenario, "Cash *is* Sovereign" (at least in the tyrannical sense). Of course, the real lesson here is not that cash should be viewed as sovereign, but rather that firms should not put themselves in a "cash poor" situation.

Proper cash management is essential to all firms! In fact, poor cash management will result in a situation where a firm is forced to reject wealth creating opportunities because it does not have the means to handle "lumpy" cash flows. For example, "cash poor" firms often have to reject positive net present value projects due to the fact that in early years the projects' cash flows are negative.

In sum, corporate executives need to eschew the myth that "Cash is Sovereign." Although proper cash management is critical, the real key to creating firm value over the long-run is to make sure that a firm generates a growing stream of earnings from its normal operating activities.

CONCLUDING COMMENTS

Operating budgets are statements of the formal plans for an organization's normal operating activities. A key aspect of operating budgets is their motivation effect on the performance levels of individuals and, in turn, organizations.

Operating budgets are prepared based on the principles of accrual accounting. With appropriate adjustments, operating income can be adjusted to obtain cash provided by operations. By adding cash flows provided by investments and financing to the cash flows from operations, a firm's total cash flows can be derived. A forecast of future cash flows is usually referred to as a cash flow budget. The primary objective of the cash flow budget is to prevent undesirable interruptions in activities due to cash shortages, while avoiding having too much cash on hand.

The present value of all future cash flows is theoretically equal to a firm's value. However, it does not follow that realized cash flows (even if limited to those from operations) provide the best gauge of firm performance and, in turn, firm value. In fact, empirical evidence shows that realized accounting earnings often provide a better indicator of firm value (measured in terms of stock market value) than realized cash flows.[10]

Operating activities are usually thought of in terms of the normal operating period of a firm. For most firms, the operating period is considered to last one year.[11] Planning and control beyond this one period time interval often involves large capital investments. The budgeting process related to these investments falls under the domain of capital budgeting, which is the subject of the next chapter.

---

10. For example, see the study by Dechow (1994).
11. For some firms the normal operating period is shorter than one year (e.g., a restaurant in a summer resort area) and for others it is longer than one year (e.g., wine manufacturers).

APPENDIX 11.1:
Consolidated Statement of Cash Flows, IBM Corporation and Subsidiary Companies

(Dollars in millions)
For the year ended December 31:

	1997	1996	1995
Cash flow from operating activities:			
Net earnings	$ 6,093	$ 5,429	$ 4,178
Adjustments to reconcile net earnings to cash provided from operating activities:			
Depreciation	4,018	3,676	3,955
Amortization of software	983	1,336	1,647
Effect of restructuring charges	(445)	(1,491)	(2,119)
Purchased in-process research and development	–	435	1,840
Deferred income taxes	358	11	1,392
Gain on disposition of fixed and other assets	(273)	(300)	(339)
Other changes that (used) provided cash:			
Receivables	(3,727)	(650)	(530)
Inventories	432	196	107
Other assets	(1,087)	(980)	(1,100)
Accounts payable	699	319	659
Other liabilities	1,814	2,294	1,018
Net cash provided from operating activities	8,865	10,275	10,708
Cash flow from investing activities:			
Payments for plant, rental machines and other property	(6,793)	(5,883)	(4,744)
Proceeds from disposition of plant, rental machines and other property	1,130	1,314	1,561
Acquisitions of Tivoli Systems, Inc. and Lotus Development Corporation – net, 1996 and 1995, respectively	–	(716)	(2,880)
Investment in software	(314)	(295)	(823)
Purchases of marketable securities and other investments	(1,617)	(1,613)	(1,315)
Proceeds from marketable securities and other investments	1,439	1,470	3,149
Net cash used in investing activities	(6,155)	(5,723)	(5,052)
Cash flow from financing activities:			
Proceeds from new debt	9,142	7,670	6,636
Short-term borrowings less than 90 days – net	(668)	(919)	2,557
Payments to settle debt	(4,530)	(4,992)	(9,460)
Preferred stock transactions – net	(1)	–	(870)
Common stock transactions – net	(6,250)	(5,005)	(4,656)
Cash dividends paid	(783)	(706)	(591)
Net cash used in financing activities	(3,090)	(3,952)	(6,384)
Effect of exchange rate changes on cash and cash equivalents	(201)	(172)	65
Net change in cash and cash equivalents	(581)	428	(663)
Cash and cash equivalents at January 1	7,687	7,259	7,922
Cash and cash equivalents at December 31	$ 7,106	$ 7,687	$ 7,259
Supplemental data:			
Cash paid during the year for:			
Income taxes	$ 2,472	$ 2,229	$ 1,453
Interest	$ 1,475	$ 1,563	$ 1,720

The financial statement in this Appendix is from IBM's 1997 Annual Report .

The notes are an integral part of this statement.

PROBLEMS

Problem 11.1

Define and discuss the importance of the: (a) Operating Budget, and (b) Cash Flow Budget.

Problem 11.2

A.   It is often argued that cash flows provide a better indicator of firm performance and, in turn, firm value than accounting income. Explain the fallacy of this argument.

B.   Many seem to believe that the difference between accounting income from operations and cash flows from operations can be reconciled by adding back accounting depreciation (plus amortization and depletion, where present) to the income. Explain why this belief is incorrect.

Problem 11.3

A large body of literature addresses the relationship between the difficulty in achieving budgets and the resulting motivational effect on performance. Some studies have shown that extremely-difficult-to-achieve budgets motivate the highest level of performance. Other studies have shown that easily-achieved budgets motivate the highest level of performance. Finally, other studies have shown that budgets which are neither too difficult nor too easy are the best performance motivators.

Required:
Provide an explanation for reconciling the mixed findings regarding motivational effect of budgets on performance.

Problem 11.4 (Adapted from CMA examination)

Alpha-Tech, a rapidly growing distributor of electronic components, is formulating its plans for 1998. Carol Jones, the firm's marketing director, has completed the sales forecast presented below.

Alpha-Tech 1998 Forecasted Sales (in thousands)			
Month	**Sales**	**Month**	**Sales**
January	$ 9,000	July	$15,000
February	10,000	August	15,000
March	9,000	September	16,000
April	11,500	October	16,000
May	12,500	November	15,000
June	14,000	December	17,000

Philip Smith, a manager in the Planning and Budgeting Department, is responsible for preparing the cash flow projection. The following information will be used in preparing the cash flow projection.

- Alpha-Tech's excellent record in accounts receivable collection is expected to continue. Sixty percent of billings are collected the month after the sale and the remaining 40 percent two months after.

- The purchase of electronic components is Alpha-Tech's largest expenditure and is estimated to be 40 percent of sales. Seventy percent of the parts are received by Alpha-Tech one month prior to sale and 30 percent are received during the month of sale.

- Historically, 75 percent of accounts payable have been paid one month after receipt of the purchased components, and the remaining 25 percent is paid two months after receipt.

- Hourly wages and fringe benefits, estimated to be 30 percent of the current month's sales, are paid in the month incurred.

- General and administrative expenses are projected to be $15,620,000 for the year. The breakdown of these expenses is presented at the top of the next column. All expenditures are paid uniformly throughout the year, except the property taxes which are paid at the end of each quarter in four equal installments.

1998 Forecasted General and Administrative Costs (in thousands)	
Salaries and fringe benefits	$ 3,200
Promotion	3,800
Property taxes	1,360
Insurance	2,000
Utilities	1,800
Depreciation	3,460
Total	$15,620

- Income tax payments are made at the beginning of each calendar quarter based on the income of the prior quarter. Alpha-Tech is subject to an effective income tax rate of 40 percent. Alpha-Tech's operating income for the first quarter of 1998 is projected to be $3,200,000. The company pays 100 percent of the estimated tax payment.

- Alpha-Tech maintains a minimum cash balance of $500,000. If the cash balance is less than $500,000 at the end of each month, the company borrows amounts necessary to maintain this balance. All amounts borrowed are repaid out of subsequent positive cash flow. The projected April 1, 1998 opening balance is $500,000.

- Alpha-Tech has no short-term debt as of April 1, 1998.

- Alpha-Tech uses a calendar year for both financial reporting and tax purposes.

Required:
Prepare a cash budget for Alpha-Tech by month for the second quarter of 1998. Ignore any interest expense associated with borrowing.

Problem 11.5 *(Adapted from CMA examination)*

Summit Equipment specializes in the manufacture of medical equipment, a field that has become increasingly competitive. Approximately two years ago, Ben Harrington, president of Summit, became concerned that the company's bonus plan, which focused on division profitability, was not helping Summit remain competitive. Harrington decided to revise the bonus plan so that it would encourage division managers to focus on areas that were important to customers and that added value without increasing cost. In addition to a profitability incentive, the revised plan also includes incentives for reduced rework costs, reduced sales returns, and on-time deliveries. Bonuses are calculated and awarded *semi-annually* on the following basis.

Profitability:	Two percent of operating income.
Rework:	Costs in excess of 2 percent of operating income are deducted from the bonus amount.
On-time delivery:	$5,000 if over 98 percent of deliveries are on time, $2,000 if 96-98 percent of deliveries are on time, and no increment if on-time deliveries are below 96 percent.
Sales returns:	$3,000 if returns are less than 1.5 percent of sales. Fifty percent of any amount in excess of 1.5 percent of sales is deducted from the bonus amount.

Note: If the calculation of the bonus results in a negative amount for a particular period, the manager simply receives no bonus, and the negative amount is *not* carried forward to the next period.

The revised bonus plan was implemented on October 1, 1993, the beginning of Summit's fiscal year. Presented below are the results for two of Summit's divisions, Charter and Mesa Divisions, for the first year under the new bonus plan.

	Charter Division		Mesa Division	
	October 1993- March 1994	April 1994- September 1994	October 1993- March 1994	April 1994- September 1994
Sales	$4,200,000	$4,400,000	$2,850,000	$2,900,000
Operating income	$462,000	$440,000	$342,000	$406,000
On-time delivery	95.4%	97.3%	98.2%	94.6%
Rework costs	$11,500	$11,000	$6,000	$8,000
Sales returns	$84,000	$70,000	$44,750	$42,500

Both of these divisions had similar sales and operating income results for the prior fiscal year which ended September 30, 1993, when the old bonus plan was in effect. Based on the 1992-93 results, the manager of the Charter Division earned a bonus of $27,060 while the manager of the Mesa Division earned $22,440.

Required:

A.   For the manager of the Charter Division,

   1.   compute the semi-annual installments and total bonus awarded for the fiscal year ended September 30, 1994.

   2.   discuss the likely behavior of this manager under the revised bonus plan.

B.   For the manager of the Mesa Division,

   1.   compute the semi-annual installments and total bonus awarded for the fiscal year ended September 30, 1994.

   2.   discuss the likely behavior of this manager under the revised bonus plan.

C.   Evaluate whether or not Ben Harrington's revisions to the bonus plan at Summit Equipment have achieved the desired results, and recommend any changes that might improve the plan.

Problem 11.6 *(Adapted from CMA examination)*

TabComp Inc. is a retail distributor for MZB-33 computer hardware and related software and support services. TabComp prepares annual sales forecasts of which the first six months for 1996 are presented below.

	TabComp Inc. **Sales Forecast** **Six Months - 1996**			
	Hardware Sales		**Software Sales**	**Total**
	Units	**Dollars**	**and Support**	**Sales**
January	130	$ 390,000	$160,000	$ 550,000
February	120	360,000	140,000	500,000
March	110	330,000	150,000	480,000
April	90	270,000	130,000	400,000
May	100	300,000	125,000	425,000
·June	125	375,000	225,000	600,000
Total	675	$2,025,000	$930,000	$2,955,000

Cash sales account for 25 percent of TabComp's total sales, 30 percent of the total sales are paid by bank credit card, and the remaining 45 percent are on open account (TabComp's own charge accounts). The cash and bank credit card sales are received in the month of the sale. Bank credit card sales are subject to a four-percent discount deducted at the time of the daily deposit. The cash receipts for sales on open account are 70 percent in the month following the sale, 28 percent in the second month following the sale, and the remaining are estimated to be uncollectible.

TabComp's month-end inventory requirements for computer hardware units are 30 percent of the next month's sales. A one-month lead time is required for delivery from the manufacturer; thus, orders for computer hardware units are placed on the 25th of each month to assure that they will be in the store by the first day of the month needed. The computer hardware units are purchased under terms of n/45 measured from the time the units are delivered to TabComp. TabComp's purchase price for the computer units is 60 percent of the selling price.

Required:

A.   Calculate the cash that TabComp Inc. can expect to collect during April 1996. Be sure to show all of your calculations.

B.   TabComp Inc. is determining the MZB-33 computer hardware units that will be ordered on January 25, 1996.

1.   Determine the projected number of computer hardware units that will be ordered.

2.   Calculate the dollar value of the order that TabComp will place for these computer hardware units.

3.   In which month will TabComp pay for these computer hardware units?

Problem 11.7 (Adapted from CMA examination)

Bullen & Company makes and sells high-quality glare filters for microcomputer monitors. John Crane, controller, is responsible for preparing Bullen's master budget and has assembled the data below for 1997.

The direct labor rate includes wages and all employee-related benefits and the employer's share of FICA. Labor saving machinery will be fully operational by March. Also, as of March 1, the company's union contract calls for an increase in direct labor wages that is included in the direct labor rate.

Bullen expects to have 10,000 glare filters in inventory at December 31, 1996, and has a policy of carrying 50 percent of the following month's projected sales in inventory.

	1997			
	January	February	March	April
Estimated unit sales	20,000	24,000	16,000	18,000
Sales price per unit	$80	$80	$75	$75
Direct labor hours per unit	4.0	4.0	3.5	3.5
Direct labor hourly rate	$15	$15	$16	$16
Direct materials cost per unit	$10	$10	$10	$10

Required:

A.   Prepare the following monthly budgets for Bullen & Company for the first quarter of 1997. Be sure to show supporting calculations.

    1.   Production budget in units.

    2.   Direct labor budget in hours.

    3.   Direct materials budget.

    4.   Sales budget.

B.   Calculate the total budgeted contribution margin for Bullen & Company for the first quarter of 1997. Be sure to show supporting calculations.

CAPITAL BUDGETING

CHAPTER OUTLINE

- Identification of Capital Projects

- Selection of Capital Projects: Naive Methods

- Selection of Capital Projects: Sophisticated Methods

- Sensitivity Analysis

- Taxes

- High Technology Investments

- Capital Investments and Managerial Incentive Plans

- Option Values and Capital Investments

INTRODUCTION

As discussed in Chapter 11, operating expenditures are directed toward supporting the firm's current operating activities, which are usually viewed in terms of a one year period. **Capital expenditures** (often called **capital investments**) are intended to benefit the firm's activities for more than one operating period. Acquisitions of plant and equipment are examples of capital expenditures. The acquisition of an entire subsidiary also can be viewed as a capital expenditure, but usually is treated separately from project level investments. Capital expenditures also are made on intangible assets of a firm (e.g., investments in human capital via training programs). The discussion in this chapter will focus on capital expenditures which are related to project level tangible fixed assets of a firm.

In an effort to plan for the upcoming activities, major corporations usually develop a forecast (plan) of capital expenditures for one or more years into the future. A listing of such anticipated capital expenditures comprises what is usually referred to as the **capital budget**.

There are two basic phases associated with the process leading up to selection of capital projects. The first phase is the **identification** of projects which are consistent with achieving the overall goals of the firm. Once various projects have been identified, the **selection** of specific projects for actual implementation is the second phase of the process. The selection phase of capital investments involves developing the detailed costs and benefits associated with the various alternatives and choosing those projects with an acceptable payoff. The selection of projects should be carried out in line with the notion that scarce resources must be allocated among competing alternatives.

Once projects have been chosen and implemented, an assessment should be conducted to decide whether they have achieved their desired performance. This assessment represents the **control** (often called postauditing) phase. The combination of the three phases of the capital expenditure process (i.e., identification, selection, and control) comprise what is commonly referred to as **capital budgeting**. This chapter will focus on the identification and selection phases of capital budgeting. The postauditing phase will be the subject of Chapter 13.

Capital investments permit the continued flow of operating activities. Hence, the importance of capital investments to the long-run success of most organizations cannot be overstated. Indeed, capital investments represent an essential ingredient to successful competitiveness at both the firm and national level.

Evidence attesting to the importance of capital expenditures at the firm level is provided by the fact that it is common for firms to announce via the popular press their anticipated and revised levels of capital expenditures. *The Wall Street Journal*, for example, contains announcements of planned corporate capital expenditures on a regular basis. The fact that such announcements can, and often do, have a direct effect on the market value of firms (e.g., see McConnell and Muscarella, 1985; and Tsay, Alt and Gordon, 1993) provides further support for the argument that capital expenditures are of key importance to firms. In addition, information on the level of capital expenditures is highlighted in the annual reports of firms in the statement of cash flows, as well as the discussion and analysis offered by management on the firm's operations and financial condition. The CEO's letter to stockholders also often singles out information concerning a firm's capital expenditures.

At the macro level, the U.S. Department of Commerce conducts quarterly surveys of planned capital expenditures by U.S. corporations. Public announcements related to planned countrywide capital expenditures also are frequently contained in the popular press.

IDENTIFICATION OF CAPITAL PROJECTS

The first step in capital budgeting is the **identification** of the various capital projects available for investments. Only after being identified can a project be selected. Hence, the importance of the identification phase of capital budgeting cannot be overstated.

In identifying various capital projects, the firm's overall objective (e.g., improving the firm's profitability ratios vis à vis other firms in the same industry) needs to be kept in mind. At the same time, it should be remembered that there are usually many paths to the same destination. Thus, once an opportunity for investment by a firm has been recognized, alternative ways of meeting this opportunity should be identified. For example, assume a firm decides that an opportunity to reduce information processing costs exists via the introduction of a new computer based information system. The issue that must be considered next concerns the various ways that a computer based information system can be configured. One alternative might be to heavily rely on a mainframe computer, with numerous support terminals and inexpensive microcomputers. An alternative option might be to heavily rely on several minicomputers and a distributed data processing system of powerful microcomputers. In other words, once an opportunity has been identified, the various options for taking advantage of that opportunity also need to be identified.

The identification phase is not only the first step in capital budgeting, but it is also the most difficult step to formally specify. There is no simple set of procedures which allows a firm to identify its various opportunities and related options. A factor which complicates this notion is that highly competitive markets, by definition, tend to drive out high return projects. Thus, the more competitive the market, the more likely the firm will not be able to identify high return capital investments.

The problems associated with the identification of high return capital investments notwithstanding, a key factor distinguishing successful firms from unsuccessful ones is the ability to identify such investments. One way to approach this task is by thinking in terms of project types. In general, capital projects can be classified according to: (1) mandatory projects, (2) cost savings projects, and (3) revenue generating projects.

Mandatory projects are must-do investments. For example, a steel company must invest in pollution abatement equipment to control their chimney stacks. Of course, there are various options available for carrying out the required pollution abatement. Nevertheless, a key feature of mandatory projects is the fact that they are externally driven. Therefore, information of an external and largely nonfinancial nature is critical to their identification.

Cost savings projects relate to investments which reduce the cost of existing activities. As such, identification of these projects begins with an examination of existing firm activities. The computer based information system noted above would be an example of a cost savings project and would depend on information which is largely of a financial, ex post, and internal nature. The importance of cost savings projects was highlighted by Bleakley (1994), where he noted that a growing number of companies are requiring significant cuts in costs as a key means of justifying capital spending. Among the firms noted by Bleakley in this regard were RJR Nabisco, Inc., Colgate-Palmolive Co., and American Telephone & Telegraph Co.

Revenue generating projects relate to investments which either increase the revenues of existing firm activities or create revenues from new activities. Identification of these activities would likely depend on market based information which is largely of a nonfinancial, ex ante, and external nature. An example of a revenue generating type project would be an investment in plant and equipment required to produce a new, high-tech product line.

Once opportunities and the related options have been identified, the next step is to choose projects for actual investments. Where investment opportunities are competing for the same resources, the objective is to select the most efficient investments. This step involves the development of the details of the various options and actually selecting projects for investment. As a result, this step is usually referred to as being the selection phase of capital budgeting. Unlike the identification phase, the selection phase does lend itself to a set of formally stated procedures.

SELECTION OF CAPITAL PROJECTS: NAIVE METHODS

The techniques used in selecting capital projects are often classified as either sophisticated or naive. Sophisticated methods explicitly consider the risk adjusted discounted cash flows associated with projects, whereas naive methods usually do not. Two naive methods are frequently used. These are the payback period and the accounting rate of return. We will discuss these two methods before looking at the more complicated sophisticated methods. As will become apparent, the naive methods of selecting capital projects rely heavily on information which can be characterized as being ex post, financial, and internal in nature.

Payback Period

The **payback period** method for selecting projects computes the number of periods (usually years) that it takes for a project to recover its initial cost, ignoring the time value of money. Algebraically, this can be expressed as follows:

$$\sum_{t=1}^{P} CF_t \geq CF_0 \qquad\qquad \text{Eq. 12.1}$$

where,

P	=	payback period,
CF_t	=	net after-tax cash flow from the project in period t,
CF_0	=	the initial after-tax cash outflow (i.e., cost) for the project.

The decision rule determining whether to accept or reject a project is stated in terms of a target payback period. That is:

If P < target payback period, accept the project.
If P = target payback period, be indifferent to the project.
If P > target payback period, reject the project.

When choosing a project from more than one option, the payback method selects the option with the shortest payback period.

An example of how to use the payback period follows. Smith Co. is evaluating the possibility of buying a new piece of equipment for $45,000 (Project A). The equipment has an estimated economic life of ten years and the net cash inflows (after considering tax effects) from the project are expected to be $8,000 for each of the first three years, $14,000 for each of the next five years, and $9,000 for each of the remaining two years. The payback period for this example would be 4 1/2 years (see Exhibit 12.1).

Two problems associated with using the payback period method are: (1) failure to consider cash flows after the payback period, and (2) failure to consider the time value of money.[1] To illustrate the first limitation, let us return to the Smith Co. The company still has a total of $45,000 to spend on capital investments, only now it is faced with choosing between Project A noted above and an alternative project, Project B, which also costs $45,000. However, Project B has an estimated economic life of six years and net cash inflows (after considering tax effects) of $7,000 for each of the first three years and $24,000 for each of the remaining three years. The payback period for Project B would be 4 years (see Exhibit 12.1). Based on the payback criterion, the firm would choose Project B over A because it has a payback period of 4 years compared to 4 1/2 years for Project A. However, it is not clear that this is the best option because Project A yields a total cash inflow of $112,000 compared to $93,000 for Project B.

To illustrate the second limitation, let us assume that Smith Co. has a third project, Project C, to consider. Project C also has a cost of $45,000 and estimated economic life of six years. Net cash inflows (after considering taxes) for Project C are $24,000 for the first year, $7,000 for each of the next three years, and $24,000 for each of the next two years. The payback period for this project would be four years, as with Project B (see Exhibit 12.1). Based on the payback criterion for selecting projects, both B and C appear equally attractive. However, the cash inflows associated with Project C would clearly be preferred to B's cash inflows since the only difference between the two is that B receives $7,000 and $24,000 in years 1 and 4, respectively, whereas C receives $24,000 and $7,000 in years 1 and 4, respectively. Thus, there is more cash inflow and a higher percentage of payback in years 1 through 3 with Project C.

---

1. Although not commonly used, it is possible to compute the payback period in terms of discounted cash flows (a concept discussed in the next section).

EXHIBIT 12.1
Smith Co.
Illustration of Payback Period

Project	Cost	Yr. (1)	Yr. (2)	Yr. (3)	Yr. (4)	Yr. (5)	Yr. (6)	Yr. (7)	Yr. (8)	Yr. (9)	Yr. (10)	Total Cash Inflows	Payback Period
A	$45,000	8,000	8,000	8,000	14,000	14,000*	14,000	14,000	14,000	9,000	9,000	$112,000	4½ yrs.
B	$45,000	7,000	7,000	7,000	24,000*	24,000	24,000					$ 93,000	4 yrs.
C	$45,000	24,000	7,000	7,000	7,000*	24,000	24,000					$ 93,000	4 yrs.

Despite its limitations, the payback period method of selecting capital expenditures is commonly used in practice. For example, in a study conducted by Scapens and Sale (1985) it was found that between 55% and 60% of both U.S. and U.K. firms use the payback period method. One reason for using the payback period is that the method provides a simple procedure for considering part of the risk or uncertainty associated with a project.[2] That is, the payback period method implicitly considers the fact that the accuracy associated with estimated cash flows diminishes as you predict further into the future. A second reason in favor of using the payback period method is that it directly facilitates the liquidity needs of a firm by placing emphasis on early cash inflows. Both risk and liquidity are key concerns to firms, which likely account for the widespread use of the payback period as a constraint, if not as the primary criterion, in selecting capital projects.

Accounting Rate of Return

The accounting rate of return (*ARR*) method for selecting projects is based on dividing the annual incremental net income derived from a project by the project's initial cost. That is:

$$ARR = \frac{\text{Average Annual Income From Project}}{\text{Project Cost}} \qquad \text{Eq. 12.2}$$

A target *ARR* is then used to decide whether to accept or reject a project. More specifically, the decision rule would be as follows:

If ARR > target *ARR*, accept the project.
If ARR = target *ARR*, be indifferent to the project
If ARR < target *ARR*, reject the project.

When choosing a project from more than one option, the *ARR* method selects that project with the highest *ARR*.

---

2.   The terms **risk** and **uncertainty** are used interchangeably throughout this chapter.

An example of how to use the accounting rate of return follows. Jones Co. is evaluating the possibility of purchasing a new building at a cost of $2,000,000. The building has an estimated economic life of 20 years and the net income (after considering taxes) from the building's use is expected to be approximately $240,000 per year. The accounting rate of return for this example would be 12% ($240,000/$2,000,000).[3]

The problems associated with computing accounting rates of return, as discussed in Chapter 8, have led many to argue against the use of such returns for selecting capital investments. Further, as with the payback period, the *ARR* method ignores the time value of money. Hence, as with the payback period method, the *ARR* method for selecting capital expenditures is the object of severe criticism.

Despite the criticisms usually leveled at the *ARR* method, many managers use it as a selection technique. For example, in the study conducted by Scapens and Sale (1985), it was found that 40% of U.S. firms and 55.6% of U.K. firms use the *ARR* method. There are at least two reasons which help explain its popularity. First, even the staunchest critics recognize that financial analysts, creditors, and investors continually use the *ARR* to measure overall firm performance. Indeed, annual financial statements of most major corporations show some form of return on investment.[4] Hence, congruency between selecting specific projects and measuring overall firm returns often leads managers to consider the *ARR* as a constraint, if not as the primary criterion, in selecting projects. The second reason that the *ARR* method is often used as a means of selecting projects has to do with the way managerial performance is measured. In many firms, managerial bonuses and incentive plans are based on data which either directly use, or relate to, accounting rates of return. In these firms the managerial reward structure encourages, often unintentionally, the selection of capital projects with the highest *ARR*.

---

3. An alternative way to compute the ARR, which is in common use, is to divide the project's net income by its average book value (i.e., the initial cost divided in half). Based on this alternative, the ARR for this example would be 24% [$240,000/($2,000,000/2)].

4. For a discussion of the various measures of return, the reader is referred to the paper by Gordon (1976).

SELECTION OF CAPITAL PROJECTS:
SOPHISTICATED METHODS

There is a large body of empirical evidence which indicates that major corporations use sophisticated techniques in selecting capital projects (e.g., see Klammer, 1973; Schall, Sundem and Geijsbeek, 1978; Rosenblatt and Jucker, 1979; Scapens and Sale, 1985; Pike, 1986, 1988). Unlike the naive methods, these techniques explicitly consider the risk adjusted discounted cash flows (DCF) associated with projects. However, the degree to which these techniques are used varies from firm to firm and from project to project. One impediment to the use of risk adjusted discounted cash flow techniques of capital budgeting is the inability of firms to accurately derive the required information. As will become apparent, sophisticated methods for selecting capital projects rely heavily on a broad spectrum of information. In fact, the nature of the information required cuts across the entire tripartite classification scheme discussed in Chapter 1. In this regard, recent developments in the area of decision support systems should help facilitate the collection and processing of the requisite information. This is especially true in light of the fact that firms can easily tie external data bases into their internal management accounting system.

Given the multitude of activities carried out by a firm and the inaccuracies associated with estimating risk adjusted discounted cash flows, there is good reason to expect that the use of sophisticated methods for selecting projects will not, in and of itself, guarantee firm success. Nevertheless, these techniques add much rigor into the analysis and screening of projects. Practitioners and theorists alike seem to agree that the use of risk adjusted discounted cash flow procedures provides a meaningful framework for approaching the selection of capital projects. As one senior corporate executive noted to the author, "We view DCF analysis as an important initial screening device which assists in, but does not by itself determine, the ultimate selection of projects."

The net present value, profitability index, and internal rate of return are the sophisticated techniques most typically used. However, before discussing these techniques, we will introduce the present value (*PV*) concept because it is fundamental to all of the sophisticated methods of selecting capital projects.

Present Value Concept

The term **present value (PV)** refers to the amount one is willing to pay today in exchange for the receipt of cash flows in the future. The process of determining the present value of future cash flows is often referred to as **discounting cash flows (DCF)** and can be thought of as the inverse of compounding. This discounting process works as follows: Assume that today you are willing to lend the bank $1.00 in exchange for its promise to repay one year from now $1.00 plus

10% annual interest. At the end of one year the amount of principal plus interest will equal $1.10. Alternatively, $1.00 is the present value of receiving $1.10 one year from now at an interest rate of 10%. Algebraically, the PV may be expressed as:

$$PV = \frac{(\$1.10)}{(1+.10)^1} = \$1.00$$

If you left your money in the bank for two years, the compounded amount would have added up to $1.21 [$1.00 x (1.10)²]. Alternatively, the present value of receiving $1.21 two years later, assuming an acceptable compound annual return of 10%, is also $1.00. This may be expressed as:

$$PV = \frac{(\$1.21)}{(1+.10)^2} = \$1.00$$

The present value of a stream of future cash receipts equals the sum of the discounted cash flows. Algebraically, the general case can be expressed as follows:[5]

$$PV = \frac{CF_1}{(1+k)^1} + \frac{CF_2}{(1+k)^2} + ... + \frac{CF_n}{(1+k)^n} = \sum_{t=1}^{n} \frac{CF_t}{(1+k)^t} \qquad \text{Eq. 12.3}$$

where,

CF_t	=	net cash flow for period t,
k	=	discount rate (i.e., opportunity cost of funds),
n	=	last year in which future cash flow will be received.

---

5. Tables for the present value of $1 and the present value of an ordinary annuity of $1 are provided in Appendix 12.1 and Appendix 12.2, respectively.

Net Present Value

The **net present value (NPV)** method is based on computing the differences between the present value of future cash inflows from a project and the project's initial cost. This method can be expressed as follows:

$$NPV = \sum_{t=1}^{n} \frac{CF_t}{(1+k)^t} - CF_0 = \frac{CF_1}{(1+k)^1} + \frac{CF_2}{(1+k)^2} + ... + \frac{CF_n}{(1+k)^n} - CF_0 \qquad \text{Eq. 12.4}$$

where,

CF_t	=	net cash flow from the project in period t,
k	=	the discount rate,
n	=	economic life of the project,
CF_0	=	initial after-tax cash outlay (i.e., cost) of the project.

The decision of whether to accept or reject a project based on the net present value method is based on the following:

If NPV > zero, accept the project.
If NPV = zero, be indifferent to the project.
If NPV < zero, reject the project.

Profitability Index

A slight variation on the net present value method is the profitability index (often called benefit-cost ratio). The **profitability index (PI)** is a measure of relative profitability calculated by dividing the present value of a project's benefits by its initial cost. Algebraically, the PI may be expressed as follows:

$$PI = \sum_{t=1}^{n} \frac{CF_t}{(1+k)^t} / CF_0 \qquad \text{Eq. 12.5}$$

where the symbols are defined as in the NPV method. The decision rule concerning whether to accept or reject a project is as follows:

If PI > 1.0, accept the project.
If PI = 1.0, be indifferent to the project.
If PI < 1.0, reject the project.

Internal Rate of Return

A third discounted cash flow method for selecting capital investments is called the internal rate of return. The **internal rate of return (IRR)** method sets the initial cost of a project equal to the project's expected cash flows and solves for the discount rate that equates the two. The derived discount rate is called the internal rate of return. Algebraically, the IRR can be derived from the following expression:

$$\sum_{t=1}^{n} \frac{CF_t}{(1+IRR)^t} - CF_0 = 0 \qquad\qquad \text{Eq. 12.6}$$

where the symbols are defined as previously. The computed IRR is compared to the opportunity cost of funds, k, in order to decide whether to accept or reject a project. The decision rule can be expressed as follows:

> **If** $IRR > k$, accept the project.
> **If** $IRR = k$, be indifferent to the project.
> **If** $IRR < k$, reject the project.

An Example of NPV, PI, and IRR

The calculations for the three discounted cash flow methods of capital budgeting are demonstrated in the following example. Gold Co. has the opportunity to invest in a capital project which has an initial cost of $100,000. After much work it has been determined that the net cash inflows (after taxes) from this project are expected to be $40,000 at the end of the first year, $50,000 at the end of the second year, and $60,000 at the end of the third year. Assuming a discount rate of 12% and no salvage value, the calculation for the net present value of the project is as follows:

$$NPV = \frac{\$40,000}{(1.12)} + \frac{\$50,000}{(1.12)^2} + \frac{\$60,000}{(1.12)^3} - \$100,000$$

$$= \$35,714 + \$39,860 + \$42,707 - \$100,000 = \$18,281$$

Since the NPV is greater than zero, the project is acceptable.

The profitability index (*PI*) for the above project can also be calculated. The *PI* would be:

$$PI = \left[\frac{\$40,000}{1.12} + \frac{\$50,000}{(1.12)^2} + \frac{\$60,000}{(1.12)^3} \right] / \$100,000 = \$118,281 / \$100,000 = 1.18$$

Since the *PI* is greater than one, this criterion would also indicate that the project is acceptable.

The internal rate of return (*IRR*) for the above project can be obtained by setting the *NPV* equal to zero and solving for the discount rate. This is done as follows:

$$\frac{\$40,000}{(1+IRR)} + \frac{\$50,000}{(1+IRR)^2} + \frac{\$60,000}{(1+IRR)^3} - \$100,000 = 0$$

The *IRR* in this example works out to be 21.64%. If the firm's cost of capital, k, is 12%, the project would be acceptable under this method as well.

Comparing NPV, PI, and IRR

As the above example indicates, the same decision will be reached when evaluating an individual project under the *NPV*, *PI*, and *IRR*. That is, if a project's *NPV* is greater than zero, its *PI* will be greater than 1 and its *IRR* will be greater than k. The decision to reject or be indifferent to a project will also coincide under all three discounted cash flow methods. The reason for these similarities is that all three methods are inherently related to the principle of maximizing the net present value of a firm (e.g., see, Rubenstein, 1973; Fama, 1977; and Myers and Turnbull, 1977).[6]

When comparing or ranking across several projects, the results may vary under the three methods. Whereas the *NPV* and *PI* methods assume that early cash inflows are reinvested based on the firm's cost of capital, the *IRR* method assumes that these cash inflows are reinvested at the *IRR* of the project. In general, the former assumption is the more realistic of the two. Another problem associated with the *IRR* method is that multiple solutions, which defy economic interpretation, will result when a project has alternating positive and negative

---

6.   In contrast, the naive methods of selecting projects do not adhere to any such underlying principle. Hence, the accept/reject signal emanating from naive methods of selection may not be consistent among one another, let alone with sophisticated methods.

cash flows. Hence, as a general rule of thumb, it is fair to say that the *IRR* method is the least desirable of the three. This fact notwithstanding, the *IRR* method is quite popular among business people due to the fact that it represents a rate of return rather than an absolute number. For example, in a study conducted in 1986, Pike (1988, p. 345) found that 75% of 100 large U.K. firms use this evaluation method.

Interdependent Projects

One of the basic assumptions inherent in the discussion thus far has been **independence of cash flows** among projects. In other words, we have assumed that the combined net cash flow for two or more projects is equal to the sum of the cash flows from all projects. In reality, this assumption may not be correct. Indeed, it is quite possible that the total cash inflows for two or more projects are less than the sum of its parts. A situation like this could easily occur if the products of the projects are substitutes for one another in the product markets. Although on an individual basis the projects may look attractive, the joint consideration could indicate that the combination of projects should not be accepted. The same type of analysis would also need to be conducted when considering new projects where cash flows would be interdependent with projects already in place.

Discount Rate

The discount rate (often called hurdle rate or cost of capital) used in the above analyses, denoted by k, is fundamental to all discounted cash flow techniques of capital budgeting. In the *NPV* and *PI* methods, k is used to derive the present value of cash flows. In the *IRR* method, k is compared to the derived internal rate of return.

The meaning of k has been the subject of a great deal of literature. In fact, few aspects of capital budgeting have received as much attention. In conceptual terms, k is the firm's opportunity cost of capital (i.e., the foregone return that could be earned by the best alternative use of funds) associated with funding capital investments. This **cost of capital** is the minimum rate a project needs to earn so that a firm's value will not be reduced.

Several approaches exist for computing k. One is to compute the marginal or project-specific cost of capital. This approach assumes that a firm raises funds for specific projects as the need arises and is based on the underlying economic principle of marginal analysis. As long as the net cash flows from a specific project exceed the related financing costs, marginal analysis argues in favor of accepting the project. The specific financing charges can be either of a debt or equity nature, depending on the circumstances. For example, if a firm is considering to finance a specific project by floating a bond issue, the cost associated with the specific bond issue would be used as k.

On a conceptual level, it is hard to argue against the logic associated with using a marginal cost of capital as the discount rate. However, on an operational basis it stretches one's imagination beyond believability to assume that major organizations raise funds on a project-specific basis. Indeed, the separation of activities and personnel related to raising funds and making capital investment decisions is well established in most major corporations. On the one hand, financial experts are responsible for raising a pool of funds. At any given moment in time, it is reasonable to assume that successful firms have funds (including a line of credit) available for investment purposes. On the other hand, the allocation of these funds is based on the merits of individual projects proposed by operating managers. In fact, projects must typically compete with each other for the allocation of funds. The process whereby corporations raise a pool of funds and allocate such funds to the most meritorious projects has led many, especially corporate executives, to argue for a weighted average cost of capital approach to computing k.

The weighted average cost of capital is determined by taking a weighted average of the firm's cost of debt and equity. The weighting process most often advocated is based on market values, given that the notion of cost of capital is itself a market determined concept. In algebraic terms, the weighted average cost of capital, k, can be computed as follows:[7]

$$k = k_b(1-T)B/V + k_e S/V$$ **Eq. 12.7**

where,

k_b =   the before tax cost of debt,

k_e =   the after tax cost of equity (usually viewed in terms of the CAPM),

---

7. The CAPM (capital asset pricing model) approach to viewing k_e is based on the firm's required return as derived from:

$$k_e = R_F + \beta_i(R_m - R_F)$$

where,

R_F =   risk free rate of return,
βi =   risk associated with firm i relative to the market,
R_m =   market rate of return.

$$T \quad = \quad \text{the firm's tax rate,}$$
$$B \quad = \quad \text{the firm's market value of debt,}$$
$$S \quad = \quad \text{the firm's market value of equity, and}$$
$$V \quad = \quad \text{total market value of firm } (B + S).$$

The use of a weighted average cost of capital implicitly assumes that the firm's capital structure (i.e., its mix between debt and equity) remains constant and that all of its projects are of roughly equal risk. The former assumption is probably reasonable for large, mature companies. However, the latter assumption concerning the equality of risk across projects is not realistic for many firms. Indeed, the riskiness of projects can vary greatly among projects within a given firm as well as a given division. In response to this situation, many firms have adopted the concept of "equivalent risk groups" for projects. The determination of k in this case would be as follows:

Risk-Adjusted Discount Rate (k)	=	Weighted Average Cost of Capital	+(-)	Risk Adjustment for the Class of Projects

It is common for firms using the equivalent risk class approach to utilize three categories: (1) projects with average risk, (2) projects with high risk, and (3) projects with low risk. The amount of risk adjustment and assignment of projects to particular risk groups are usually handled on an ad hoc basis in consultation with corporate experts. In some firms, the notion of risk classes has been applied at the division (subunit) level. That is, where it is believed that corporate divisions can be thought of as typically investing in projects of either an average, high, or low risk, a divisional cost of capital, k, is sometimes utilized. Of course, this approach assumes that the various projects in a given division are of roughly equal riskiness.

In recent years many firms have used what appear to be excessively high discount rates. Apparently, firms tend to use high discount rates to adjust for various potential problems such as overly optimistic cash inflow estimates, low estimates of initial project costs, and hidden agency costs arising from asymmetric information and conflict of interests between project sponsors (i.e., agents) and resource allocators (i.e., principals).

SENSITIVITY ANALYSIS

Capital budgeting decision making is well suited to the techniques associated with sensitivity analysis. For example, in evaluating a particular project it is often helpful to consider whether the selection of a project is sensitive to the discount rate, k, utilized. One way of addressing this concern is by computing the NPV of a project for a range of discount rates. This approach represents a simple "what if" type analysis in terms of the effect of k on NPV. A graph plotting the relationship between NPV and k can accompany this type of analysis.

To illustrate the above point, assume that Baker Co. has an opportunity to invest in a computer that costs $120,000, which is expected to generate net cash flow savings of $60,000, $55,000, and $45,000 at the end of years 1, 2, and 3, respectively. (All figures are adjusted for taxes, and salvage value is assumed to be zero.) The firm is uncertain as to the appropriate k to use in a project of this sort and hence decides to consider a range of discount rates varying from 10% to 20%, in increments of 1%. The computation of the NPV under the various discount rates is provided in Exhibit 12.2 and the relationship between NPV and k is shown graphically in Figure 12.1.

As long as the appropriate k for the project under consideration is 16% or less, the NPV is positive and hence the project is worth acquiring. If the firm believes that the appropriate k for this project is somewhere around 12%, the decision to accept the project is not very sensitive to a minor error. In contrast, if the appropriate k is believed to be closer to 16% or 17%, the decision to accept this project is quite sensitive to the appropriate k. The same type of sensitivity analysis could be applied to variables other than discount rates. One such variable might be the project's salvage value. Consider the same cash flows as above, only now assume that the computer's cost is $150,000, the discount rate is 10%, and the salvage value at the end of year 3 is estimated to be between $10,000 and $35,000, in increments of $5,000. Exhibit 12.3 provides a table for this example. As is evident from Exhibit 12.3, the decision to accept or reject this project is indeed sensitive to the salvage value chosen within the range specified.

Although the use of sensitivity analysis in capital budgeting is not new, the availability of inexpensive microcomputer software which can handle such problems has opened up the door for its wide scale use. Most spreadsheet packages (e.g., Lotus 1-2-3) have the capability of quickly generating the information required for a sensitivity analysis. Printed copies of this material are also easily obtained from the software packages. Hence, what was once only at the disposal of those having programming capabilities and access to large computers is now readily available to all capital budgeting managers.

EXHIBIT 12.2
Baker Co.
NPV for Various Levels of K

K	NPV
10%	$13,809.17
11	11,596.90
12	9,447.20
13	7,357.67
14	5,326.01
15	3,350.05
16	1,427.69
17	(443.03)
18	(2,264.01)
19	(4,037.06)
20	(5,763.89)

FIGURE 12.1
Baker Co.
Graph of NPV and K Relationship

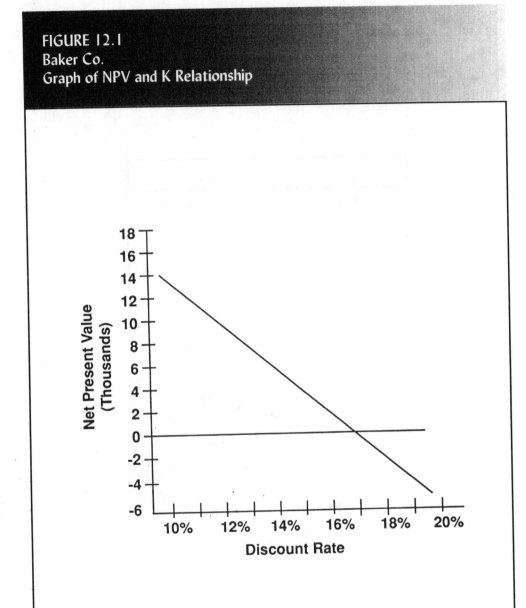

EXHIBIT 12.3
Baker Co.
NPV and Various Levels of Salvage Value

Salvage Value	NPV
$10,000.00	$(8,677.68)
15,000.00	(4,921.11)
20,000.00	(1,164.53)
25,000.00	2,592.03
30,000.00	6,348.61
35,000.00	10,105.18

TAXES

Up to this point we assumed that a project's costs and future cash flows were on an after-tax basis. We will now relax this assumption by explicitly considering taxes. There are two basic reasons why profit-oriented firms currently need to consider taxes in making capital investment decisions. First, the tax effects of depreciation need to be taken into consideration. Second, the taxable cash flows generated from a capital project's operation need to be adjusted by the firm's operating income taxes to arrive at the net cash flow after taxes. Each of these will be addressed in turn.[8] It should become obvious that the firm's management accounting system plays a critical role in accumulating the data required to compute the tax effects of capital expenditure decisions.

Depreciation on an investment reduces a firm's taxable income, thereby serving as a tax shield. The net effect of such a tax shield is to reduce a firm's taxes (which indirectly increases the firm's net cash flows) by an amount equal to an asset's depreciation multiplied by the firm's tax rate. The amount of depreciation allowed by the tax code of the Internal Revenue Service is derived from the modified accelerated cost recovery system (MACRS), which places assets into one of several categories. For each of the classes, a yearly recovery percentage is prescribed for determining the MACRS depreciation amount.[9] These percentages are generally applied to the total property base. Salvage value and useful life are not relevant for depreciation purposes.

Once the tax effects of depreciation have been considered, the investment's cash flow after taxes for each period can be computed. More to the point, the future net cash flows after taxes generated from a project are derived by deducting the project's operating income taxes from gross cash flows. In this regard, the tax liability for each year is computed based on the accrual accounting income (which includes a deduction for depreciation expense) derived from a capital project.

---

8.   A third issue which corporations have needed to consider over the years is the investment tax credit (ITC). Although not in effect at the time of writing this book, the ITC is a tax incentive which has had many appearances in the U.S. tax code (as well as the tax code of numerous other countries) and is likely to reappear. An ITC is essentially a direct credit to a firm's tax liability based on the level of new capital investment.

9.   For book purposes, firms typically use either straight-line or accelerated depreciation methods.

HIGH TECHNOLOGY INVESTMENTS

The discussion thus far has assumed a traditional economics based approach to .capital investments In recent years, many have argued that this approach is inappropriate for some specialized categories of capital investments. One such category, which has received much attention, concerns high technology investments. Indeed, some have even gone as far as to argue that a key reason underlying the fact that many U.S. firms have lost their competitive edge in the international marketplace is due to their reliance on traditional capital investment selection techniques.

High technology investments usually involve large initial cash outflows and long periods before resulting operating activities begin to generate positive cash flows. Figure 12.2 contrasts the cash flow profile from traditional investments with the cash flow profile from high technology investments. As illustrated in that figure, when compared to regular investments, high technology investments often require larger initial cost outlays and a longer time before positive cash inflows are received. However, in return, large cash inflows, over a long time period, often result.

Because of the cash flow pattern associated with high technology investments, the use of traditional DCF selection techniques presents a bias against such investments. This bias is due to the fact that the discounting process places an exponentially decreasing value on future cash flows. This concern is especially severe for firms which use excessively high discount rates as a means of considering difficult-to-quantify factors. In a related fashion, where firms use a short payback period (e.g., two years) constraint (or criterion) in selecting projects, another strong bias exists against high technology investments. This latter bias is due to the fact that large cash flows received after the first few years are ignored.

FIGURE 12.2
Cash Flow Profiles for
Regular vs. High Technology Investments

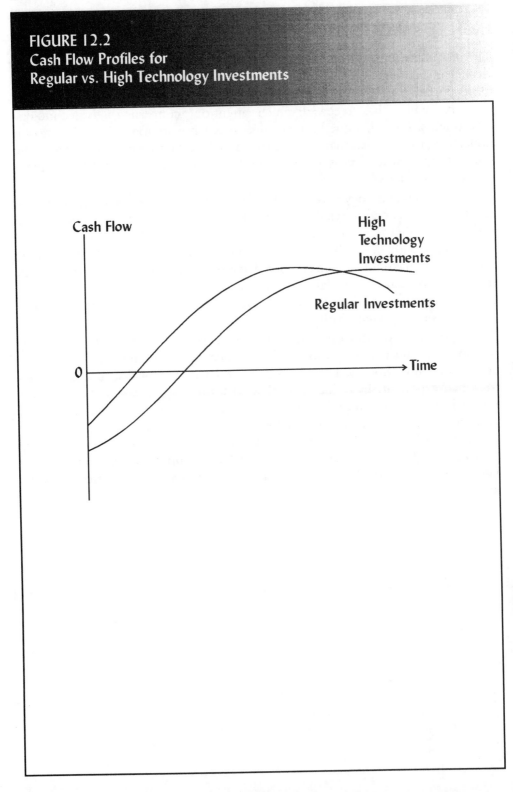

Of course, the issues discussed above are not really problems with the traditional economics based approach to selecting capital projects, but rather result from their inappropriate application. More to the point, the DCF techniques (e.g., net present value) discussed earlier in this chapter, clearly argue for considering all cash flows and discounting such cash flows at the firm's cost of capital. In addition, these techniques implicitly argue that opportunity cost concepts need to be considered. In this latter regard, it is important to recognize that a decision by a firm not to invest in a high technology investment may well mean that "business as usual" will not continue. For example, where the high technology investment produces a higher quality product, with a quicker delivery time, a non-investing firm may lose a large share of its existing market to a competing firm which does make the investment. Hence, there may be a large opportunity cost associated with not investing. Therefore, by investing in the new technology, the firm avoids this opportunity cost. One way to incorporate this latter cost into the analysis is to add it to the cash flows resulting from the high technology investment. Where this is done, it may well be that otherwise unattractive high technology investments look attractive.[10]

CAPITAL INVESTMENTS AND MANAGERIAL INCENTIVE PLANS

As discussed elsewhere in this book, agency conflicts may lead managers to act in a fashion which is not in the best interest of the firm's owners. Capital investments is one area which has received much attention in this regard. More to the point, it is often argued that the long-term payoff from many capital investments (e.g., high technology investments) lead managers to make less than optimal capital investment decisions due to their concern for short-run performance. In order to offset this short-run focus, most major corporations have adopted long-term managerial incentive plans. Although these plans take on many forms, the key objective of such incentive plans is to encourage managers to make decisions that have a positive effect on the firm's long-run success. In an empirical study by Larcker (1983), it was found that long-term accounting based incentive plans are positively associated with the capital expenditure level of firms. In another study by Gaver and Gaver (1993), a similar, although less supportive, association was found.

---

10. Lee (1991) provides an interesting discussion of how United Architects, Inc., an architectural firm in southern California, justified investments in CADD (computer aided design and drafting) technology by considering lost contribution margins.

OPTION VALUES AND CAPITAL INVESTMENTS

The sophisticated methods of capital budgeting discussed thus far take a traditional economics view toward capital investments. They assume that the decision at hand is to invest now or not at all. Hence, as long as the $NPV > 0$, or the $IRR > k$, or the $PI > C$, it pays to invest. A more realistic approach assumes that most capital investment decisions can be deferred for at least some time period. Hence, given that at least some part of nearly all capital investments is irreversible (i.e., a sunk cost) and new information on most investment opportunities arrives over time, the appropriate decision is often focused on whether to invest now or later, rather than invest now or never. In other words, waiting to invest may well be the optimal decision.

The more realistic approach to capital investments takes into consideration the dynamic nature of a capital investment in an uncertain environment. In essence, deciding whether to invest now or later assumes there is a value associated with the option to defer an investment. This option value can be thought of as part of the opportunity cost of investing today. The option value associated with deferring a real (fixed) investment is similar to an option value associated with capital stock and in particular the value of an **American Call Option** (i.e., a right to buy stock at a specified price prior to an expiration date). An illustration of how to compute the option value associated with a real investment is provided below.

Assume a U.S. firm, R-Tech., Inc., is considering an investment opportunity in a new product to be sold in China. The product has a five year life horizon and the investment will cost $8,000,000 today. Further, the firm uses a cost of capital of 20% for projects of this type.

The expected net cash flows from the investment (assumed to be received at the end of the year) will be either a constant $1,500,000 per year or a constant $4,500,000 per year, with an equal probability. The firm can invest now and receive the five years of cash flows or it can defer the investment and make the decision sometime in the future. The true cash flows to be received will be revealed at the end of the first year. However, deferring the investment will not extend the product's life horizon due to competitive and technological factors (i.e., in five years from today this product will be obsolete) nor will it change the cost of this investment. Further, once the investment is made it is considered totally irreversible (i.e., the $8,000,000 investment all becomes a sunk cost). If the firm considers this investment in a traditional manner, the expected cash flows (assuming a risk neutral investor) per year would be $3,000,000 [i.e., (.5)($1,500,000) + (.5)($4,500,000)] for five years and the project's NPV would equal $971,836 [i.e., $\sum_{t=1}^{5}$ ($3,000,000) / $(1.20)^t$ - $8,000,000].

Hence, the decision would be to invest.

As noted above, if the firm decides to defer the investment for one year and lose the net cash flow for the first year, it would learn whether or not the $1,500,000 or $4,500,000 net cash flows would be received over the remaining life of the investment. (In this example, the firm has no incentive to defer the investment for more than one year, since all the information concerning the investment will be revealed by the end of the first year.) If the firm defers the investment and the lower cash flows of $1,500,000 surface as being the correct ones, the investment would not be made because the *NPV* would equal -$4,116,898 [i.e., $\sum_{t=1}^{4}$ ($1,500,000) / (1.20)^t) - $8,000,000]. Alternatively, if the higher cash flows of $4,500,000 turn out to be correct, the *NPV* would equal $3,649,306 [i.e., $\sum_{t=1}^{4}$ (4,500,000) /(1.20)^t) - $8,000,000] and the investment would be made at the end of the first year. The option value associated with deferring this investment can be derived by taking the present value of the difference between investing now and the *NPV* of waiting, which is $2,069,252 [i.e., ($3,649,306/1.2) - ($971,836)].

In terms of a decision rule, if the *NPV* of making the investment today minus the option value of deferring the investment is greater than zero, the investment should be made today. Alternatively, if this value is less than zero, as in the above example (i.e., $971,836 - $2,069,252 < 0), then the investment should be deferred. Of course, for some investments it will pay to wait to invest (as in the above example), in other cases the investment will be most attractive today rather than waiting, and still in other cases it will never pay to invest.

The above example is simple enough to intuitively demonstrate the notion underlying the option value associated with waiting to invest in real assets. However, as the cash flow profile from the investment becomes more complicated, the problem needs to be formulated in a more sophisticated manner. Fortunately, the Black and Scholes (1973) model for valuing stock options provides a basic approach for valuing options in real assets. Consequently, the option pricing approach to making capital investment decisions is gaining wide-scale acceptance among academicians and, to a lesser extent, among practitioners.[11]

---

11. For a rigorous approach to using option pricing models for capital investment decisions, the reader is referred to the book by Dixit and Pindyck (1994).

Whereas the option value associated with waiting to invest can lead to the postponement of an investment, another type of option value could be pushing in exactly the opposite direction. For some investments, there is a strategic value associated with making a seemingly unattractive investment. The reason being that some investments may be a necessary first step toward future investments. Let us return to the previous example where R-Tech, Inc. is considering an investment in a product to be sold in China. Prior to this investment, the company is not doing any business in China. Nevertheless, the firm believes there are numerous potential business opportunities in China. The key, in this regard, is to get a foot into the Chinese marketplace. Accordingly, even if the initial product venture discussed above were to lose money, it may well be that the experience gained will lead to some sort of successful business venture down the road. In other words, the firm sees the initial product venture as a necessary, although possibly not sufficient, first step to doing business in China over the long-run. Thus, the first investment is seen as having a strategic value in that it gives the option for successfully doing business in China in the future. This strategic investment option value is demonstrated by modifying the above illustration.

Assume R-Tech, Inc. is considering the new product project discussed earlier. Only now, the decision is to invest now or never due to exogenous factors (i.e., there is no option to defer this initial investment). Further, the cash flow profile associated with this investment is now considered to be either $1,500,000 or $2,500,000, with equal probability for the project's five year time horizon. The project's cost is still considered to be $8,000,000 and the discount rate to be used for this product is still 20%. Hence, the expected cash flows would be $2,000,000 [i.e., ($1,500,000)(.5) + ($2,500,000)(.5)]. Based on traditional capital investment techniques, the project would be rejected because the NPV would equal - $2,018,776 [i.e., $\sum_{t=1}^{5}$ ($2,000,000) / (1.20)^t - $8,000,000]. However, the firm estimates that after two years of doing business in China it will have gained enough experience with the Chinese marketplace such that other opportunities will become available. (These opportunities will not be available without the initial investment.) Although difficult to quantify in specific detail at this time, the firm believes that there is at least a 40% probability that after two years it will be able to invest in new projects that have at least a $15,000,000 *NPV*. Hence, there is currently a strategic investment option value worth $4,166,667 [i.e., ($15,000,000)(.4) / (1 + .20)^2]. This strategic option value would be added to the original *NPV*, thereby making the initial investment attractive as of today because the new *NPV* would be equal to $2,147,891 (i.e., $4,166,667 - $2,018,776).[12]

---

12. Although beyond the scope of this book, it is possible to consider both the strategic investment option value and the option value to wait (from the previous section) simultaneously.

CONCLUDING COMMENTS

The survival of a firm is the result of many factors. However, there is little doubt that expenditures on long term investments play a critical role in the success of an organization. These expenditures are usually referred to as capital investments and the process relating to the planning and control of such investments is usually referred to as capital budgeting. Capital budgeting is, in essence, the long-run counterpart to short-run profit planning discussed in Chapter 2. Indeed, the estimated and actual periodic cash flows are inseparable from the short-run profit planning and control process.

The selection of capital investments is often discussed in terms of naive and sophisticated techniques. Whereas sophisticated methods are based on a risk adjusted discounted cash flow approach, naive methods tend to ignore the time value of money and risk. Given the inaccuracies associated with estimating risk adjusted discounted cash flows, sophisticated methods are not a guarantee for organizational success. Nevertheless, their use, often in conjunction with naive methods, is prevalent among major organizations.

The control side of capital budgeting is often referred to as postauditing. Chapter 13 is devoted to this topic.

APPENDIX 12.1:
Present Value of 1 (t = period received, k = discount rate) = $\dfrac{1}{(1+k)^t}$

Period (t)	1%	2%	3%	4%	5%	6%	7%	8%	9%	10%	11%	12%
1	0.990	0.980	0.971	0.962	0.952	0.943	0.935	0.926	0.917	0.909	0.901	0.893
2	0.980	0.961	0.943	0.925	0.907	0.890	0.873	0.857	0.842	0.826	0.812	0.797
3	0.971	0.942	0.915	0.889	0.864	0.840	0.816	0.794	0.772	0.751	0.731	0.712
4	0.961	0.924	0.888	0.855	0.823	0.792	0.763	0.735	0.708	0.683	0.659	0.636
5	0.951	0.906	0.863	0.822	0.784	0.747	0.713	0.681	0.650	0.621	0.593	0.567
6	0.942	0.888	0.837	0.790	0.746	0.705	0.666	0.630	0.596	0.564	0.535	0.507
7	0.933	0.871	0.813	0.760	0.711	0.665	0.623	0.583	0.547	0.513	0.482	0.452
8	0.923	0.853	0.789	0.731	0.677	0.627	0.582	0.540	0.502	0.467	0.434	0.404
9	0.914	0.837	0.766	0.703	0.645	0.592	0.544	0.500	0.460	0.424	0.391	0.361
10	0.905	0.820	0.744	0.676	0.614	0.558	0.508	0.463	0.422	0.386	0.352	0.322
11	0.896	0.804	0.722	0.650	0.585	0.527	0.475	0.429	0.388	0.350	0.317	0.287
12	0.887	0.788	0.701	0.625	0.557	0.497	0.444	0.397	0.356	0.319	0.286	0.257
13	0.879	0.773	0.681	0.601	0.530	0.469	0.415	0.368	0.326	0.290	0.258	0.229
14	0.870	0.758	0.661	0.577	0.505	0.442	0.388	0.340	0.299	0.263	0.232	0.205
15	0.861	0.743	0.642	0.555	0.481	0.417	0.362	0.315	0.275	0.239	0.209	0.183
16	0.853	0.728	0.623	0.534	0.458	0.394	0.339	0.292	0.252	0.218	0.188	0.163
17	0.844	0.714	0.605	0.513	0.436	0.371	0.317	0.270	0.231	0.198	0.170	0.146
18	0.836	0.700	0.587	0.494	0.416	0.350	0.296	0.250	0.212	0.180	0.153	0.130
19	0.828	0.686	0.570	0.475	0.396	0.331	0.277	0.232	0.194	0.164	0.138	0.116
20	0.820	0.673	0.554	0.456	0.377	0.312	0.258	0.215	0.178	0.149	0.124	0.104
21	0.811	0.660	0.538	0.439	0.359	0.294	0.242	0.199	0.164	0.135	0.112	0.093
22	0.803	0.647	0.522	0.422	0.342	0.278	0.226	0.184	0.150	0.123	0.101	0.083
23	0.795	0.634	0.507	0.406	0.326	0.262	0.211	0.170	0.138	0.112	0.091	0.074
24	0.788	0.622	0.492	0.390	0.310	0.247	0.197	0.158	0.126	0.102	0.082	0.066
25	0.780	0.610	0.478	0.375	0.295	0.233	0.184	0.146	0.116	0.092	0.074	0.059

APPENDIX 12.1 (continued)

Period (t)	13%	14%	15%	16%	17%	18%	19%	20%	21%	22%	23%	24%
1	0.885	0.877	0.870	0.862	0.855	0.847	0.840	0.833	0.826	0.820	0.813	0.806
2	0.783	0.769	0.756	0.743	0.731	0.718	0.706	0.694	0.683	0.672	0.661	0.650
3	0.693	0.675	0.658	0.641	0.624	0.609	0.593	0.579	0.564	0.551	0.537	0.524
4	0.613	0.592	0.572	0.552	0.534	0.516	0.499	0.482	0.467	0.451	0.437	0.423
5	0.543	0.519	0.497	0.476	0.456	0.437	0.419	0.402	0.386	0.370	0.355	0.341
6	0.480	0.456	0.432	0.410	0.390	0.370	0.352	0.335	0.319	0.303	0.289	0.275
7	0.425	0.400	0.376	0.354	0.333	0.314	0.296	0.279	0.263	0.249	0.235	0.222
8	0.376	0.351	0.327	0.305	0.285	0.266	0.249	0.233	0.218	0.204	0.191	0.179
9	0.333	0.308	0.284	0.263	0.243	0.225	0.209	0.194	0.180	0.167	0.155	0.144
10	0.295	0.270	0.247	0.227	0.208	0.191	0.176	0.162	0.149	0.137	0.126	0.116
11	0.261	0.237	0.215	0.195	0.178	0.162	0.148	0.135	0.123	0.112	0.103	0.094
12	0.231	0.208	0.187	0.168	0.152	0.137	0.124	0.112	0.102	0.092	0.083	0.076
13	0.204	0.182	0.163	0.145	0.130	0.116	0.104	0.093	0.084	0.075	0.068	0.061
14	0.181	0.160	0.141	0.125	0.111	0.099	0.088	0.078	0.069	0.062	0.055	0.049
15	0.160	0.140	0.123	0.108	0.095	0.084	0.074	0.065	0.057	0.051	0.045	0.040
16	0.141	0.123	0.107	0.093	0.081	0.071	0.062	0.054	0.047	0.042	0.036	0.032
17	0.125	0.108	0.093	0.080	0.069	0.060	0.052	0.045	0.039	0.034	0.030	0.026
18	0.111	0.095	0.081	0.069	0.059	0.051	0.044	0.038	0.032	0.028	0.024	0.021
19	0.098	0.083	0.070	0.060	0.051	0.043	0.037	0.031	0.027	0.023	0.020	0.017
20	0.087	0.073	0.061	0.051	0.043	0.037	0.031	0.026	0.022	0.019	0.016	0.014
21	0.077	0.064	0.053	0.044	0.037	0.031	0.026	0.022	0.018	0.015	0.013	0.011
22	0.068	0.056	0.046	0.038	0.032	0.026	0.022	0.018	0.015	0.013	0.011	0.009
23	0.060	0.049	0.040	0.033	0.027	0.022	0.018	0.015	0.012	0.010	0.009	0.007
24	0.053	0.043	0.035	0.028	0.023	0.019	0.015	0.013	0.010	0.008	0.007	0.006
25	0.047	0.038	0.030	0.024	0.020	0.016	0.013	0.010	0.009	0.007	0.006	0.005

APPENDIX 12.2:
Present Value of an Ordinary Annuity of 1 (t = period received, k = discount rate) = $\dfrac{1}{k} - \dfrac{1}{k(1+k)^t}$

Period (t)	1%	2%	3%	4%	5%	6%	7%	8%	9%	10%	11%	12%
1	0.990	0.980	0.971	0.962	0.952	0.943	0.935	0.926	0.917	0.909	0.901	0.893
2	1.970	1.942	1.913	1.886	1.859	1.833	1.808	1.783	1.759	1.736	1.713	1.690
3	2.941	2.884	2.829	2.775	2.723	2.673	2.624	2.577	2.531	2.487	2.444	2.402
4	3.902	3.808	3.717	3.630	3.546	3.465	3.387	3.312	3.240	3.170	3.102	3.037
5	4.853	4.713	4.580	4.452	4.329	4.212	4.100	3.993	3.890	3.791	3.696	3.605
6	5.795	5.601	5.417	5.242	5.076	4.917	4.767	4.623	4.486	4.355	4.231	4.111
7	6.728	6.472	6.230	6.002	5.786	5.582	5.389	5.206	5.033	4.868	4.712	4.564
8	7.652	7.325	7.020	6.733	6.463	6.210	5.971	5.747	5.535	5.335	5.146	4.968
9	8.566	8.162	7.786	7.435	7.108	6.802	6.515	6.247	5.995	5.759	5.537	5.328
10	9.471	8.983	8.530	8.111	7.722	7.360	7.024	6.710	6.418	6.145	5.889	5.650
11	10.368	9.787	9.253	8.760	8.306	7.887	7.499	7.139	6.805	6.495	6.207	5.938
12	11.255	10.575	9.954	9.385	8.863	8.384	7.943	7.536	7.161	6.814	6.492	6.194
13	12.134	11.348	10.635	9.986	9.394	8.853	8.358	7.904	7.487	7.103	6.750	6.424
14	13.004	12.106	11.296	10.563	9.899	9.295	8.745	8.244	7.786	7.367	6.982	6.628
15	13.865	12.849	11.938	11.118	10.380	9.712	9.108	8.559	8.061	7.606	7.191	6.811
16	14.718	13.578	12.561	11.652	10.838	10.106	9.447	8.851	8.313	7.824	7.379	6.974
17	15.562	14.292	13.166	12.166	11.274	10.477	9.763	9.122	8.544	8.022	7.549	7.120
18	16.398	14.992	13.754	12.659	11.690	10.828	10.059	9.372	8.756	8.201	7.702	7.250
19	17.226	15.678	14.324	13.134	12.085	11.158	10.336	9.604	8.950	8.365	7.839	7.366
20	18.046	16.351	14.877	13.590	12.462	11.470	10.594	9.818	9.129	8.514	7.963	7.469
21	18.857	17.011	15.415	14.029	12.821	11.764	10.836	10.017	9.292	8.649	8.075	7.562
22	19.660	17.658	15.937	14.451	13.163	12.042	11.061	10.201	9.442	8.772	8.176	7.645
23	20.456	18.292	16.444	14.857	13.489	12.303	11.272	10.371	9.580	8.883	8.266	7.718
24	21.243	18.914	16.936	15.247	13.799	12.550	11.469	10.529	9.707	8.985	8.348	7.784
25	22.023	19.523	17.413	15.622	14.094	12.783	11.654	10.675	9.823	9.077	8.422	7.843

APPENDIX 12.2 (continued)

Period (t)	13%	14%	15%	16%	17%	18%	19%	20%	21%	22%	23%	24%
1	0.885	0.877	0.870	0.862	0.855	0.847	0.840	0.833	0.826	0.820	0.813	0.806
2	1.668	1.647	1.626	1.605	1.585	1.566	1.547	1.528	1.509	1.492	1.474	1.457
3	2.361	2.322	2.283	2.246	2.210	2.174	2.140	2.106	2.074	2.042	2.011	1.981
4	2.974	2.914	2.855	2.798	2.743	2.690	2.639	2.589	2.540	2.494	2.448	2.404
5	3.517	3.433	3.352	3.274	3.199	3.127	3.058	2.991	2.926	2.864	2.803	2.745
6	3.998	3.889	3.784	3.685	3.589	3.498	3.410	3.326	3.245	3.167	3.092	3.020
7	4.423	4.288	4.160	4.039	3.922	3.812	3.706	3.605	3.508	3.416	3.327	3.242
8	4.799	4.639	4.487	4.344	4.207	4.078	3.954	3.837	3.726	3.619	3.518	3.421
9	5.132	4.946	4.772	4.607	4.451	4.303	4.163	4.031	3.905	3.786	3.673	3.566
10	5.426	5.216	5.019	4.833	4.659	4.494	4.339	4.192	4.054	3.923	3.799	3.682
11	5.687	5.453	5.234	5.029	4.836	4.656	4.486	4.327	4.177	4.035	3.902	3.776
12	5.918	5.660	5.421	5.197	4.988	4.793	4.611	4.439	4.278	4.127	3.985	3.851
13	6.122	5.842	5.583	5.342	5.118	4.910	4.715	4.533	4.362	4.203	4.053	3.912
14	6.302	6.002	5.724	5.468	5.229	5.008	4.802	4.611	4.432	4.265	4.108	3.962
15	6.462	6.142	5.847	5.575	5.324	5.092	4.876	4.675	4.489	4.315	4.153	4.001
16	6.604	6.265	5.954	5.668	5.405	5.162	4.938	4.730	4.536	4.357	4.189	4.033
17	6.729	6.373	6.047	5.749	5.475	5.222	4.990	4.775	4.576	4.391	4.219	4.059
18	6.840	6.467	6.128	5.818	5.534	5.273	5.033	4.812	4.608	4.419	4.243	4.080
19	6.938	6.550	6.198	5.877	5.584	5.316	5.070	4.843	4.635	4.442	4.263	4.097
20	7.025	6.623	6.259	5.929	5.628	5.353	5.101	4.870	4.657	4.460	4.279	4.110
21	7.102	6.687	6.312	5.973	5.665	5.384	5.127	4.891	4.675	4.476	4.292	4.121
22	7.170	6.743	6.359	6.011	5.696	5.410	5.149	4.909	4.690	4.488	4.302	4.130
23	7.230	6.792	6.399	6.044	5.723	5.432	5.167	4.925	4.703	4.499	4.311	4.137
24	7.283	6.835	6.434	6.073	5.746	5.451	5.182	4.937	4.713	4.507	4.318	4.143
25	7.330	6.873	6.464	6.097	5.766	5.467	5.195	4.948	4.721	4.514	4.323	4.147

PROBLEMS

Problem 12.1

It is common for major U.S. firms to use sophisticated methods of capital budgeting in selecting projects. In other countries (e.g., Japan), however, these techniques are less frequently used.

Required:
Explain why firms in some countries tend to use sophisticated methods of capital budgeting more regularly than firms in other countries.

Problem 12.2

The problem provided in the section on option values illustrates the case where the investment should be deferred. Modify the illustrations to show: (a) the case where it pays to make the investment today, and (b) the case where it never pays to invest.

Problem 12.3

"Strategic planning is essentially capital budgeting" quipped an executive. Explain the rationale underlying this quote.

Problem 12.4 (Adapted from CMA examination)

Cording Manufacturing is a small company that is currently analyzing capital expenditure proposals for the purchase of equipment. The capital budget is limited to $500,000, which Cording believes is the maximum capital it can raise.

Richard King, an outside financial advisor, is preparing an analysis of four projects that Walter Minden, Cording's president, is considering. King has projected the future cash flows for each potential purchase. The information concerning the four projects is given below.

	Project A	Project B	Project C	Project D
Projected cash outflow	$200,000	$190,000	$250,000	$210,000
Equipment cost				
Projected cash inflows				
Year 1	$ 50,000	$ 40,000	$ 75,000	$ 75,000
2	50,000	50,000	75,000	75,000
3	50,000	70,000	60,000	60,000
4	50,000	75,000	80,000	40,000
5	50,000	75,000	100,000	20,000

Required:

A.   Since Cording Manufacturing's cash is limited, Walter Minden thinks that the payback method for calculating investments would be the best method for choosing the assets to purchase.

   1.   Explain what the payback method measures and how it is used. Include in your explanation several benefits and limitations of the payback method.

   2.   Calculate the payback period for each of the four assets, rounding to one decimal place.

B.   Richard King believes that a venture capitalist may be interested in lending funds to Cording Manufacturing in order to purchase all of the assets that are economically desirable. King would like to compare the projects using the net present value method and the excess present value index (profitability index) method. An appropriate hurdle rate for Cording is 12 percent. All cash flows occur at the end of the year. Tax considerations should be ignored.

	Present Value Factors at 12%	
Period	Present Value of $1	Present Value of an Annuity of $1
1	0.893	0.893
2	0.797	1.690
3	0.712	2.402
4	0.636	3.038
5	0.567	3.605

1. Calculate the net present value for each asset.

2. Calculate the profitability index for each asset.

C. Assume that the venture capital funds as discussed in Requirement B can be obtained. Which projects, if any, would you recommend funding?

Problem 12.5 (Adapted from CMA examination)

Miranda Wells joined Sycamore Corporation four months ago as a financial analyst and has been assisting Jake Richter, the controller, in evaluating capital projects. Shortly, Wells will be making her first presentation to the management committee responsible for selecting capital projects, and she has been working diligently to ensure that her analysis is correct. The management committee will be considering the two mutually exclusive projects at this meeting. Both projects require the same initial investment and have the same project lives. Wells has used several capital budgeting methods to evaluate each project.

	Project A	Project B
Accounting rate of return	34%	26%
Internal rate of return	16%	19%
Net present value	$2.6 million	$3.5 million
Payback period	4 years	5 years

After completing her analysis, Wells discussed the results with Richter. She believes Project B is superior to Project A and intends to recommend Project B to the management committee. Richter replied, "I agree with you that Project B appears to be the better choice; however, the group will select Project A as they have been encouraged by the head of the committee to make their decision based on the accounting rate of return. Since none of the other calculations are negative, that 34 percent accounting rate of return will sway their thinking."

Wells was discouraged by Richter's remarks. She contemplated leaving the accounting rate of return calculation out of the analysis she presented to the committee but realized that was not a good solution as the committee would surely request it.

Required:

A. For each of the four capital budgeting methods used by Miranda Wells to evaluate the two projects at Sycamore Corporation, explain the merits and limitations of each method.

B. Explain why both Miranda Wells and Jake Richter believe that Project B is superior to Project A.

C. Identify three qualitative considerations that generally should be considered in capital budget evaluations.

13

POSTAUDITING
CAPITAL INVESTMENTS

CHAPTER OUTLINE

- Objectives of Postauditing

- Process of Postauditing

- Performance Effects

- Managing Risk

- Abandonment Decision

- Option Value

- Illustration of Postauditing

INTRODUCTION

As already noted in Chapter 12, the accounting, economics, and finance literature is replete with discussions on how capital projects should be selected. This literature by and large argues that the sophisticated methods of capital budgeting (e.g., *NPV*, *IRR*, and *PI*) are preferable to the naive methods (e.g., *ROI*, Payback Period). Empirical studies show that more and more firms have heeded this call for using sophisticated methods as the major criteria for selecting projects, often combined with a payback period constraint. Unfortunately, the control side of the capital budgeting process has been seriously neglected by a large number of firms.

The control of capital investments involves the postauditing of such projects. The term **postauditing** refers to the assessment or monitoring of projects to determine whether or not they are accomplishing their intended purpose. The objectives, process, and performance effects of postauditing will be among the topics covered in this chapter. It will be argued that the postauditing of capital assets represents an important managerial accounting technique that can help firms achieve world class status. In fact, the position taken in this chapter is that ". . . once projects are chosen, the control phase needs to be set in motion" (Gordon and Pinches, 1984, p. 85). This position is consistent with that taken by many others (e.g., Emmanuel and Otley, 1985).

OBJECTIVES OF POSTAUDITING

There are several objectives which underlie the *raison dêtre* for postauditing capital projects, as illustrated in Figure 13.1.[1] First, postauditing provides a financial control mechanism. Both inflows and outflows of cash associated with a capital investment project are monitored through postauditing. Corrective measures relating to a particular project can (and should) be identified through this financial control mechanism.

---

1. The discussion in this section is based partly on the paper by Gordon and Myers (1991).

FIGURE 13.1
Objectives of Postauditing

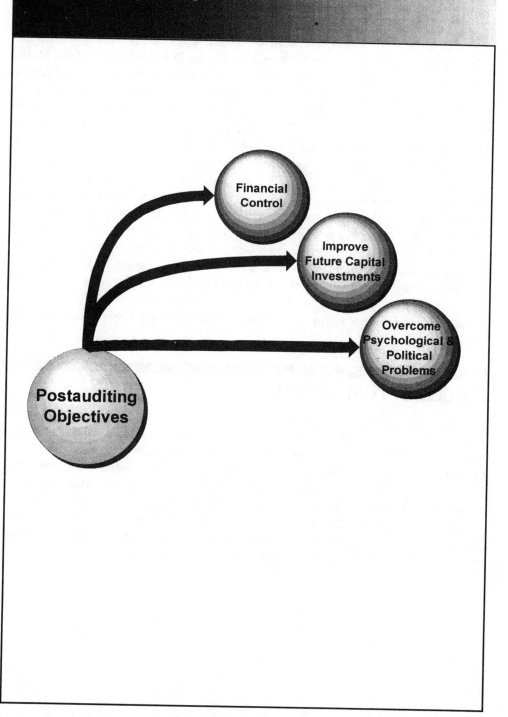

The second objective of postauditing is to provide input to future capital expenditures. By monitoring past investments, a firm gains insight into improving future investment decisions. This point is especially true for similar or related investments. For example, assume a U.S. firm recently invested in a capital project to produce a new power tool product. Since the product was intended to be sold in several countries outside the U.S. as well as within the U.S., the decision to invest in the capital project included estimates of the global demand for the new product. As a result of monitoring the global demand for the new product, it is determined that estimates of the European demand were grossly overstated due to newly developed products from competitive firms in Europe. This knowledge could be of great importance to future capital investment decisions related to other similar new products.

A third objective underlying the postauditing of capital assets has to do with overcoming the psychological and political problems associated with proposing and terminating projects. Of course, the penalties associated with postauditing should not be so severe as to completely discourage managers from investing in high risk, and potentially high return, projects. In terms of proposing projects, the mere knowledge that postauditing will (or may) occur tends to keep estimates associated with projects at a more realistic level. In other words, postauditing introduces a degree of accountability not otherwise present. In terms of terminating projects, postauditing provides a mechanism (although not a guarantee) for eliminating projects which otherwise might be "too political to touch."

PROCESS OF POSTAUDITING

The process of postauditing capital investments involves a comparison of actual results with the anticipated results. This comparison should take place in a manner which is consistent with the way projects were selected. Hence, if projects were selected based on discounted cash flow techniques over the expected life of the project (i.e., sophisticated methods of capital budgeting), then actual cash flows should be compared to expected cash flows. Surprisingly, empirical studies indicate that many firms select projects based on discounted cash flow techniques, but monitor the very same projects based on accounting numbers. Conceptually, such an approach is seriously flawed.

Another aspect of the postauditing process which needs to be considered is the regularity with which postauditing occurs. Empirical evidence in this regard seems to suggest that many firms do a one-time postaudit of their capital projects. In some cases, the one-time postaudit occurs at the end of the project's life and in other cases it occurs after some predetermined time period, such as two years after the start of the project. From a cost/benefit perspective, postauditing every project each year will make little sense. Nevertheless, some sort of regular, periodic review of at least some projects seems appropriate if the objectives of postauditing noted above are to be accomplished. In this regard, Gordon and Myers (1991) found that firms tend to view the benefits of regularly postauditing strategic capital investments as being greater than those derived from other types of capital investments.[2]

The two aspects of the postauditing process discussed above can be thought of in terms of the two-by-two matrix shown in Figure 13.2. One dimension of this matrix has to do with the comparability of the data used in postauditing projects with the data used in the sophisticated methods of selecting such projects. The second dimension has to do with the regularity of postauditing. For a firm to be following a sophisticated postauditing process, the evaluation data should be comparable to the selection data and done on a regular, periodic basis. Hence, in terms of Figure 13.2, firms operating in cell IV are considered to be using sophisticated postauditing techniques.

PERFORMANCE EFFECTS

During the past few years, several empirical studies have investigated the performance effects of postauditing capital assets. The motivation for these studies has been partly due to the fact that earlier studies have produced mixed results regarding the relationship between the use of sophisticated capital budgeting selection techniques and firm performance (e.g., see Christy, 1966; Haka, Gordon, and Pinches, 1985; Kim, 1982; Klammer, 1973; Pike, 1984, 1988).

The study conducted by Myers, Gordon, and Hamer (1991) investigated the effect on firm performance of initiating sophisticated postauditing procedures. All firms included in the study used risk adjusted discounted cash flow (i.e., sophisticated) methods for selecting projects. Firm performance in this study was measured in terms of Tobin's q. In a follow-up study, Gordon, Loeb, and Myers (1994) examined the same issue using accounting rates of return to measure firm performance (rather than Tobin's q). In both studies, firms were deemed to be using sophisticated postaudit procedures if they conducted regular,

---

2.   For a further discussion of the way firms actually conduct postaudits, the reader is
       referred to the papers by Gordon and Myers (1991) and Gordon and Smith
       (1992).

FIGURE 13.2
Sophisticated Postauditing Procedures[a]

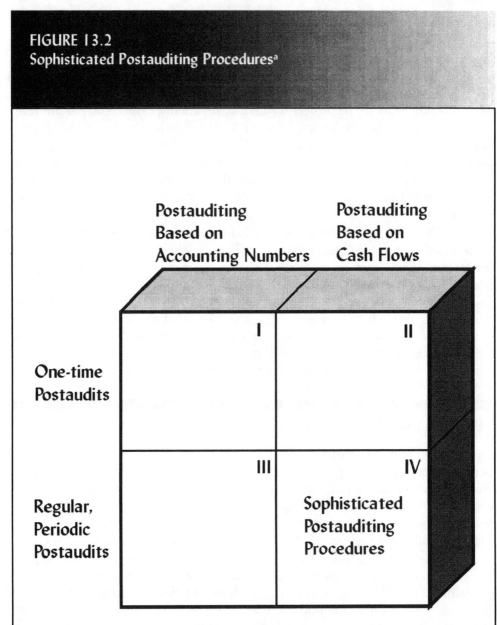

---

[a] It is assumed that firms invest in capital projects based on risk-adjusted discounted cash flow techniques.

periodic reviews of the cash flows from projects (i.e., they fell into cell IV of Figure 13.2).

The findings from the Myers, Gordon, and Hamer (1991), and Gordon, Loeb, and Myers (1994) studies provide strong support for the argument that sophisticated postauditing of capital projects is significantly associated with the improvement of firm performance. These studies did not, however, attempt to derive the factors which account for the positive link between the use of sophisticated postauditing and firm performance. In contrast, the study conducted by Gordon and Smith (1992) focused on examining the factors which could account for the postauditing-performance link. One key finding from the Gordon and Smith study is that the positive firm performance-postauditing link was significantly influenced by (i.e., contingent upon) the degree of asymmetric information between central and lower level managers. The intuitive explanation for this finding is that the greater the degree of asymmetric information, the greater the relative potential benefits to central management from postauditing. Hence, principal-agent relationships apparently play an important role in determining the value of postauditing capital investments. Another important finding of the Gordon and Smith study was that ". . . having a postaudit system which is not sophisticated enough is associated with lower firm performance than having a system which is too sophisticated" (p. 754). The intuitive explanation for this latter finding seems to be that the extra costs of having a postauditing system which is "too sophisticated" are much less than the downside costs of having a postauditing system which is "too pedestrian."

The combination of the above three empirical studies, which were all based on U.S. firms, strongly suggests that postauditing can play an important role in improving firm performance. Empirical research on firms from countries other than the U.S. corroborates this conclusion. Neale (1991a), for example, found that postauditing provides benefits to U.K. firms, especially where such firms were facing turbulent environments. Neale et al. (1994) found that postauditing provides benefits to Norwegian firms, especially in terms of improving the quality of future decisions. Apparently, an increasing number of managers have recognized the potential benefits of postauditing as evidenced by the increasing number of firms initiating such procedures. In this latter regard, Gordon and Myers (1991) found that a large percentage of the U.S. firms initiated postauditing procedures during the period from 1980-1986. Pike (1988) had similar empirical findings regarding U.K. firms and Neale (1991b; 1993) found this trend for U.K. firms to be continuing through the late 1980s. These findings notwithstanding, there remains a large number of firms which, at best, give only lip service to the postauditing phase of capital budgeting.

MANAGING RISK

A problem which confronts many firms, especially those competing on a global basis, is determining the acceptable degree of risk related to a capital project. In this regard, the old adage "nothing ventured, nothing gained" contains an important message. In other words, there is a direct relationship between the expected return and riskiness of a project. If firms are not willing to accept any risk then they might as well close down and invest their money in risk-free treasury bills. At the other extreme, too much risk can easily lead to financial disaster. Thus, the goal is to take some risk, but not too much. Stated differently, firms need to manage the riskiness of their capital investments.

One important way firms can manage the riskiness of their capital investments is through postauditing. Effective postauditing can help firms identify projects which should be either improved or abandoned early on in their lives. As such, postauditing allows firms to take chances (risks) on projects, but at the same time minimizes those risks. Indeed, effective postauditing of capital assets represents an important means by which firms can achieve "world class" status.

ABANDONMENT DECISION

The postauditing emphasis thus far has been on feedback control. **Feedback control** is a process whereby actual results are compared to expected results, with the difference being the basis for potential action. Postauditing can also help to trigger the feedforward control process. **Feedforward control** is a process whereby newly determined expected results are compared to earlier expected results, with the difference being the basis for potential action. One outcome of feed forward control could be the recognition that earlier expectations about forthcoming cash flows were overly optimistic. In such a case, revised estimates of a project's expected future discounted cash flows may suggest that the best course of action is to abandon the project.

The decision to abandon a capital project should be based on a present value analysis. If the present value of the expected future discounted cash flows from a capital project is less than the project's current abandonment value, the proper decision would be to abandon the project. In algebraic terms, the basic abandonment decision could be expressed as follows:

If $PV < AV$, abandon capital project   **Eq. 13.1**

where,

$$PV = \sum_{t=1}^{n} \frac{CF_t}{(1+k)^t}$$

CF_t	=	net cash flow in period t,
k	=	firm's cost of capital,
n	=	remaining economic life of project,
AV	=	current abandonment value of project.

The importance of a postauditing system to making effective abandonment decisions was empirically examined in a study by Smith (1993). The findings from the Smith study indicate that firms are more likely to derive net benefits from an aggressive policy of abandoning projects (i.e., retirement of assets) when they use sophisticated postauditing procedures (i.e., cell IV of Figure 13.1) than when they use a less sophisticated postauditing system.

OPTION VALUE

As discussed in the previous chapter, strategic capital investments often provide an opportunity for future investments (i.e., a "strike" position) which would not otherwise be available. Hence, there is an **option value** associated with investing in these strategic investments. Due to the irreversible nature of capital investments, there is also an option value associated with deferring certain capital investments (Stark, 1990). Hence, for some projects there are option value incentives to both invest and to defer investments. Postauditing can play an important role in reconciling these two conflicting signals. More to the point, effective postauditing can help a firm exercise the strike value associated with an acquired project as quickly as possible, while at the same time allow a firm to recognize the need for reversing the investment in a project (i.e., either shutdown or disinvest) as quickly as possible. Thus, effective postauditing should, on balance, move the option value conflict noted above in favor of investing rather than deferring investments.

ILLUSTRATION OF POSTAUDITING

An illustration of postauditing is presented in this section. The emphasis will be on the postauditing process and utilizing the information gleaned from that process.

The Laur Company, which owns and operates a chain of restaurants, has recently made a capital investment in a new restaurant called Laur 23. The investment was made based on the data shown in the first row of Exhibit 13.1.

EXHIBIT 13.1
Laur 23 Capital Investment (in 000s)

	Cost	CF_1[a]	CF_2	CF_3	CF_4	. . . . . .	CF_{30}
(1) Initial Estimates	$3,000	$600	$600	$600	$600		$600
(2) Results to Date	$3,400	$350	$450				
(3) Revised Estimates				$500	$500		$500

[a] CF = net cash inflow after taxes.

The new restaurant is in its second year of operation and the actual results to date are shown in the second row of Exhibit 13.1. The Laur Co. has recently received an offer, in writing, to buy its newest restaurant from a large restaurant chain. The offer consists of an immediate cash payment of $2,500,000. Revised estimates for the project's remaining life, should Laur Co. decide not to sell, are given in the third row of Exhibit 13.1. In considering capital projects of the type under review in this example, Laur Co. estimates its cost of capital to be 15% and looks for projects which meet a payback constraint of no more than 5 years.

Before discussing the postauditing of the Laur 23 project, it is important to recognize why Laur Co. accepted this project in the first place. Given the information provided in the first row of Exhibit 13.1, the NPV of the project was

determined to be $939,587 [i.e., $NPV = \sum_{t=1}^{30} \dfrac{(\$600,000)}{(1+.15)^t} -$

$3,000,000 = $939,587]. The IRR of the initial project was determined to be 19.91%. The payback period initially estimated for this project was 5 years [i.e.,

$\sum_{t=1}^{5} (\$600,000)$ = $3,000,000]. Hence, the Laur 23 project was considered an

attractive capital investment at the time of initiation.

Company policy for projects of the sort considered here is to conduct a postaudit every two years. As shown in Exhibit 13.1, actual costs of initiating the project exceeded estimates by $400,000 and the net cash inflows in the first two years were less than expected by $250,000 and $150,000, respectively. These latter results have prompted increased advertising for Laur 23, which is expected to boost remaining net cash inflows to $500,000 per year. Needless to say, actual results to date and revised estimates of the future indicate that the project is far less profitable than initially thought and taking a longer time period to pay itself back. Nevertheless, the company cannot go back in time. Hence, the only relevant consideration at this juncture is whether to continue operating Laur 23 or abandon the project.

If the company decides to sell (abandon) the restaurant, its best option is the offer in hand for $2,500,000. The decision not to sell will result in an estimated $500,000 net cash inflow for the next 28 years. At a 15% discount rate, the PV of the remaining project is equal to $3,266,754 [i.e.,

$PV = \sum_{t=1}^{28} \dfrac{(\$500,000)}{(1+.15)^t}$] and the AV is equal to $2,500,000 (i.e., the offer in

hand). Since the $PV > AV$, the project would not be abandoned.

Although the above is an extremely simplified example, it does highlight several key aspects of the postauditing process. First, a comparison of actual and expected results may help to improve an existing project. In the above example, the lower than expected cash flows in the first two years led to increased advertising. Second, postauditing and abandonment decisions go hand in hand with one another.[3] In the above example, the decision not to abandon Laur 23 could easily switch to abandon if the offer and/or future cash flows from the project changed. Third, the results from postauditing existing projects should be an integral part of future investments. Regarding the above example, Laur Co. would be wise to keep in mind, for future new restaurant opportunities, that cost estimates were understated and future net cash inflows overstated for Laur 23.

The fourth aspect of the postauditing process highlighted by the above example is the fact that the benefits of postauditing are increased by a sophisticated system in terms of a periodic review and in a fashion which is comparable to the way capital projects are selected. If Laur Co. only conducted a post-completion audit of Laur 23 (i.e., at the end of the project's life), it may not have increased the related advertising and net cash inflows beyond the second year might be substantially lower than the $500,000 now predicted. Further, if Laur Co. utilized accounting numbers rather than cash flow figures, such accrual items as depreciation expenses could provide misleading signals regarding the desirability of keeping, rather than abandoning, the project.

CONCLUDING COMMENTS

Major corporations spend much time and effort in selecting capital projects. In contrast, the control side of the capital budgeting process is often ignored or given inadequate attention. A key argument in this chapter has been that postauditing cannot only help weed out unsuccessful projects but, equally important, can assist in the selection of future projects. Indeed, an aggressive postauditing system will permit firms to seek out high return projects while at the same time keeping the risk associated with these projects at a manageable level.

Recent empirical studies suggest two important findings. First, there is a significant positive link between firm performance and the use of sophisticated postauditing procedures. Second, firms are beginning to recognize this positive performance-postauditing link as evidenced by the growing number of firms initiating postauditing procedures during the past decade. For strategic capital projects, postauditing is probably best handled in terms of groups, or bundles, of assets required to achieve strategic goals. In this regard, Hendricks et al. (1992) provide an excellent discussion of how Caterpillar uses "bundle monitoring" to evaluate strategic initiatives.

---

3.   Although beyond the scope of this book, abandonment values also affect capital investment decisions. For an excellent discussion on how abandonment and capital investment decisions are interrelated, including consideration of uncertainty and temporal dependence of cash flows, the reader is referred to the paper by McCabe and Sanderson (1984).

PROBLEMS

Problem 13.1

Briefly discuss the objectives of postauditing capital investments. Also discuss the benefits and costs of postauditing capital investments.

Problem 13.2

An executive noted that "special issues need to be considered in postauditing capital assets of a multinational corporation (i.e., a corporation that operates in more than one country) as compared to a firm which limits its operations to one country."

Required:
Explain the above quote.

Problem 13.3

As discussed in this chapter, there is evidence to suggest that firm performance is positively affected by the postauditing of capital assets. Nevertheless, there is also a cost to such postauditing. Since postauditing is actually a means of gathering information on existing capital projects, the costs and benefits of postauditing are logically considered from an information economics perspective.

Required:
A.   Discuss the argument presented above concerning the information economics perspective towards postauditing.

B.   From an information economics perspective, explain why it may be perfectly logical for a firm to postaudit large capital investments more frequently than small capital investments.

Problem 13.4

EcraM Corporation started a new line of hi-tech stereos two years ago. At that time, it was estimated that the project would require an initial cash outlay of $7,000,000 and would generate net cash inflows of $1,600,000 per year for the following ten years. The company's cost of capital is 10% and it has a policy of rejecting projects that cannot meet a payback constraint of no more than 5 years. The company also has a policy of conducting a postaudit of capital projects every two years.

The first postaudit of the above noted project showed that the initial cash outlay exceeded the estimate by $1,500,000 and the actual net cash inflows for the first two years were $1,400,000 and $1,300,000, respectively. As a result of the postauditing, the company is considering a one time increase in its advertising expenditures by $2,000,000 and to drop two of the unprofitable products within the new line of stereos. As a consequence of these actions, the revised estimates show that the future cash inflows would be $1,500,000 for the remaining eight years. Alternatively, the company could sell the new line of stereos and receive (based on a definite offer) $5,000,000 from an overseas investor.

Required (Show all work):
Should the company abandon the project?

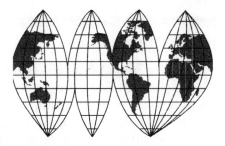

14

MANAGEMENT ACCOUNTING SYSTEMS AS AGENTS OF ORGANIZATIONAL CHANGE

CHAPTER OUTLINE

■ Organizational Change Framework

■ Illustrative Support for Framework

INTRODUCTION

The degree to which an organization survives depends, in large part, on how adaptable it is to its external environment. For organizations operating in stable environments, such adaptability requires only a moderate effort. Alternatively, for organizations operating in highly dynamic environments, such adaptability requires significant and difficult planning to be successful. Yet, the significance and difficulty connected with adapting to changing environments in no way mitigates the need for such adaptation. On the contrary, many organizations are now facing highly turbulent economic, political, and social environments at a time when such organizations are playing their largest and most important role in society. More people than ever, both internal as well as external to the organization, are affected by the failure of today's large global organizations to adapt to such environments. Thus, many organizations are on the horns of the following dilemma. On the one hand, it is increasingly difficult for organizations to keep up with rapidly changing environments. On the other hand, it is intrinsically important for organizations to be able to adapt to such environments.

The primary objective of this chapter is to provide a conceptual framework for viewing management accounting systems as agents for implementing organizational change. Illustrative support for the framework will also be provided in this chapter. This support is based on an abundance of empirical evidence. The framework contained in this chapter differs from most other work in accounting in at least three important, although related, ways. First, it explicitly addresses the relationship between management accounting and organizational change. Second, by emphasizing the proactive, as opposed to reactive, role of management accounting in facilitating organizational change, it sheds new light on the relationship between accounting and organizational design issues. Third, it provides a link between the behavioral and organizational design aspects of the role of accounting in organizational change.

ORGANIZATIONAL CHANGE FRAMEWORK

A large part of the literature on organizational change has concentrated on the notion of changing the behavior of individuals within an organization. Lewin's (1947, 1952) classic work in the area discussed an *unfreezing-changing-refreezing* model in studying the behavioral change processes in groups. Other literature has discussed the notion of organizational change largely in terms of an organization's structural characteristics and its environment. Much of this latter literature has taken a contingency focus, arguing that the appropriate organizational structure required to facilitate organizational change is partly a function of the type of environment facing the firm (e.g., Burns and Stalker, 1961; Khandwalla, 1977; Perrow, 1970; Thompson, 1967; Woodward, 1965). Taking a more dynamic perspective, Toffler (1970) argues that frequently changing environments require continual organizational change, in terms of one temporary organization structure after another.

Weick's (1974) discussion of organizational change points out the need for organizations to be adaptable. Wildavsky (1972) argued that the ideal organization would be self-evaluating. Such an organization, according to Wildavsky (1972), would monitor its own activities and try to prevent individuals from building vested interests in existing activities. Hedberg et al., (1976) continued Wildavsky's line of argument by pointing out that organizations which face changing environments need to be erected in "tents" not "palaces." Whereas palaces put primary emphasis on the status quo, tents place primary emphasis on the organization's need and ability to change.

MacKenzie (1974b) also argues that organizational change and organizational structure are inextricably entwined. Indeed, he ultimately argues that organizational change is actually structural change. Thus, a theory of organizational change, according to MacKenzie, requires a theory of structural change. By focusing on the micro-processes of group intra-relationships, MacKenzie (1974b) argues that a group structure represents a need satisfying interaction pattern between the participants or parts of the group. If we let $X_n = (X_1, X_2, \ldots X_n)$ be the list of participants interacting in a group, there are $[n \, (n - 1)]/2$ possible pairs of interactions or channels (i.e., a channel represents an interaction pattern between two participants). MacKenzie (1970), describes a group structure by a matrix of the interactions, in terms of sending and receiving information between every pair of participants. The notion of structure being composed of simple two way interaction patterns can, of course, be expanded to include various types of relationships. In the final analysis, MacKenzie's argument is that structural change, and in turn organizational change, occurs whenever the interaction patterns, in terms of sending and receiving information, between individuals in the organization change. Thus, at the most fundamental level, MacKenzie's view of organizational change is the result of sending and receiving messages among individuals. The logic of this approach toward organizational change is both intuitively appealing and rigorous.[1]

The accounting literature addressing the subject of organizational change is largely based on the contingency relationships among an organization's environment, structure and accounting systems. However, a reactive, rather than proactive, role usually has been assigned to the accounting system in this literature. That is, the accounting system usually has been viewed as being a

---

1.   Other organization theorists have discussed organizational structure in terms of interaction patterns among individuals making up the organization. However, MacKenzie has provided a much more rigorous treatment of the subject than other work in the area.

function of the organization's environment and structure rather than as an agent of change. Golembiewski (1964), in one of the earliest papers discussing the relationship between accounting and organization theory, explicitly notes that accounting systems are a function of organization theory. In contrast, the paper by Gordon and Narayanan (1984) points out that management accounting systems and organization structure are more appropriately viewed as being in tandem with each other and simultaneously affected by environmental conditions.

Hedberg and Jonsson (1978), in their discussion of the role of information systems for organizations in changing environments, assigned a more proactive role to the accounting system in helping firms adapt to changing environments. Although focusing on the adaptive role of accounting, Gordon and Miller (1976) also note that accounting systems could take a proactive role in facilitating organizational change. Viewing management accounting systems as change agents is both logical and straightforward in the context of MacKenzie's work as noted above. Indeed, sending and receiving messages, which is at the heart of MacKenzie's organizational change perspective, is the fundamental activity of management accounting systems. As such, whether planned or not, management accounting systems effect the interaction patterns of individuals.[2]

The management accounting system creates changes in the interaction patterns of individuals using (i.e., receiving) information because it affects the user's ability to carry out decisions (from both a planning and control perspective). This user, or decision-oriented perspective, is well accepted in the management accounting literature (as discussed in Chapter 1). The management accounting system also creates changes in the interaction patterns of those individuals providing (i.e., sending) information via the process referred to in the accounting literature as *information inductance*. Prakash and Rappaport (1997), who originally coined the term, defined information inductance in terms of the way the behavior of an information sender is influenced by the information communicated.

---

2.   Of course, the argument that the MAS can act as an agent of organizational change in no way mitigates the fact that there are other agents of organizational change.

Figure 14.1 illustrates the key concepts of the MAS organizational change framework discussed above. As indicated in the figure, the MAS is an integral part of the organization's structure because it directly affects the interaction patterns of individuals via the sending and receiving of information. Further, as individuals interact to make relevant organizational decisions, they are accomplishing specific activities. The sequential process of accomplishing these activities leads to a revised MAS-organizational structure configuration. This process of moving from one MAS-organizational structure configuration to another, when placed in the context of the organization's environmental conditions and overall strategies, comprises the continual process of organizational change.

ILLUSTRATIVE SUPPORT FOR FRAMEWORK

The MAS-organizational change framework summarized above is based on many loosely specified relationships. Accordingly, it is difficult, if not impossible, to empirically examine the framework based on traditional statistical testing procedures (e.g., econometrics). Nevertheless, there are many strands of the framework running through a large body of case studies which clearly support the argument that management accounting systems do indeed serve as agents of organizational change. The purpose of this section is to highlight two areas of management accounting where this evidence is both compelling and timely. The two areas highlighted, both of which have been discussed in earlier chapters of this book, are organizational performance measures and activity based costing.[3] The tact taken in discussing each of these two areas is to provide an illustrative scenario, based on an abundance of empirical evidence. Each scenario will show how the MAS can serve as an agent of organizational change within the context of the framework provided in Figure 14.1.

---

3.   There are many other areas of management accounting (e.g., budgeting, transfer pricing) which provide equally compelling evidence on the role of MAS as agents of organizational change.

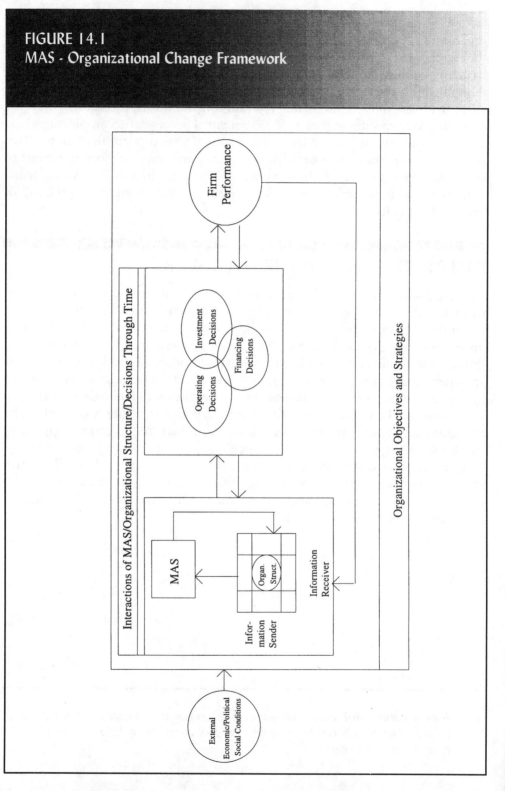

FIGURE 14.1
MAS - Organizational Change Framework

Organizational Performance Measures

Few areas of managerial accounting have received as much attention, over a sustained period of time, as the topic of organizational performance measures. In this text, Chapter 8 addressed the issue of financial performance measures. Chapter 9 focused on nonfinancial performance measures. However, regardless of which type of measure is being considered (i.e., financial or nonfinancial), it is well accepted that different performance measures induce different behavior, and thus interaction patterns in terms of information sending and receiving, among the individuals being measured. To see this point, consider the scenario described below.

Assume a firm's Vice-President of Operations is having her/his performance measured based on return on assets (i.e., operating income divided by total assets). In this case, the Vice-President would likely focus on the firm's income and investments. Information processing, in terms of the interaction patterns among individuals, are also focused on operating and investment decisions. Now assume the firm decides that it wants its Vice-President of Operations to give more attention to financing, as well as operating and investment, decisions. One way to accomplish this change is to begin measuring the Vice President's performance based on residual income (i.e., net income less a charge for the use of capital) instead of return on assets.

The newly installed performance measure will create a situation whereby the MAS will be required to solicit and communicate an explicit charge (i.e., cost of capital) for using funds. This charge will be sent to the Vice-President in question, who in turn will likely begin having increased interactions with the finance group responsible for determining the financing charges to be placed into the MAS (i.e., the interest charge on debt which is used to derive net income, as well as the cost of equity charge used to derive residual income). In addition, the Vice-President in question will likely start thinking differently about projects than before the new measure went into effect. In other words, since some projects reduce the firm's average return on assets, but increase its residual income (i.e., those which have a return greater than the cost of capital, but less than the existing average return), the Vice-President will now look at projects differently than before residual income was installed as a performance measure.[4] Of course, the Vice-President in question will communicate (via meetings, discussions and memos) this difference in view to the managers working with him/her. In the final analysis, this shift in performance measurement will create numerous changes in the interaction patterns among individuals in the firm until a new status quo is reached. Hence, the process of organizational change has

---

4.   Although maximizing a firm's average return on assets is not a desirable goal, there is substantial evidence that shows firms do indeed try to maximize on this measure (e.g., see Gordon and Iyengar, 1996).

occurred as a result of the change in the performance measure being communicated by the MAS.

Although the scenario described above is hypothetical in nature, the recent developments concerning economic value added (which is a stylized form of residual income) provide strong evidence of the scenario's validity. In fact, based on the large number of articles published in the various journals, and discussions with numerous business executives by this author, there is no doubt that the organizational change process described in the above scenario is both realistic and currently occurring.

Activity Based Costing

As discussed in Chapter 5, there are numerous problems associated with allocating indirect costs. One solution to many of these problems, as discussed in Chapter 6, is the use of activity based costing (ABC). The ABC advocates essentially argue that by assigning indirect costs to those activities which cause their occurrence and allocating the costs associated with each activity based on its own cost driver, improved indirect cost allocations and, in turn, decision making, will result. Whether or not one agrees with this argument (see Chapter 6 for the pros and cons of this argument), there can be little disagreement on the fact that ABC has been adopted by numerous organizations (to one extent or the other) around the world.

The adoption of ABC provides another excellent example of how the MAS can serve as an agent of organizational change via the model presented above. ABC focuses attention on defining the organization's key activities, the cost of such activities, and the way to allocate costs (based on cost drivers) according to these activities. In addition, ABC also focuses attention on managing the organization's activities. In other words, ABC places the cost management focus on activities. Traditional cost management systems focus attention at a much more aggregate level (e.g., departments). By shifting the cost management focus to activities, the interaction patterns among individuals, in terms of sending and receiving management accounting type information, are also changed. To see how this change would occur, consider the following example.

A medium size, general purpose, auto service and repair company is currently allocating its indirect costs to specific jobs based on direct labor hours. Prices for its services and repairs are initially set based on full costs, plus a percentage mark-up for profits. These initial prices are adjusted for market conditions, but the general philosophy of the firm is that it should be possible to achieve a profit on all its products (i.e., services and repairs). Although the company has been in business for over 20 years, the competition for customers has become fierce in the past few years. The intensity of competition is in large part due to the chains that perform limited, high turnover automobile services and repairs. These chains perform services and repairs quickly, at a low cost, and without an appointment. The manager of the company in question recently has been receiving complaints from many old customers over the charge for particular services and repairs. As a result, a decision is made by the company to have its controller conduct an ABC study.

The ABC analysis has revealed the fact that there are many indirect costs which are not volume driven, let along direct labor hour driven. For example, some jobs require the ordering of special parts whereas other jobs only require standard stock parts. Further, some jobs rely on high technology machinery, which is operated by specially trained technicians in the service department, whereas other jobs are easily completed with hand tools (such as screwdrivers and wrenches) and only require the services of para-professional mechanics. After carefully analyzing the operations of the service and repair company, it is decided that indirect costs are best viewed in terms of the following four activities: (1) routine service maintenance activities, such as oil changes and rotation of tires, (2) high technology related activities, such as computer based tune-ups and engine diagnostics, (3) highly technical, labor intense activities, such as repairing a clutch or leaky head gasket, and (4) special purchase orders for auto parts (especially for foreign cars). The cost drivers for these activities, respectively, are determined to be: (1) the number of standard hours (or part thereof) for completing the job, (2) the dollar value of the machinery used in the service, (3) the average salary level of the company's certified auto mechanics, and (4) the number of special purchase orders. Accordingly, the company decides to change the way it will manage its activities and allocate the costs associated with the activities. In other words, the company decided to install an ABC system based on the analysis provided above.

As a result of the shift to an ABC system, the following changes in the company have occurred. First, indirect costs have been grouped into one of the four activities noted above, rather than all being lumped into one category. Second, the service and repair shop has been physically reorganized in relation to the four activities noted above. For example, all of the company's high technology machinery is now located in the middle of the shop, rather than being placed in various parts of the shop. The oil changing and tire rotation services are now located in the part of the shop that is most accessible to the shop's main outside door, rather than in the back of the shop. Third, indirect costs for particular services and repairs are now allocated based on the four cost drivers noted above, and as a result the charges for indirect costs now vary significantly from job to job. For example, low technology, high volume jobs (e.g., oil changes) now receive a very low charge for indirect costs relative to the old system. In contrast, high technology, low volume jobs (e.g., highly specialized repairs to exotic foreign sport cars) now receive a high charge for indirect costs relative to the old system. Fourth, the interactions among those who make decisions to invest in high technology machinery, and those responsible for operating and allocating the costs of such machinery to particular jobs, is much more closely coordinated. Fifth, the marketing strategy for the company's services has shifted from a blanket emphasis on service quality to a mixed strategy of quality for some products and low cost for other products. All of these changes have resulted in changes in the interaction patterns, via changes in the sending and receiving of information, among individuals in the company. Thus, we have another example of how the MAS can serve as the agent of organizational change.

Although the scenario described above is hypothetical, the plethora of cases and survey studies on the subject of ABC leaves no doubt of the scenario's validity. Indeed, the finding that organizational change has occurred as described by some aspect of the framework provided in Figure 14.1, is one of the key findings of many of these studies.

CONCLUDING COMMENTS

One constant confronting organizations is the fact that survival requires change. The nature of the change required depends on numerous factors, including the external environment (i.e., the economic, political and social environment), as well as the nature of the firm's specific business activities. The interactions among individuals running the business are also of key importance in determining the way organizations adapt to change. Indeed, it has been argued that, at the most basic level, organizational change is actually the result of changes in the interaction patterns, via the sending and receiving of information, making up the organization.

Management accounting systems are essentially concerned with sending and receiving information. As such, management accounting systems are at the heart of organizational change as illustrated in Figure 14.1. In fact, the MAS-organizational change process is occurring in all organizations whether or not planned. Accordingly, it seems appropriate for organizations to recognize this latter fact and to explicitly consider the MAS-change agent phenomenon.

PROBLEMS

Problem 14.1

To survive, modern organizations need to be flexible enough to meet new customer demands, technological advances, and the unanticipated actions of competitors. In other words, organizations need to be able to confront new situations. Indeed, organizational change has become one of the cornerstones of modern corporations.

Required:

A.   Define the concept of organizational change.

B.   Give two examples of organizational changes currently taking place in the global market place.

Problem 14.2

Many believe that management accounting systems should adapt to organizations, and not the other way around (i.e., organizations should not adapt to the management accounting system). However, the empirical evidence seems to show that it is a two-way path.

Required:

Provide an explanation for the fact that organizations need to adapt to the MAS, as well as have the MAS adapt to the organization.

Problem 14.3

Mary Capelli, the new controller for a medium size manufacturer of high technology equipment, just left a meeting with the company's President and the Senior Vice-President of Operations. One of the topics discussed at the meeting was the rapid change taking place in the firm's industry. During the meeting, the Vice-President suggested that the company needed to do a better job monitoring the changes taking place in the industry. Mary was asked to think about ways to modify the firm's management accounting system to provide such a monitoring system.

Required:

In outline form, provide a list of some of the items that Mary should consider in responding to the Vice-President's request.

Problem 14.4 *(Adapted from CMA examination)*

Bio-Cure Inc. (BCI) was established five years ago by several medical scientists who developed a potential cure for the AIDS disease. As a by-product of their experimentation, they also developed several other vaccines that could have relatively significant market potential. BCI was originally funded by the founding scientists who planned BCI's activities at periodic brainstorming sessions.

During the past year, BCI was in need of additional financing to continue its research efforts as the company's products have not yet been brought to market. A major financial institution brought BCI and a venture capital group together. The venture capital group provided a sizable capital infusion for a controlling interest in BCI. As part of its normal management procedures to control its investments, the venture capital group developed a formal strategic plan for BCI, which included a mission statement and strategic goals for each functional area of BCI. The president of the venture capital group forwarded the strategic plan by mail to BCI's management.

Required:

A.   Identify at least three advantages of planning through brainstorming sessions.

B.   Identify at least three advantages of formal organizational planning.

C.   Provide at least three reasons why the management group of Bio-Cure Inc. is likely to resist the change in planning technique.

D.   Recommend at least two ways that communication could have been improved, thereby making the change in planning technique more acceptable to Bio-Cure Inc.'s management group.

Problem 14.5 *(Adapted from CMA examination)*

Masefield Corporation is a diversified manufacturing company that has been in business since 1965. The company's current organizational structure is represented by the first chart on the following page. This structure has been in place for approximately ten years and has proved to be satisfactory.

Masefield recently hired a new vice president for Textiles, Scott Parker. Parker has an extensive background in sales which complements the vice president for Plastics whose background has been in manufacturing. Parker believes that Masefield would be more effective if it were reorganized according to the second organizational chart presented on the following page.

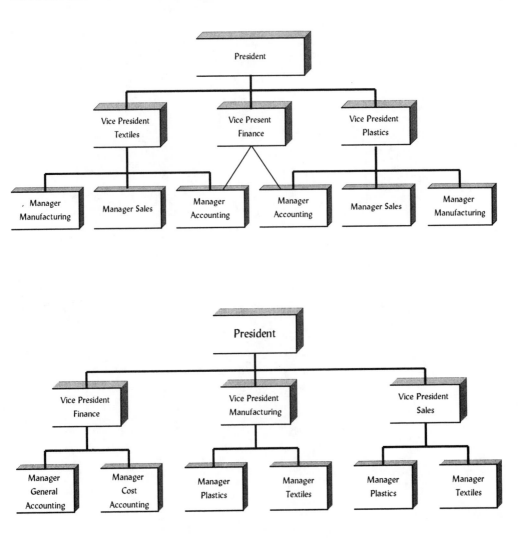

Required:

A.   Identify the key difference between the two types of organizational structures depicted by the two charts.

B.   Compare the two organizational structures by discussing at least two advantages and at least two disadvantages to the organization of the

    1.   current organizational structure.

    2.   proposed organizational structure.

C.   Discuss the circumstances that would favor each form of organizational structure.

GLOSSARY

Absorption costing. A cost accumulation system whereby inventories are charged with fixed as well as variable manufacturing costs.

Accounting rate of return (ARR). (See **Return on investment.**)

Accounts receivable collection period. The average time it takes a firm to collect credit sales.

Activity. An act or task directed at accomplishing a specific goal.

Activity based costing (ABC). A two-stage procedure for allocating indirect costs to various activities. In the first stage, the activities which cause an organization to incur indirect costs are identified and the related costs for each activity are pooled together. In the second stage, the costs of each activity are allocated to the cost objective based on the cost driver associated with the activity.

Activity based management (ABM). The process by which a firm manages its activities.

Agency theory. The field of economics and law which is concerned with the delegation of decision making authority by a principal to an agent.

Asymmetric information. Information available to managers and owners, but not principals.

Backflush costing. A costing system where the costs of producing a product are not computed (i.e., flushed out) until the product is sold.

Batch costing. A costing system whereby costs are accumulated based on a batch of mass produced units.

Budget. A formal plan for future activities, usually expressed in financial terms.

Budgeting. The process by which budgets are prepared.

By-products. Products, not intentionally produced, resulting from joint costs.

Capital budget. The budget for capital investments.

Capital expenditures or **capital investments**. Expenditures which are intended to benefit the firm's activities for more than one operating period.

Cash flow budget. The budget related to cash flows.

Cash recovery rate. A measure of performance which is derived by dividing operating cash flows by gross investments.

Constant returns to scale. The points on the production function where outputs increase in equal proportion to inputs.

Contingency theory. An approach toward managerial accounting which argues that the appropriateness of a management accounting system depends on the specific organization and the circumstances under which the organization operates.

Contribution margin. The difference between revenues and variable costs.

Contribution margin paradox. The notion that a positive contribution margin does not guarantee that a firm will not lose money.

Contribution margin ratio. The contribution margin divided by revenues.

Control. A process which consists of assessing whether the allocation of organizational resources has accomplished the desired objectives.

Conversion costs. The direct labor and indirect costs required to convert raw materials into a final product.

Cost based transfer price. A transfer price derived from the costs of the intermediate product.

Cost center. An organizational arrangement whereby the performance of a subunit and its managers is evaluated in terms of costs.

Cost objective. The purpose for which a cost is being measured.

Cost of capital. The minimum rate a project needs to earn so that a firm's value will not be reduced (i.e., the opportunity cost of funds).

Cost-plus pricing. A procedure for pricing which begins by determining a product's costs and adding a markup (i.e., a plus) to cover profits.

Cost savings projects. Capital investments which reduce the cost of existing activities.

Current ratio. Current assets divided by current liabilities.

Data. Signs and symbols that are gathered and processed, providing they are understood by the sender.

Data base. Various data within the decision support system which is utilized in conducting planning and control activities.

Data base management systems. Software used to create, maintain, retrieve, and update the data base.

Decentralization. An organizational structure based on subunits, whereby subunit managers have decision making autonomy.

Decision making. A process which includes the activities associated with planning and control.

Decision support system. A computer based information system designed to support managerial decision making.

Decreasing returns to scale. The points on the production function where outputs increase less rapidly than increases in inputs.

Direct costs. Costs which are directly related to the cost objective.

Direct method. A method for allocating reciprocal service departments' costs which ignores the reciprocal relationships among service departments.

Discount rate. The rate used in discounting future cash flows in order to determine their present value.

Dividend payout ratio. Dividends paid divided by net income.

Economic value added. (See **Residual income**).

Economics of internal organization. A perspective which argues that firms organize in ways to create internal markets that serve as substitutes for external markets to run their economic activities.

Effective. Accomplishing a given task or objective. Being effective is a necessary, but not sufficient, requirement for being efficient.

Efficient. Deriving the maximum output from a given level of input or, alternatively, using the minimum level of input (i.e., resources) to derive a given level of output.

Equivalent units of production. The common denominator used to compute the unit cost of producing a product under a process costing system.

Feedback control. A process whereby actual results are compared to expected results, with the difference being the basis for potential action.

Feedforward control. A process whereby newly expected results are compared to earlier expected results, with the difference being the basis for potential action.

Fixed costs. Costs which remain the same for a specified period of time, regardless of the changes in the level of production.

Flexible manufacturing system (FMS). An arrangement whereby production facilities and activities can be quickly and easily reconfigured.

Increasing returns to scale. The points on the production function where outputs increase more rapidly than increases in inputs.

Incremental budgeting. A budgeting process which assumes that the budget consists of a base portion plus (or minus) some incremental (or decremental) portion.

Incremental costs. The additional costs associated with producing additional units of a product.

Incremental revenues. The additional revenues associated with selling additional units of a product.

Indirect costs. Costs which cannot be directly related to the cost objective. These costs are often referred to as overhead costs.

Information. A subset of data which increases the knowledge of the person receiving the data.

Information economics. The area of economics concerned with assessing the costs and benefits of gathering, processing, and using information.

Information inductance. The way an information sender is influenced by the information communicated.

Internal rate of return (IRR). The discount rate that equates the present value of future cash inflows from a project to the project's initial cost. The IRR is also a method for selecting capital investments based on the IRR.

Inventoriable costs. Costs which are charged to the firm's inventory.

Inventory Turnover Ratio. Cost of goods sold divided by average inventory.

Investment center. An organizational arrangement whereby the performance of a subunit and its managers is evaluated in terms of a rate of profit per unit of investment.

Job order costing. A costing system whereby costs are accumulated by jobs.

Joint costs. Costs associated with the inseparable production process of two or more products.

Joint products. Two or more products resulting from an inseparable production process.

Just-in-time (JIT). A production system whereby the goods in one stage of the production-sales cycle are completed just prior to being needed at the next stage.

Least squares method. A method for estimating the parameters in a regression model, which minimizes the sum of the squared errors.

Main products. Products resulting from joint costs which represent the primary products derived from the inseparable production process.

Management accountant. An individual who helps develop, implement, and use the management accounting system.

Management accounting system (MAS). The formal information system concerned with supporting managerial accounting related activities.

Managerial accounting. The area of accounting concerned with the design and use of information systems that support managerial planning and control.

Managerial economics. The application of economic theory, especially microeconomic theory, to managerial decision making (i.e., planning and control).

Mandatory projects. Must-do capital investments.

Marginal cost. The additional cost associated with producing one additional unit of a product. (Technically, marginal cost is the first derivative of the total costs function. However, operationally the derivative concept is interpreted in terms of a one unit change in production.)

Marginal revenue. The additional revenue associated with selling one additional unit of a product. (Technically, marginal revenue is the first derivative of the total revenues function. However, operationally the derivative concept is interpreted in terms of a one unit change in sales.)

Market based transfer price. A transfer price derived from the price charged by an external market supplier.

Market value added. The difference between the market value and accounting book value of a firm.

Model base. Subroutines within the decision support system which are utilized to carry out planning and control activities.

Model base management system. Software necessary to update, retrieve, maintain, and integrate the various subroutines in the model base.

Negotiated transfer price. A transfer price derived through negotiations between the buying and selling subunits.

Net present value. A method for selecting capital investments based on the difference between the present value of future cash inflows from a project and the project's initial cost.

Nonstrategic decisions. Decisions which range from highly programmable to semiprogrammable steps, involve small to medium amounts of resource commitments, and are usually made by lower to middle level managers.

Open system. A system that interacts with its environment.

Operating budget. The budget for current operating activities.

Opportunity cost. The value, and thus implicit cost, associated with the foregone opportunity to use resources in the best alternative.

Option value. The value associated with the opportunity to take some future action.

Overhead costs. See **Indirect costs**.

Payback period. A method for selecting capital investments based on the number of periods it takes for a project to recover its initial cost.

Period costs. Costs which are treated as operating expenses of the period.

Planning. A process consisting of the following basic stages: (1) setting organizational objectives; (2) identifying opportunities and/or problems related to these objectives; and (3) selecting a given course of action to be pursued.

Postauditing. The assessment or monitoring of capital investments to determine whether or not they are accomplishing their intended purpose.

Present value. The amount one is willing to pay today in exchange for the receipt of cash flows in the future.

Price elasticity of demand. The relationship between the percentage change in the number of units sold and the percentage change in the price of the product.

Process costing. A costing system whereby costs are accumulated by production processes.

Product. A physical good or service which represents the output of a firm (or subunit).

Production function. The relationship between a firm's inputs and outputs.

Productivity. A ratio of outputs to inputs.

Profit center. An organizational arrangement whereby the performance of a subunit and its managers is evaluated in terms of profits.

Profitability index (PI). A method for selecting capital investments based on the ratio of the present value of future cash inflows of a project divided by the project's initial cost.

Reciprocal method. A method for allocating reciprocal service departments' costs which considers the simultaneous relationships among service departments.

Regression analysis. A statistical technique for examining the relationship between a dependent variable and one or more independent variables.

Relevant costs. Costs that affect the decision under consideration.

Relevant range. The likely range of operations.

Residual income (RI). A measure of performance which is derived by deducting a capital charge (derived from multiplying the cost of capital by the investments utilized to generate profits) from accounting profits.

Responsibility accounting. An accounting system which is based on the notion of holding individuals responsible for a specific set of activities.

Return on investment (ROI) or **accounting rate of return (ARR)**. A measure of performance which is derived by dividing accounting profits by the accounting value of investments.

Revenue generating projects. Capital investments which either increase the revenues of existing firm activities or create revenues from new activities.

Standard cost system. A cost system whereby direct and indirect manufacturing costs are initially estimated. These estimates are referred to as standards and form the basis for product costing.

Step method. A method for allocating reciprocal service departments' costs that allocates the costs of the service department that spends more effort (in terms of dollars) on other service departments. This process continues in sequential fashion until all service departments' costs are fully allocated.

Strategic cost management. The notion of managing costs within the context of a firm's strategy.

Strategic decisions. Decisions which have long-term effects on an organization, involve senior executives, impact a significant portion of the organization's resource commitments, and do not lend themselves to a set of programmable steps.

Strategy. The way a firm positions itself in the long-run relative to its competitors.

Sunk costs. Costs that have been incurred, but which are not relevant to the decision under consideration.

Target costing. A procedure for managing costs, such that, given a price, a desirable profit level is achieved.

Throughput time. The time required to move a product through the entire production cycle, from start to final sale.

Times Interest Earned Ratio. Operating income divided by interest expense.

Tobin's q. A measure of performance which is derived by dividing the market value of a firm by the replacement cost of its tangible assets.

Total quality control. A philosophy toward production which emphasizes high quality and continuous improvement.

Transfer pricing. An area of economics and management accounting concerned with establishing the price one subunit charges another subunit within the same organization for the internal transfer of intermediate products.

Variable costing. A cost accumulation system whereby inventories are charged only with variable manufacturing costs.

Variable costs. Costs which go up or down with increases or decreases in the production level of a particular good or service.

Variances. The difference between actual and standard (or budgeted) costs or revenues.

Working capital. Current assets minus current liabilities.

Zero base budgeting. A budgeting process where the entire budget is open for scrutiny and evaluation.

REFERENCES

Al-Eryani, M.F., P. Alam, and S.H. Akhter, "Transfer Pricing Determinants of U.S. Multinationals," *Journal of International Business Studies* (Third Quarter 1990), pp. 409-25.

Amey, L., "Tomkins on Residual Income," *Journal of Business, Finance and Accounting* (Spring 1975), pp. 55-68.

Antle, R.A., and J.S. Demski, "The Controllability Principle in Responsibility Accounting," *The Accounting Review* (October 1988), pp. 700-718.

Archibald, N.D., "Letter to Stockholders," Black & Decker, Inc., *1995 Annual Report* (February 22, 1996).

Argyris, C., *The Impact of Budgets on People* (Ithaca, NY: Controllership Foundation, Inc., 1952).

Armitage, H., and A. Atkinson, "The Choice of Productivity Measures in Organizations," in *Measures for Manufacturing Excellence*, (Boston, MA: Harvard Business School Press, 1990), pp. 91-126.

Armitage, H., and R. Nicholson, *Activity Based Costing: A Survey of Canadian Practice,* Society of Management Accountants, (1993).

Ask, U., and C. Ax, "Trends in the Development of Product Costing Practices and Techniques-A Survey of the Swedish Manufacturing Industry," 15th Annual Congress of the European Accounting Association, (1992).

Baiman, S., "Agency Research in Management Accounting: A Survey," *Journal of Accounting Literature* (1982), pp. 154-213.

Bedingfield, J., and L. Rosen, *Government Contract Accounting* (Washington, D.C.: Federal Publications, Inc., 1985).

Bleakley, F.R., "As Capital Spending Grows, Firms Take a Hard Look at Returns from the Effort," *Wall Street Journal* (February 8, 1994), pp. A2, A6.

Bonczek, R.H., C.W. Holsapple, and A.B. Whinston, *Foundation of Decision Support Systems* (New York: Academic Press, 1981).

Boschen, J.F., and K. J. Smith, "You Can Pay Me Now and You Can Pay Me Later: The Dynamic Response of Executive Compensation to Firm Performance," *Journal of Business,* Vol. 68, No. 4 (1995), pp. 577-608.

Brief, R.P. and R.E. Lawson, "The Role of the Accounting Rate of Return in Financial Statement Analysis," *The Accounting Review* (April 1992), pp. 411-426.

Briner, R., M. Akers, J. Truitt, and J. Wilson, "Coping with Change at Martin Industries," *Management Accounting* (January 1989), pp. 45-49.

Brownell, P., "Participation in the Budgeting Process: When it Works and When it Doesn't," *Journal of Accounting Literature,* Vol. 1, No. 2 (1982), pp. 124-153.

Burns, T., and G. Stalker, *The Management of Innovation* (London: Tavistock, 1961).

Byrd, V., "The Business Week 1000," *Business Week* (March 28, 1994), pp. 63-142.

Caldwell, C.W., and J.K. Welch, "Applications of Cost-Volume-Profit Analysis in the Governmental Environment," *The Government Accountants Journal* (Summer 1989), pp. 3-8.

Chan, K.H. and L. Chow, "International Transfer Pricing for Business Operations in China: Inducements, Regulation, and Practice," *Journal of Business Finance and Accounting* (October / December 1997), pp. 1269-1289.

Chandler, A., *Strategy and Structure: Chapters in the History of the Industrial Enterprise* (Cambridge, MA: MIT Press, 1962).

Chandler, C., "Japan's Woes Stir Talk Its Firms May Modify Time-Honored Ways," *Wall Street Journal* (April 30, 1992), pp. A1, A8.

Chenhall, R.H., and D. Morris, "The Impact of Structure, Environment, and Independence On the Perceived Usefulness of Management Accounting Systems," *The Accounting Review*, Vol. 61, No. 1 (1986), pp. 16-35.

Christy, G.A., "Capital Budgeting—Current Practices and Their Efficiency" (Eugene, Oregon: Bureau of Business and Economic Research, University of Oregon, 1966).

Clark, John M., *Studies in the Economics of Overhead Costs* (Chicago: The University of Chicago Press, 1923).

Clarke, P.J., "Management Accounting Practices in Irish Manufacturing Businesses: A Pilot Study," *Irish Accounting and Finance Association Proceedings*, (1992), pp. 17-34.

Clarke, P., "Bringing Uncertainty Into the CVP Analysis," *Accountancy* (England, September 1986), pp. 105-107.

Coase, R.H., "The Nature of the Firm," *Economica* (November 1937), pp. 386-405.

Cohen, S., and M. Loeb, " Improving Performance Through Cost Allocation," *Contemporary Accounting Research*, Vol. 5, No. 1 (1988), pp. 70-95.

Cohen, S., and M. Loeb, "Implicit Cost Allocation and Bidding for Contracts," *Management Science* (September 1990), pp. 1133-1138.

Cooper, R.R. and R. Slagmulder, "Cost Management Beyond the Boundaries of the Firm," *Management Accounting* (March 1998), pp. 19, 20.

Cornick, M.,W. Cooper, and S. Wilson, "How Do Companies Analyze Overhead," *Management Accounting* (June 1988), pp. 41-43.

Cost Management Group of the Institute of Management Accountants, "Second Annual Activity Based Costing Survey," *Cost Management Update* (October 1991).

Cost Management Group of the Institute of Management Accountants, "Strategic Cost Management: Companies That Try It Don't Give Up," *Cost Management Update* (July 1997), pp. 1, 4.

Cyert, R., and J. March, *A Behavioral Theory of the Firm* (Englewood Cliffs, NJ: Prentice Hall, 1963).

Dechow, P.M., "Accounting Earnings and Cash Flows as Measures of Firm Performance: The Role of Accounting Accruals," *Journal of Accounting and Economics*, Vol. 18 (1994), pp. 3-42.

Demski, J., "Cost Allocation Games," in S. Moriarity (ed.), *Joint Cost Allocation* (Center for Economic and Management Research, University of Oklahoma, 1981), pp. 142-173.

DiCamillo, G.T., "Letter to Shareholders," *Polaroid Corporation's 1995 Annual Report* (March 19, 1996).

DiCamillo, G.T., "Letter to Stockholders, Customers, and Friends" *Polaroid Corporation's 1996 Annual Report* (March 19, 1997).

Draper, N.R., and H. Smith, *Applied Regression Analysis*, 2nd Ed. (New York, N.Y.: John Wiley & Sons, Inc., 1981).

Duncan, K. and K. Moores, "Residual Analysis: A Better Methodology for Contingency Studies in Management Accounting," *Journal of Management Accounting Research* (Fall 1989), pp. 89-103.

Dyckman, T.R., "The Investigation of Cost Variances," *Journal of Accounting Research* (Autumn 1969), pp. 215-244.

Eccles, R., "Control with Fairness in Transfer Pricing," *Harvard Business Review* (November-December 1983), pp. 149-161.

Egginton, D., "Divisional Performance Measurement: Residual Income and the Asset Base," *Management Accounting Research* (1995), Vol. 6, No. 3, pp. 201-222.

Emmanuel, C. and D.T. Otley, *Accounting for Management Control* (Van Nostrand Reinhold, 1985).

Fama, E.F., "Risk-Adjusted Discount Rates and Capital Budgeting Under Uncertainty," *Journal of Financial Economics* (August 1977), pp. 3-24.

Fisher, A.B., "Creating Stockholder Wealth," *Fortune* (December 11, 1995), pp. 105-116.

Fisher, F.M. "Accounting Data and Economic Performance of Firms," *Journal of Accounting and Public Policy*, Vol. 7, No. 4 (Winter 1988) pp. 253-260.

Fisher, F.M., and J.J. McGowan, "On the Misuse of Accounting Rates of Return to Infer Monopoly Profits," *American Economic Review* (March 1983), pp. 82-97.

Fisher, J., "Implementing Target Costing," *Journal of Cost Management* (Summer 1995), pp. 50-59.

Frey, K. and L.A. Gordon, "ABC, Strategy, and Firm Performance," (Working Paper, 1998).

Friedman, M., "The Methodology of Positive Economics," *Essays in Positive Economics,* pp. 1-43. (Chicago: University of Chicago Press, 1953).

Friedman, M., "The Social Responsibility of Business is to Increase Profits," *The New York Times Magazine* (September 13, 1970).

Gaumnitz, B.R., and F.P. Kollaritsch, "Manufacturing Cost Variances: Current Practice and Trends," *Journal of Cost Management* (Spring 1991), pp. 58-64.

Gaver, J.J., and K.M. Gaver, "The Association Between Performance Plan Adoption and Corporate Capital Investment: A Note," *Journal of Management Accounting Research* (Fall 1993), pp. 145-158.

General Accounting Office (GAO), "Streamlining Zero-Base Budgeting Will Benefit Decision Making" (Report to Congress, 1979).

General Accounting Office (GAO), "International Taxation: Updating Information on Transfer Pricing" (Testimony before the Committee on Governmental Affairs, U.S. Senate, 1993), *GAO/T-GGD-93-16.*

Gilmartin, R.V., "Chairman's Message," *Merck & Co., Inc. 1997 Annual Report* (March 1, 1998).

Golembiewski, R.T., "Accountancy as a Function of Organization Theory," *The Accounting Review*, April 1964, pp. 333-341.

Gordon, L.A., "Accounting Rate of Return vs. Economic Rate of Return," *Journal of Business, Finance and Accounting* (Autumn 1974a), pp. 343-356.

Gordon, L.A., "Allocating Service Departments' Costs: Methodology and Case Study," *Accounting and Business Research* (Winter 1974b), pp. 3-8.

Gordon, L.A., "The Return on Investment and the Cost of Capital," *Management Accounting* (February 1976), pp. 37-40.

Gordon, L.A., "Federal Capital Expenditures and Public Policy: The Budgeting Link," *Journal of Accounting and Public Policy,* Vol. 2, No. 1 (1983), pp. 1-4.

Gordon, L.A., R. Cooper, H. Falk, and D. Miller, *The Pricing Decision* (NY: NAA, 1981).

Gordon, L.A., S. Haka, and A. Schick, "Strategies for Information Systems Implementation: The Case of Zero Base Budgeting," *Accounting, Organizations and Society*, Vol. 9, No. 2 (1984), pp. 111-123.

Gordon, L.A., and M. Hamer, "Rates of Return and Cash Flow Profiles: An Extension," *The Accounting Review* (July 1988), pp. 514-521.

Gordon, L.A. and R.J. Iyengar, "Return on Investment and Corporate Capital Expenditures: Empirical Evidence," *Journal of Accounting and Public Policy* (Winter 1996), pp. 305-325.

Gordon, L.A., M. Loeb, and M. Myers, "A Note on Postauditing and Firm Performance," *Managerial and Decision Economics*, Vol. 15 (1994), pp. 177-181.

Gordon, L.A., and D. Miller, "A Contingency Framework for the Design of Accounting Information Systems," *Accounting Organizations and Society,* Vol. 1, No. 1 (1976), pp. 59-69.

Gordon, L.A. and M. Myers, "Postauditing Capital Projects: Are You in Step with the Competition?" *Management Accounting* (January 1991), pp. 39-42.

Gordon, L.A., and .V.K. Narayanan, "Management Accounting Systems, Perceived Environmental Uncertainty and Organization Structure: An Empirical Investigation," *Accounting, Organizations and Society*, Vol. 9, No. 1 (1984), pp. 33-47.

Gordon, L.A., and G.E. Pinches, *Improving Capital Budgeting Decisions: A Decision Support System Approach* (Boston, MA: Addison Wesley, 1984).

Gordon, L.A., and F. Sellers, "Accounting and Budgeting Systems," *The Journal of Accounting and Public Policy* (Winter 1984), pp. 259-292.

Gordon, L.A., and K.J. Silvester, "Stock Market Reaction to News Concerning Activity-Based Costing Adoptions" (Working Paper, 1993).

Gordon, L.A., and K. Smith, "Postauditing Capital Expenditures and Firm Performance: The Role of Asymmetric Information," *Accounting, Organizations and Society*, Vol. 17, No. 8 (1992), pp. 741-757.

Gordon, L.A., and A.W. Stark, "Accounting and Economic Rates of Return: A Note on Depreciation and Other Accruals," *Journal of Business, Finance and Accounting* (Summer 1989), pp. 425-432.

Gosselin, M., "The Effect of Strategy and Organizational Structure on the Adoption and Implementation of Activity-Based Costing," *Accounting, Organizations and Society*, Vol. 22, No. 2 (1997), pp. 105-122.

Govindarajan, V., and R.N. Anthony, "How Firms Use Cost Data in Pricing Decisions," *Management Accounting* (July 1983), pp. 30-36.

Griner, E.H., and A.W. Stark, "Cash Recovery Rates, Accounting Rates of Return, and the Estimation of Economic Performance," *Journal of Accounting and Public Policy,* Vol. 7, No. 4 (1988), pp. 293-312.

Griner, E.H., and A.W. Stark, "On the Properties of Measurement Error in Cash-Recovery-Rate-Based Estimates of Economic Performance," *Journal of Accounting and Public Policy* (Fall 1991), pp. 207-223.

Haka, S., L.A. Gordon, and G.E. Pinches, "Sophisticated Capital Budgeting Selection Techniques and Firm Performance," *The Accounting Review* (October 1985), pp. 651-669.

Harcourt, G.C., "The Accountant in a Golden Age," *Oxford Economic Papers* (March 1965), pp. 66-80.

Hayes, D., "The Contingency Theory of Managerial Accounting," *The Accounting Review* (January 1977), pp. 22-39.

Healy, P., "The Effect of Bonus Schemes on Accounting Decisions," *Journal of Accounting and Economics,* Vol. 7, No. 1-3 (April 1985), pp. 85-107.

Hedberg, B. and S. Jonsson, "Designing Semi-Confusing Information Systems for Organizations in Changing Environments," *Accounting, Organizations and Society,* 1978, Vol. 3, No. 1, pp. 47-64.

Hedberg, B., C. Nystrom and W. Starbuck, "Camping on Seesaws: Prescriptions for a Self-Designing Organization," *Administrative Science Quarterly,* March 1976, pp. 41-65.

Hendricks, J., R. Bastian, and T. Sexton, "Bundle Monitoring of Strategic Projects," *Management Accounting,* (February 1992), pp. 31-35.

Hirshleifer, J., "On the Economics of Transfer Pricing," *Journal of Business* (July 1956), pp. 172-184.

Hopwood, A.G., "An Empirical Study of the Role of Accounting Data in Performance Evaluation," *Journal of Accounting Research,* Vol. 10, Supplement (1972), pp. 156-182.

Howell, R.A., J.D. Brown, S. Soucy, and A. Seed, *Management Accounting in the New Manufacturing Environment* (Montvale, New Jersey: National Association of Accountants, 1987).

Ijiri, J., "Convergence of Cash Recovery Rate," in *Quantitative Planning and Control* (eds. Y. Ijiri, and A. Whinston) (New York: Academic Press, Inc., 1979), pp. 259-267.

Ijiri, J., "Recovery Rate and Cash Flow Accounting," *Financial Executive* (March 1980), pp. 54-60.

Innes, J., and F. Mitchell. "A Survey of Activity-based Costing in the U.K.'s Largest Companies," *Management Accounting Research,* Vol. 6, No. 2 (June 1995), pp. 137-153.

Jensen, R.E., H. Arnet, W. Frank, G. Jones, G. Luoma, R. Manes and B. Oliver, "Report of the Committee on Nonfinancial Measures," *The Accounting Review* (Supplement to 1971), pp. 164-211.

Johnson, H.T., and R.S. Kaplan, *Relevance Lost: The Rise and Fall of Management Accounting* (Boston: Harvard Business School Press, 1987).

Kaplan, R.S., "The Significance and Investigation of Cost Variances: Survey and Extensions," *Journal of Accounting Research* (Autumn 1975), pp. 311-337.

Kaplan, R.S., and D. Norton, "The Balanced Scorecard—Measures that Drive Performance," *Harvard Business Review* (January-February 1992), pp. 71-79.

Kaplan, R.S. and D. Norton, "Putting the Balanced Scorecard to Work," *Harvard Business Review* (September-October 1993), pp. 134-147.

Kaplan, R.S. and D. Norton, "Using the Balanced Scorecard as a Strategic Management System," *Harvard Business Review* (January-February 1996), pp. 75-85.

Kelly, G., "Accounting and Economic Rates of Return: Additional Australian Evidence," *Journal of Accounting and Public Policy* (Winter 1996), pp. 347-372.

Khandwalla, P., *The Design of Organizations,* (NY: Harcourt Brace Jovanovich, Inc.) 1977.

Kim, S.H., "An Empirical Study of the Relationship Between Capital Budgeting Practices and Earnings Performance," *Engineering Economist* (Spring 1982), pp. 185-196.

Klammer, T.P., "The Association of Capital Budgeting Techniques with Firm Performance," *Accounting Review* (1973), pp. 353-364.

Kolodny, R., M. Lawrence, and A. Ghosh, "In Search of Excellence . . . For Whom?," *Journal of Portfolio Management* (Spring 1989), pp. 56-60.

Krumwiede, K.R. and W.G. Jordon, "Fewer Companies Believe that ABC is Necessary," *Cost Management Update,* No. 81 (January 1998), pp. 1-3.

Lambert, R., and D.F. Larcker, "Executive Compensation, Corporate Decision-Making and Shareholder Wealth: A Review of the Evidence," *Midland Corporate Finance Journal,* Vol. 2 (Winter 1985a), pp. 6-22.

Lambert, R. and D.F. Larcker, "Golden Parachutes, Executive Decision Making and Shareholder Wealth," *Journal of Accounting and Economics*, Vol. 7, No. 1-3 (1985b), pp. 179-203.

Landeman, M., and F.W. Schaeberle, "The Cost Accounting Practices of Firms Using Standard Costs," *Cost and Management* (July-August 1983), pp. 21-25.

Larcker, D.F., "The Association Between Performance Plan Adoption and Corporate Capital Investment," *Journal of Accounting and Economics,* Vol. 5, No. 1 (1983), pp. 5-30.

Lawrence, P., and J. Lorsch, *Organization and Environment* (Harvard University Press, 1967).

Lee, J.Y., "Investing in New Technology to Stay Competitive," *Management Accounting* (June 1991), pp. 45-48.

Lee, J.Y. and B.G. Jacobs, "Kunde Estate Winery," *CMA Magazine* (April 1993), pp. 15-19.

Lev, B., "The Curse of Great Expectations," *Wall Street Journal* (November 30, 1992), p. A12.

Lewin, Kurt, "Frontiers in Group Dynamics," *Human Relations*, 1: 2-38.

Lewin, Kurt, "Group Decision and Social Change" in G.E. Swanson, T. Newcomb and E. Hartley (eds.), *Readings in Social Psychology* (NY: Holt, Rinehart and Winston), pp. 459-473.

Livingstone, J.L., and G.L. Salamon, "Relationship between the Accounting and the Internal Rate of Return Measures. A Synthesis and an Analysis," *Journal of Accounting Research* (Autumn 1970), pp. 199-216.

Locke, E.A., K.N. Shaw, L.M. Saab, and G.P. Latham, "Goal Setting and Task Performance: 1969-1980," *Psychology Bulletin* (July 1981), pp. 125-152.

Loeb, M.P., and K. Surysekar, "On the Optimality of Cost-based Contracts in Sole Source Procurement," *Management Accounting Research* (forthcoming).

Macintosh, N.B., "A Contextual Model of Information Systems," *Accounting, Organizations and Society,* Vol. 6, No. 1 (1981), pp. 39-52.

Mackenzie, K.D., "A Set Theoretic Analysis of Group Interactions," *Psychometrika* (1970), pp. 23-42.

Mackenzie, K. D., "Measuring a Person's Capacity for Interaction in a Problem Solving Group," *Organizational Behavior and Human Performance* (October 1974a), pp. 149-169.

Mackenzie, K. D., "Organizational Change," in *Contemporary Management: Issues and Viewpoints* (Englewood Cliffs, NJ: Prentice-Hall, Inc.) 1974b, pp. 223-243. Ed. J. McGuire.

Mackenzie, K.D., *A Theory of Group Structure, Volume I, Basic Theory* (Gordon and Breach, 1976).

Marriott, J.W., "Letter to Shareholders," *Marriott Corporation's 1995 Annual Report* (March 4, 1996).

McCabe, G.M., and G.N. Sanderson, "Abandonment Value in Capital Budgeting: Another View," *Management Accounting* (January 1984), pp. 32-36.

McConnell, J.J. and C.J. Muscarella, "Corporate Capital Expenditures Decisions and the Market Value of the Firm," *Journal of Financial Economics* (September 1985), pp. 399-422.

Merchant, K.A., and J. Manzoni, "The Achievability of Budget Targets in Profit Centers: A Field Study," *The Accounting Review* (July 1989), pp. 539-558.

Merz, M. and A. Hardy, "ABC Puts Accountants on Design Team at HP," *Management Accounting* (September 1993), pp. 22-27.

Mia, L., "The Role of MAS Information In Organizations: An Empirical Study," *The British Accounting Review,* Vol. 25, No. 3 (1993), pp. 269-285.

Mia, L. and R.H. Chenhall, "The Usefulness of Management Accounting Systems, Functional Differentiation and Managerial Effectiveness," *Accounting, Organizations and Society,* Vol. 19, No. 1 (1994), pp. 1-13.

Monden, J., and K. Hamada, "Target Costing and Kaizen Costing in Japanese Automobile Companies," *Journal of Management Accounting Research* (Fall 1991), pp. 16-34.

Morgan, M.J., "A Case Study in Target Costing: Accounting for Strategy," *Management Accounting,* U.K. (May 1993), pp. 20-23.

Murphy, K., "Top Executives Are Worth Every Nickel They Get," *Harvard Business Review* (March-April 1986), pp. 125-132.

Myers, M., L.A. Gordon, and M. Hamer, "Postauditing Capital Assets and Firm Performance: An Empirical Investigation," *Managerial and Decision Economics,* Vol. 12 (1991), pp. 317-327.

Myers, S.C., and S.M. Turnbull, "Capital Budgeting and the Capital Asset Pricing Model: Good News and Bad News," *Journal of Finance* (May 1977), pp. 321-333.

National Association of Accountants, *Objectives of Management Accounting* (New York: NAA, 1982).

Neale, C.W., "The Benefits Derived from Post-Auditing Investment Projects," *Omega,* Vol. 19, No. 2,3 (1991a), pp. 113-120.

Neale, C.W., "A Revolution in Post-Completion Audit Adoption," *Management Accounting,* U.K. (November 1991b), pp. 44-46.

Neale, C.W., "Linkages Between Investment, Post-Auditing Capital Expenditure, and Corporate Strategy," *Management Accounting,* U.K. (February 1993), pp. 20-22.

Norkiewcz, A., "Nine Steps to Implementing ABC," *Management Accounting* (April 1994).

Nowak, W.A. and A. Jaruga, "On A Conceptual Framework for Financial Accounting: The Case of Polish Accounting Systems." Presented at the *21st Annual Congress of the European Accounting Association, Antwerp, Belgium* (April 1998).

Otley, D.T., "Budget Use and Managerial Performance," *Journal of Accounting Research,* Vol. 16, No. 1 (1978), pp. 122-149.

Otley, D.T., "The Contingency Theory of Management Accounting: Achievement and Prognosis," *Accounting, Organizations and Society,* Vol. 5, No. 4 (1980), pp. 413-28.

Peasnell, K.V., "Some Formal Connections Between Economic Values and Yields and Accounting Numbers," *Journal of Business Finance and Accounting* (Autumn 1982), pp. 361-381.

Peasnell, K.V., "Using Accounting Data to Measure the Economic Performance of Firms," *Journal of Accounting and Public Policy* (Winter 1996), pp. 291-303.

Perrow, C., *Organizational Analysis: A Sociological View* (London: Tavistock, 1970).

Pike, R.H., "Sophisticated Capital Budgeting Systems and Their Association with Corporate Performance," *Managerial and Decision Economics* (June 1984), pp. 91-97.

Pike, R.H., "The Design of Capital Budgeting Procedures and the Corporate Context," *Managerial and Decision Economics*, Vol. 7 (1986), pp. 187-195.

Pike, R.H., "An Empirical Study of the Adoption of Sophisticated Capital Budgeting Practices and Decision-Making Effectiveness," *Accounting and Business Research* (Autumn 1988), pp. 341-351.

Platt, L., "Letter to Shareholders," *Hewlett Packard Company's 1995 Annual Report* (December 15, 1995).

Pouliot, J., "High Tech Budgeting," *Management Accounting* (May 1991), pp. 30-31.

Prakash, P. and A. Rappaport, "Information Inductance and Its Significance for Accounting," *Accounting, Organizations and Society*, Vol. 2, No. 1, pp. 29-38.

Pugh, D., D. Hickson, C. Hinnings, K. MacDonald, C. Turner, and T. Lupton, "A Conceptual Scheme for Organizational Analysis," *Administrative Science Quarterly* (June 1963), pp. 289-315.

Reece, J.S., and W.R. Cool, "Measuring Investment Center Performance," *Harvard Business Review* (May/June 1978).

Ronen, J., and J.L. Livingstone, "An Expectations Theory Approach to the Motivational Imports of Budgets," *The Accounting Review* (October 1975), pp. 671-685.

Rosenblatt, M.J., and J.V. Jucker, "Capital Expenditure Decision Making: Some Tools and Trends," *Interfaces* (February 1979), pp. 63-69.

Rubenstein, M.E., "A Mean-Variance Synthesis of Corporate Financial Theory," *Journal of Finance* (March 1973), pp. 167-181.

Sakurai, M., "Past and Future of Japanese Management Accounting," *Journal of Cost Management* (Fall 1995), pp. 21-30.

Salamon, G.L., "Cash Recovery Rates and Measures of Firm Profitability," *The Accounting Review* (April 1982), pp. 292-302.

Salamon, G.L., "Accounting Rates of Return," *American Economic Review* (June 1985), pp. 495-504.

Scapens, R.W., "A Neoclassical Measure of Profit," *The Accounting Review* (April 1978), pp. 448-469.

Scapens, R.W., "Profit Measurement In Divisionalised Companies," *Journal of Business Finance and Accounting*, Vol. 6, No. 3 (1979), pp. 281-306.

Scapens, R. J., and J. T. Sale, "An International Study of Accounting Procedures in Divisionalised Companies and Their Association with Organizational Variables," *The Accounting Review* (April 1985), pp. 231-247.

Schall, L.D., G.L. Sundem, and W.R. Geijsbeek, "A Survey and Analysis of Capital Budgeting Methods," *Journal of Finance* (March 1978), pp. 281-287.

Selto, F.H., "Implementing Activity Based Costing," *Journal of Cost Management* (Summer 1995), pp. 36-49.

Shim, E., and E. Sudit, "How Manufacturers Price Products," *Management Accounting* (February 1995), pp. 37-39.

Simon, H.A., "Rational Decision Making in Business Organizations," *American Economic Review* (September 1979), pp. 493-513.

Smith, J.F., "Letter to Shareholders," *General Motors 1996 Annual Report* (January 28, 1997).

Smith, K.J., "Investment Monitoring Systems, Abandonment of Capital Assets, and Firm Performance," *Journal of Management Accounting Research* (Fall 1993), pp. 281-299.

Sprague, R.H., Jr., and E.D. Carlson, *Building Effective Decision Support Systems* (Englewood Cliffs, NJ, Prentice Hall, 1982).

Stark, A.W., "Irreversibility and the Capital Budgeting Process," *Management Accounting Research,* Vol. 1, No. 3 (1990), pp. 167-180.

Stark, A.W. "Problems in Measuring the Cash Recovery Rate and Measurement Error in Estimates of the Firm IRR," *European Accounting Review* (1993), pp. 199-218.

Stauffer, T.R., "The Measurement of Corporate Rates of Return: A Generalized Formulation," *Bell Journal of Economics and Management Science* (Autumn 1971), pp. 434-469.

Tank, A., "Information for Strategic Decisions," (U.S.A.: The Conference Board Report Number 1027, 1993).

Thompson, J., *Organizations in Action*, (McGraw-Hill, NY, 1967).

Toffler, A., *Future Shock* (NY: Random House), 1970.

Tomkins, C., "Another Look at Residual Income," *Journal of Business, Finance and Accounting* (Spring, 1975a), pp. 39-53.

Tomkins, C., "Residual Income—A Rebuttal to Professor Amey's Arguments," *Journal of Business, Finance and Accounting* (Summer, 1975b), pp. 161-168.

Trotman, A., "Letter to Shareholders, Customers, and Friends," *Ford Motor Company's 1995 Annual Report* (March 14, 1996).

Tsay, Y.Z., F. Alt and L.A. Gordon, "The Market Reaction to Announced Deep Cuts in Capital Expenditures," *Managerial and Decision Economics*, Vol. 14, No. 1 (1993), pp. 1-14.

Tully, S., "America's Best Wealth Creators," *Fortune* (November 28, 1994), pp. 43-162.

Tully, S., "The Real Key to Creating Wealth," *Fortune* (September, 1993), pp. 38-40, 42, 45, 48, 50.

Tyson, T., L. Weisenfeld, and D. Stout, "Running Actual Costs vs. Standard Costs," *Management Accounting* (August 1989), pp. 54, 56.

Vancil, R.F., *Decentralization: Management Ambiguity By Design* (Homewood, IL: Dow Jones-Irwin, 1978).

Weick, J., "Conceptual Trade-Offs in Studying Organizational Change," in *Contemporary Management: Issues and Viewpoints* (Prentice-Hall, Inc., Englewood Cliffs, NJ), 1974, pp. 244-251. Ed. J. McGuire.

Welch, J.F., P. Fresco, E.F. Murphy and J.D. Opie, "Letter to Share Owners and Employees," *General Electric Corporation's 1997 Annual Report* (April 20, 1998).

Whitwam, D.R., "Letter to Shareholders," *Whirlpool Corporation's 1995 Annual Report* (February 1, 1996).

Wildavsky, A., "The Self-Evaluating Organization," *Public Administration Review* (September/October, 1972), pp. 509-520.

Williamson, O.E., "The Modern Corporation: Origins, Evolution, Attributes," *Journal of Economic Literature* (December 1981), pp. 1537-1568.

Williamson, O.E., "Corporate Finance and Corporate Governance," *Journal of Finance*, Vol. 43, No. 3 (1988), pp. 567-591.

Woodward, J., *Industrial Organization: Theory and Practice* (London: Oxford University Press, 1965).

Zimmerman, J., "The Costs and Benefits of Cost Allocations," *The Accounting Review* (July 1979), pp. 504-521.

INDEX